CW00684047

Rethinking Terrorism

Terrorism, Violence and

Rethinking World Politics

Series Editor: Professor Michael Cox

In an age of increased academic specialization where more and more books about smaller and smaller topics are becoming the norm, this major new series is designed to provide a forum and stimulus for leading scholars to address big issues in world politics in an accessible but original manner. A key aim is to transcend the intellectual and disciplinary boundaries which have so often served to limit rather than enhance our understanding of the modern world. In the best tradition of engaged scholarship, it aims to provide clear new perspectives to help make sense of a world in flux.

Each book addresses a major issue or event that has had a formative influence on the twentieth-century or the twenty-first-century world which is now emerging. Each makes its own distinctive contribution as well as providing an original but accessible guide to competing lines of interpretation.

Taken as a whole, the series will rethink contemporary international politics in ways that are lively, informed and – above all – provocative.

Rethinking Terrorism

Colin Wight

First published 2015 by
PALGRAVE

Palgrave in the UK is an imprint of Macmillan Publishers Limited, registered in England, company number 785998, of 4 Crinan Street, London, N1 9XW.

Palgrave Macmillan in the US is a division of St Martin's Press LLC, 175 Fifth Avenue, New York, NY 10010.

Palgrave is a global imprint of the above companies and is represented throughout the world.

Palgrave® and Macmillan® are registered trademarks in the United States, the United Kingdom, Europe and other countries.

ISBN 978-0-230-57377-2   ISBN 978-1-137-54054-6 (eBook)
DOI 10.1007/978-1-137-54054-6

This book is printed on paper suitable for recycling and made from fully managed and sustained forest sources. Logging, pulping and manufacturing processes are expected to conform to the environmental regulations of the country of origin.

A catalogue record for this book is available from the British Library.

A catalog record for this book is available from the Library of Congress.

Contents

Foreword

It is worth recalling that in those far distant, almost innocent days following the end of the Cold War, volumes on terrorism hardly figured at all on the bookshelves of any self-respecting academic. There were studies galore on globalization; almost a roomful on the unipolar moment; row upon row on anything to do with epistemology; and for those who claimed to have a somewhat closer relationship with the real world, a fair number of studies on the growing role played by international institutions all lumped together (somewhat incongruously) under the catch-all heading of 'global governance'. But not very much on terrorism. In part this was linked to the then dominant view that because peace was breaking out in many of the world's top trouble spots – from South Africa to Northern Ireland – there was little point devoting too much time to something that was fast going out of business. But something else was also going on; more subtle perhaps, but no less important: namely the emergence of an increasingly influential liberal paradigm in international relations that plainly found it very difficult to come to terms with terrorism. It was just too difficult and uncomfortable. Uncomfortable because terrorism was brutal, violent and anything but liberal; uncomfortable because when states – even supposedly liberal ones – were faced with terrorism they invariably responded in a most illiberal way; and uncomfortable because terrorism as a practice ran directly counter to the idea that the world was then moving in a more peaceful, liberal direction. Since 9/11, a number of fine analysts have transformed themselves into world-class experts on the subject; and many, like Richard English and Jonathan Powell (both with backgrounds in Northern Ireland), have done a truly remarkable job in explaining just what modern terrorism is about and how it might be addressed by intelligent policy-makers. But for those of us with a memory going back far enough – and who even taught in places like Queen's University Belfast, where terrorism was more than just a far distant idea – terrorism before 9/11 was not something that was ever much debated in refereed journals or at learned symposia. It just didn't figure. It was, to coin a phrase, the 'Cinderella' of the 'Academic Ball'.

It is one the many great strengths of Colin Wight's brilliant new book on terrorism that he takes the discussion about terrorism on to an entirely new conceptual plane. His story begins, though does not end, with 9/11. As he points out, not only did the attack coming out of a clear blue sky 'thrust the issue of international terrorism onto the agenda of global politics in previously unimagined ways'; it also changed the world, invariably making it a less secure, more dangerous, and altogether more fractious place. Nevertheless, it is worth recalling that immediately following the attacks it was fashionable amongst some academics to play down the significance of what had happened; even to argue that it was nowhere near as significant as that other 'Black Swan' event known as the end of the Cold War. Indeed, I remember one or two pieces I wrote at the time criticizing those who thought that far too much was being made of the whole thing by those who were apparently chasing the headlines rather than thinking like a fully paid-up member of the international relations community. But a decade or more on, with two failed wars behind us in Afghanistan and Iraq, several thousand terrorists plying their trade from Syria to northern Nigeria, with states breaking down at regular intervals in the Middle East and North Africa, and with more atrocities planned in Europe and the United States, the idea that terrorism represented an insignificant, transient phenomenon with little of importance to detain the genuine scholar has by now been consigned into that proverbial dustbin of history where it clearly deserves to remain.

But as Wight notes, even if there are now many more terrorists to think about, there is still no consensus or 'collective agreement' on what terrorism means or whether we should even be using the highly contested term 'terrorist' at all. Certainly, 'thinking theoretically about terrorism' has proven to be no easy job. However, one has to try. Moreover, if we are to make sense of terrorism we have to transcend the categories much beloved of the press and politicians, and begin to think of terrorism not as the individual act of fanatics, psychopaths and monsters (easy enough to do as the mangled bodies continue to pile up), but rather as a form of violent protest against the existing order of things.

But there is, Wight insists, something self-perpetuating about terrorism. Indeed, in his account, terrorism and the state are inextricably locked together in what might almost be described as a macabre dance of death. Born out of violence, the modern state – defined here as the sole source of the legitimate use of violence in society – has no alternative but to deal with terrorism by employing any and all means possible so as to restore the state to normal. The terrorists respond in kind. The state counters. And so the cycle goes on – until one or other of the two combatants decides that it is no longer feasible, or worthwhile, carrying on in the old way.

Therein, though, lies the true dilemma today. What if particular kinds of war between certain kinds of terrorists and the forces of 'law and order' go on and on; do not come to an end as all 'normal' wars are supposed to? Indeed, what happens if, in fact, there is nothing to negotiate about? No compromise deal to be negotiated behind closed doors? What then? With the Islamic State on the rise, the whole edifice of the Westphalian system under threat in parts of the Middle East, and with many disaffected young men and women looking for meaning and purpose in a world in which they apparently can find neither, these are questions that have to be asked, even if there are no easy answers. If nothing else, Colin Wight's landmark volume could not have come at a more propitious moment. Analytically rigorous, hard-headed and honest, it is one of those very rare books that will (unlike many on the subject) easily stand the test of time. That is a mark of its true quality – as much as it is testament to the tragedy of our time.

Professor Michael Cox
Director LSE IDEAS
London School of Economics and Political Science

Acknowledgements

The origins of this book demonstrate the ways in which the best-formulated plans can always be overturned by unexpected events that happen on the other side of the world. In July 2001, I was working at the Department of International Politics at the University of Wales Aberystwyth. I had been teaching a course on Terrorism, Violence and the State for over four years and approached my then Head of Department, Ken Booth, requesting permission to drop the course. It was always a highly popular course with students, and when constructing it I had always intended to look at the relationship between the development of the state, theories of the state, protest against the state and political violence. By July 2001, however, I had become bored with the course and thought that it was time to move my teaching into alternative areas. Ken was happy to agree, so the course was dropped from the curriculum. By the end of September 2001, the context surrounding this decision had changed. And in terms of mere student recruitment, dropping a course on terrorism looked like a perverse decision. My mind was made up, and Ken kept his word.

What followed from this was the development of Critical Terrorism Studies at Aberystwyth, as the department moved to fill the gap in research and teaching surrounding terrorism. In fact Jeroen Gunning, who was the first appointment to this nascent group of scholars, initially taught my course, adapting it, of course, to his research agenda. In this small way, I can claim some small role in the development of Critical Terrorism Studies. Although the relationship between terrorism and the state was always fundamental to my approach to the subject, this was not how critical terrorism studies developed this relationship. This was something that disturbed me and in many ways this book is a direct response to the way Critical Terrorism Studies incorporated the state into their analysis, and that is the first point of acknowledgement.

The second acknowledgement is to the many students who took the course over the years I ran it. In particular, when I had taught the course, part of the assessment was a group task that involved the students identifying a terrorist group, examining the context of that group, looking at their aims and objectives and providing a security briefing on the chosen group. In the final year of the course, one of the groups chose al-Qaeda. All of these presentations were videoed, and I still have the VHS version of those presentations on my shelf in Sydney. But equally, all of those students will attest to the fact that we never dealt with terrorism as merely Islamic terrorism – in fact, it played a minor role. Terrorism was a significant tactic long before al-Qaeda or IS burst onto the scene, and I suspect it will outlast them. Nonetheless, I would like to thank all of the students who took my terrorism course over the years, for the constant probing, questioning and disagreements. I suspect many of them will remain unconvinced by my arguments, but they have shaped those arguments.

Thirdly, I would like to acknowledge the support and encouragement I have received from colleagues over the years it has taken me to write this book. In no particular order, this would include Tim Dunne, Ken Booth, MiljaKurki, Heikki Patomaki (who will be pleased to see me putting critical realism to work), Richard Jackson, Ruth Blakeley, Nick Wheeler and Jeroen Gunning. Of course, all the usual caveats about ultimate responsibility apply.

Finally, it would be remiss of me to forget the staff at Palgrave who have displayed patience that defies description, as I constantly told them the manuscript was on its way. The correct response would have been 'so is Christmas', and that may have been what they uttered in scheduling meetings. Nonetheless, their patience with me is appreciated. In particular, in this respect I should thank Stephen Kennedy, who retired in 2014, just as the final manuscript was delivered. Steve pushed and cajoled me, in ways in which only he can. He won't know how many ISA meetings I avoided attending just so I didn't have to face him again with my pitiful pleas of workloads, family commitments, and so on. But then again, he might. Steve has not just been a commissioning editor in the formulation of this book, but an intellectual equal, and he is someone who knows more about most subjects that most authors would care to admit. This book would not be published if it were not for his persistence.

C. W.
May 2015

Introduction

'When I use a word,' Humpty Dumpty said, in a rather scornful tone, 'it means just what I choose it to mean, neither more nor less.'

'The question is,' said Alice, 'whether you *can* make words mean so many different things.'

'The question is,' said Humpty Dumpty, 'which is to be master – that's all.'

Lewis Carroll, *Alice in Wonderland*

Events that produce significant changes in the international political system are rare, and difficult to discern (Buzan and Lawson, 2014). Westphalia, the two world wars and the end of the Cold War are possible candidates, but history makes fools of those prone to premature declarations of 'new world orders'. The terrorist attacks of 11 September 2001 (henceforth 9/11) are another widely accepted candidate for an event that is said to have changed the conduct of international politics. Here was a supposed epoch-changing event played out in real time on TV screens and broadcast on radios across the globe. Apart from the musings of some conspiracy theorists, the meaning of 9/11 is relatively clear. Once the second plane, United Airlines Flight 175 from Boston, crashed into the south tower of the World Trade Center, the events of 9/11 became unmistakably understandable as 'terrorist attacks' (Thompson, 2004; Wright, 2006a). This horrific event, supposedly singular in its form, thrust the issue of international terrorism on to the agenda of global politics in previously unimagined ways.

9/11 is often claimed to be a catalyst for a series of system-defining changes that we are currently undergoing. The overturning of the Taliban regime in Afghanistan in 2002; the war on terror; the Bush doctrine of pre-emptive war; the Iraq war; the concerted attempt to export democracy to the Middle East;

and the emergence of non-state actors as significant agents on the global stage, all represent but a few of the supposed major developments directly related to 9/11 (Chandrasekaran, 2007). In addition, the emergence of the so-called Islamic State in Iraq in 2014 provides further evidence that the forces unleashed post-9/11 could yet be system-redefining in ways that are not yet fully clear. Yet a heavy sense of paradox pervades the global unanimity surrounding the meaning of 9/11. For despite the fact that the majority of the global populace understood the events of 9/11 as 'terrorist attacks' and are happy to continue to talk in these terms, there is no consensus on what terrorism is. There is no global political consensus, nor any academic consensus. We all seem to know what we mean when 'we' use the term terrorism but there is no collective agreement on what it means.

Academics are well versed in the problematics of 'essentially contested' concepts (Gallie, 1964: 157–91). And doubtless Walter Bryce Gallie's analysis can be usefully applied to the definition of terrorism. Yet in terms of political practice, the issues go well beyond any semantic contestation. It is not simply the case that we are unable to reach a consensus on the definition of terrorism, but that we are unwilling to do so. We are collectively unwilling to define terrorism because it suits our political purposes to deploy the label in circumstances of our choosing. As such, the use of the term terrorism is as much a political weapon as are acts of terrorism. In addition, both the practice of terrorism and the political deployment of the term are forms of political communication. When groups, or individuals, seek to use terrorism as a tactic the aim is to convey a political message. Likewise, when groups or individuals label an act as terrorism, they also seek to communicate something specific about the act.

Importantly, in addition to its communicative aspect, terrorism is also a form of political violence. Indeed, for many people it is the most heinous form of violence. This explains why the deployment of the term carries so much rhetorical force. To accuse someone of terrorism serves to label not only that specific act as beyond the pale, but also constitutes an attempt to delegitimize the cause that led to it. Terrorism cannot be accommodated, understood or explained; it can simply be confronted. The only rational response to terrorism is the use of terror against it. Yet, as a form of political violence, terrorism is also motivated by political circumstances; hence, those who engage in it must believe that acts of terrorism serve those political ends. Some commentators have doubted that 9/11 falls under this rubric, describing the events of 9/11 as a form of 'apocalyptic nihilism' residing outside politics and any expectation of attaining political objectives. 9/11 was not about the communication of any political message, but about destruction. According to Michael Ignatieff, 9/11 literally represents a longing for 'nothing'; at least nothing understandable in political terms (Ignatieff, 2001). There has always been a tendency to treat terrorism in this way. For some, terrorism is an evil beyond understanding, a sui generis act beyond the realms of political calculation. Such a view makes apologists of those who would seek to understand it, since terrorism is not something that can be understood.

Much of the literature on terrorism, albeit with some notable exceptions, follows this trend, with a focus primarily on description as opposed to explanation. This book travels a different path and attempts to think theoretically about contemporary forms of terrorism. Some in the field doubt that terrorism can be theorized in this way. Louise Richardson, for example, claims that terrorism is a microphenomenon and hence not susceptible to explanation (Richardson, 2006a: 2). Likewise, Andrew Silke suggests that since 'good science ... is all about prediction', terrorism cannot be subject to scientific investigation, and hence explanation (Silke, 2004: 11). This way of thinking confuses terrorism as phenomenon with terrorism as event. To paraphrase Kenneth Waltz, a theory of terrorism will explain why it recurs and will indicate some of the conditions that make terrorism more or less likely, but will not predict the occurrence of particular terrorist acts (Waltz, 1979: 69). What a theory of terrorism hopes to explain is why there is such a phenomenon, not why individual acts of terrorism are committed.

Thinking theoretically about terrorism, however, is no easy task. How can one draw generalities or tendencies out of something that cannot even be defined? How can something so particular and sui generis be given a theoretical form? The answer is context. Terrorism can only be understood in a theoretical context that brings together the modern state, political violence and alternative forms of non-violent protest against the state. Terrorism cannot be understood outside the context of the state. As a form of political communication, terrorism is always effectively a violent (or threat of) critique of existing political arrangements.

The institution at the heart of contemporary political arrangements is the state. Or as political theorist Carl Schmitt put it, 'the
concept of the political already presupposes the concept of the
state' (Schmitt, 1996: 19). As such, all forms of political protest
take place within the context of the modern nation state and can
only be understood in relation to this context. What this means for
our understanding of contemporary terrorism is nicely captured
by Philip Bobbitt, who argues that '[e]very constitutional order
invokes a unique form of terrorism' (Bobbitt, 2002: 548). Thus,
as the state undergoes change so too does the form of terrorism.

Political protest against the state can take non-violent forms.
Civil disobedience, for example, constitutes a form of protest
against the state that explicitly, at least at the theoretical level,
rejects the use of violence. What, however, explains the resort to
violence as against the adoption of non-violent forms of protest? One answer given in the literature lies in the psychologies
and pathologies of individuals (Post, 2007; Reich, 1990). Such an
approach may help explain individual cases, but it cannot explain
all cases, still less the support that terrorists must necessarily enjoy
among the wider populace. The number of individuals prepared
to engage in direct terrorist acts is comparatively small when compared to the numbers prepared to offer a wide range of varied
support. Given the large numbers giving tacit or explicit support
to groups using terrorism, it seems clear that psychological explanations of terrorism based on individuals require supplementing
with more structural accounts.

Contra these individualist explanations, this book attempts to
develop a structural explanation that provides a context within
which acts of terrorism might be understood. At the heart of
this explanation is the self-perpetuating, yet contradictory, nexus
of terrorism, violence and the state. Violence and the state are
inextricably linked. The modern state was born out of violence
and, according to Max Weber's influential definition, is defined in
terms of it being the sole source of the legitimate use of violence
in society. Although Weber's definition of the state is well known
and often cited, it is worth quoting at length to examine exactly
what it entails for the understanding of terrorism:

> 'Every state is founded on force,' said Trotsky at Brest-Litovsk.
> That is indeed right. If no social institutions existed which
> knew the use of violence, then the concept of 'state' would be

eliminated, and a condition would emerge that could be designated as 'anarchy,' in the specific sense of this word. Of course, force is certainly not the normal or the only means of the state – nobody says that – but force is a means specific to the state. Today the relation between the state and violence is an especially intimate one. In the past, the most varied institutions – beginning with the sib [kin or blood relations] – have known the use of physical force as quite normal. Today, however, we have to say that a state is a human community that (successfully) claims the monopoly of the legitimate use of physical force within a given territory. Note that 'territory' is one of the characteristics of the state. Specifically, at the present time, the right to use physical force is ascribed to other institutions or to individuals only to the extent to which the state permits it. The state is considered the sole source of the 'right' to use violence. Hence, 'politics' for us means striving to share power or striving to influence the distribution of power, either among states or among groups within a state ... Like the political institutions historically preceding it, the state is a relation of men dominating men, a relation supported by means of legitimate (i.e. considered to be legitimate) violence. If the state is to exist, the dominated must obey the authority claimed by the powers that be. (Weber, 1965: 1)

One implication of this is that states that fail to control the use of political violence are essentially not functional states. Indeed, for Weber, the use of violence by non-state actors challenges the very existence of the state. Another implication is that although states may use alternative forms of control other than violence, the right to use force is unique to the state. No other social institution can legitimately use violence. Finally, in order to remain functional states, states must suppress forms of violence that threaten to disrupt them. It follows from this that insofar as terrorists use violence as a form of political communication they necessarily present themselves as a threat to any given state. Or, in the case of contemporary international terrorism, it is a direct challenge to the contemporary global political order that has been constructed on the basis of this particular model of the state.

It is also important to see how this particular notion of the state is firmly embedded within a European context, which then spread, through the use of violence, to the rest of the world.

Empires, imperialism and colonization all played a role here, using violence to carve up territories and force indigenous populations to adopt this model of the state. Certainly, the particular form of states across the globe varies from democratic to authoritarian modes of governance, but what unites them is the fact that all forms of modern political organization accept the state's claim on the legitimate use of violence. This highlights something important about the contemporary political situation and the place of contemporary terrorism within it. For what is at stake here is not a clash of civilizations (Huntington, 1996), but the altogether more problematic issue of competing visions of what shape politics, and thus the state, should take. This struggle has taken many forms, but the emergence of radical political Islam, and the terrorism that has accompanied it, presents itself as a challenge to the notion of politics embedded with the modern state. The emergence of the Islamic State is simply the most visible demonstration of this phenomenon, and we can expect to see more such examples as our cherished definitions of politics, and thus the state, come under attack (Bobbitt, 2002: 521–46).

Almost all books on terrorism begin with a torturous discussion of the problems of definition. This is not an issue that can be sidestepped, and any book with terrorism in the title must tackle this issue head-on. Because terrorism necessarily involves a political standpoint, and engenders such extreme emotions, the search for a definition precise enough to provide meaningful analytical purchase, yet general enough to obtain agreement from all participants, is extremely difficult. Many analysts simply retreat into the rather trite and oft-repeated phrase, 'one man's terrorist is another man's freedom fighter'. This is an unacceptable position to hold; for moral, political and analytical reasons.

Analytically, to adopt this position and still continue to talk of terrorism can only produce the worst kind of scholarship. For under this approach, the assumptions underpinning the deployment of the term are always hidden. Without at least a very basic definition of terrorism, however flawed, the reader can only be left floundering as the meaning changes from sentence to sentence. Politically and morally, it suggests that decisions about the rightness of an act are simply subjective matters decided by each individual in terms of nothing other than their own political preferences. The causes we support are fighting for freedom; those we do not are terrorism.

Yet, the very idea that terrorism and freedom fighting can be counterposed in this way is a serious error. Freedom fighting describes an 'end' that groups, or individuals, strive to achieve. Terrorism is a practice, or means, to an end. It is entirely possible that one can support the political aspirations of a group attempting to free themselves from oppression, yet not support the means (terrorism) that they use to achieve it. In fact, what underpins most contemporary uses of the term terrorism is the belief that some forms of non-state actor political violence can be justified (freedom fighting) and some not (terrorism). Political violence, however, is not all of a kind, and we need to explore the nature of terrorism as a particular form of that violence. Moreover, the relationship between an academic definition of terrorism and one deployed by publics, politicians and practitioners is a particularly problematic area. Here some position on the philosophy of social science can be of help.

All research begins with ontology, and ontology is at the heart of problem of defining terrorism. The cliché that terrorism it is a bit like pornography and you will know it when you see it has a grain of truth to it. A Realist philosophy of social science can help here (Manicas, 2006; Sayer, 2000). Terrorism is no mere empirical fact, or thing, that simply requires appropriate observation and cataloguing of its process and modes of operation. As a social fact terrorism is constituted, in part, by the beliefs of the actors engaged in the complex web of that practice. However, although the concepts and beliefs of actors engaged in any given social practice are integral to any understanding of that practice, they do not exhaust it. Far less can social scientists assume that the actors have a comprehensive understanding of their situations. Everyday understandings of terrorism are essential to any social-scientific account of terrorism, but they cannot set the limits of that understanding. If this were the case then social science would be otiose. Moreover, to attempt to ground academic accounts of terrorism solely in the definitions employed by actors involved in the practice is to privilege just those actors' accounts at the expense of a more considered scientific investigation of the term. It also deprives the academic of critical purchase on those accounts; how is it possible to criticize the deployment of the term if the very definition of that term is drawn from those that that deploy it?

This means that those definitions that attempt to draw exclusively on official accounts are doomed to fail. Nothing illustrates this better than the outright refusal of the Organization of the Islamic Conference (*Taipei Times*, 2002) to countenance any definition of terrorism that portrayed Palestinian groups as terrorists. The reasons for this were clear. According to the delegates, the political violence that did emerge from groups such as the Palestine Liberation Organization (PLO), Hamas and Hezbollah was driven by deep and long-standing frustration at Israeli occupation and policies. I suspect most people would agree with this assessment of the plight of the Palestinians, but it confuses the belief in the justice of the cause with the means of addressing it. One can support a particular cause without supporting the means employed to redress it. Some violent acts emerging from Palestinian groups can be classified as terrorism, whilst some are not. Nonetheless, although academic accounts of terrorism do not need to be bound by public uses of the term, they must, since those beliefs are (in part) constitutive of it, at least be able to provide an account of why the beliefs are incorrect. As such, there is little point in academic definitions of terrorism that have no public purchase, no matter how sophisticated they may be. Academic accounts must be able to take those public beliefs and place them in a broader context in order to make sense of the error underpinning those beliefs. The broader context for terrorism is the state and its relationship to violence.

Most studies of terrorism miss the fundamental point that the concept of terrorism already implies the concept of the state. Terrorism cannot be defined in the absence of some or other account of the state. And the state can only be understood in terms of its history. The history of the development of the modern state can be understood as a long process of appropriation and accumulation (of territory, peoples and resources) achieved through the use of violence; a process that had winners and losers (Poggi, 1990). The success of the modern state in this process blinds us to this history; we accept states as the dominant and legitimate form of political organization. Noting the place of violence in the development of the modern state, however, allows us to situate that violence as an integral aspect of the state. Understood this way, terrorism and other forms of non-state violence can be interpreted as reactions to this process, and rejections of the claim to state legitimacy. Terrorism and state reactions to it can only be adequately understood if this point is grasped, and although groups deploying terrorism have specific political objectives, the underlying structural battle is over nothing less than the ownership of violence. Of course, the battle over control of the ownership of violence is clear when insurgency and revolution are involved. But in terrorism it takes a distinctive form because the violence is intentionally directed against non-state actors.

This book rethinks terrorism by linking it to the state. It explores the relationship between the state and protest against the state, in violent and non-violent forms. In placing the state at the *centre* of the analysis I aim to arrive at a deflationary account of terrorism that places severe restrictions on the use of the term. The book is primarily interested in the impact terrorism has on the international political system, which involves groups or individuals whose terrorist activities transcend national boundaries. Under conditions of globalization, most forms of terrorism now have international consequences, even if the sources of it derive from domestic conditions. The book also explores the nature of the state, and other forms of resistance against the state, but it does so primarily as a means of placing terrorism in context.

It has often been thought that the state represents a sharp dividing line between the academic division of labour between international relations (IR) and political science (broadly conceived). Thus, for example, political science concerns itself with what goes on inside the state and IR with what goes on outside the state (Walker, 1993). Of course, well before globalization became the leitmotif of the contemporary age, some analysts have challenged this hard and fast distinction. International terrorism is itself a performative act that challenges the artificial boundary between politics and IR. But more than this, a comprehensive understanding of terrorism requires the integration of politics, culture, identity, the economy and sociology.

The modern nation state is a particular form of political configuration, and in order to understand this form, we must treat the state historically. States did not just emerge into the world, fully formed. Indeed, for most of human history societies functioned without even a very primitive form of state. The modern state can only be understood in its historical context. An important aspect of any treatment of the state is to consider it in terms of its relationships to other forces and actors, and in particular, an analysis of the role of violence in its development and maintenance.

Of course, violence is not the only form of political control used by states, and indeed many modern Western states have developed sophisticated forms of control over their populations such that the role of violence in the maintenance of the state remains all but hidden. An analysis of the history of the state, however, allows us to relocate this violence as an integral aspect of the state itself. And it should come as no surprise that that which was founded on violence should itself be subject to violent challenges.

The Argument in Brief

Rethinking terrorism requires us to place it into three contexts. First, the development, shape and form of the modern state. Second, terrorism is a form of political protest that stands in a relation to other forms of political protest. Third, terrorism is a form of political violence, and we should be careful to distinguish between differing types of political violence. All violence inevitably induces terror, but the production of terror is not always terrorism. Of these three contexts, the history, function and form of the state is most important in terms of understanding terrorism.

If the book hangs on one point it is this; terrorism can only be understood in the context of the state. The state emerges and has developed through the use of violence. The violent aspects of the state are not incidental to it but are structurally a necessary part of the state. The state is the political apparatus of modern societies that claims the sole right to use violence legitimately. Violent reactions to the state are not simply protests against certain policies, but at the same time they are existential challenges to the idea of the state itself. This helps to explain why the state reacts so violently to the use of violence by non-state actors against it. But it also helps explain why non-state actors resort to violence against the state. Violence begets violence. Of course we abhor this situation, but given the structural role of violence in the state, it should come as no surprise when some critics of the state use violence against it. Such uses of violence represent direct challenges to the claim of the state to monopolize the ownership of violence.

This is important, because placing the state at the centre of analysis in terms of terrorism allows me to introduce the concept of 'state actors' as an alternative to the more common term of innocents, or non-combatants. The term innocent is morally loaded and difficult to delineate in complex contemporary societies.

In particular, in democracies where populations vote their state leaders into positions of authority, it becomes possible to argue that that population is directly responsible for the acts committed by political leaders. After all, in representative democracies these leaders 'represent' the people. As such, how then can the people be 'innocent'? The term non-combatants, on the other hand, is too restrictive and, taken literally, implies that attacks on political leaders, for example, would not be terrorism. The use of non-state actors, for now defined as those actors not directly involved in the maintenance of the state, is not without its problems, but it has the virtue of ensuring the state takes its place at the heart of any consideration of what is, or is not, terrorism.

The modern state takes many forms. Some states claim to be well-functioning democracies, allowing clearly articulated and accessible channels of dissent. Other states look much like democracies, and often function as if they were, but in certain instances the principles of democracy are overridden in order to reimpose political order. Political protest in these states often leads to military coups, martial law and the suspension of democracy. Other states make no pretence to be democracies and are ruled by autocratic leaders who clamp down harshly on protest against their rule. The validity of any form of protest against any given state can only be assessed in relation to the practices of that state and how those protesting understand its legitimacy. Given that all states were historically constituted through the use of violence and ultimately resort to violence to maintain their predominant place in the social order, it should come as no surprise that some protesters will turn to violence to tackle perceived injustices imposed on them by states.

Political protest also comes in many forms. It is best considered as a continuum running from forms of protest that are considered part and parcel of the democratic process to terrorism at the other extreme. Most democracies have well-understood mechanisms through which protest can be registered; letter writing, petitions, meetings, lobbying, strikes, and so on. When such protests fail, some in the protest group may decide to engage in civil disobedience, which for the time being can be understood as protest articulated through the deliberate breaking of some law, or set of laws. Civil disobedience, however, can quickly turn into direct action, or more radical forms of protest. Within direct action, riots and lawbreaking can quickly lead to the overturning of regimes or all-out revolution. If the protest becomes protracted protesters may use a range of tactics, and insurgency is best understood as a violent protest that takes place over a period of time, as opposed to riots, which are often short in duration. Riots, however, can be considered part of an insurgent tactic to destabilize a regime.

Terrorism, which for now I will define as *the use, or threat, of violence by non-state actors against non-state actors to communicate a political message in pursuance of political ends*, can be one tactic employed by those protesting against the state. I am aware of the potential criticisms of this definition, but for now I will simply deliver a promissory note to flesh it out in the rest of the book. I draw an important semantic distinction between *groups that use terrorism* and *terrorist groups*. The idea of *terrorist groups* makes little sense and implies that the aim of the group is terrorism. But terrorism is a specific form of political violence and is one tactic among many used by groups protesting against the state (understood for now as the locus of authority in a prevailing political order). Terrorism is rarely, if ever, an end in itself. Terrorism is a means some groups choose to advance their cause, but terrorism is not the cause itself. Put simply, there are no groups whose aim is simply the pursuance of terrorism.

Likewise, as a specific form of political violence aimed at achieving an end that is not reducible to the means of achieving that end, then terrorism has to be placed in the context of alternative forms of political violence. As part of the generic concept of political violence, terrorism obviously shares much in common with other forms of political violence. But we should be careful to tease out the differences between differing forms of political violence. The aim here is to provide a very narrow definition of terrorism that has the effect of deflating figures surrounding terrorism and the threat it poses to individuals, states or the international order. A recent opinion poll conducted by the Chicago Council on Global Affairs demonstrates why this is so important, with Americans more worried about the threat of global terrorism than they are about the potential threat to their civil liberties through government monitoring programs designed, allegedly, to deal with terrorist threats (Verton, 2014). This is an alarming trend and represents one of the most pernicious aspects of the post-9/11 discourse surrounding terrorism. Academics have a responsibility here to provide accurate assessments of the threat of terrorism, and they can only do so if they can reach agreement of what terrorism is. Only if this can be achieved can the inflationary account of terrorism that has emerged since 9/11 be countered.

Plan of the Book

In Chapter 1, I examine the historical development of the modern state. This is not meant to be an exhaustive account, the aim being only to ensure a sufficient understanding of the various conflicts and processes that have led to the particular form the modern state takes in contemporary societies, and in particular, an appreciation of the role of violence in that history. My focus on violence is deliberate, and obviously any comprehensive account of the development of the modern state would deal with a range of alternative factors. However, given the argument of the book, placing violence at the centre of analysis allows me to situate that aspect of the modern state that is most important when considering terrorism and other forms of political protest. It is also important to understand that states differ in form and that these differences are the result of historical formations and practices. The modern state was born out of, and constituted through, violence. Understanding this process allows us to see terrorism as situated on a continuum of political violence that is not external to the state, but constitutive of it. Readers well versed in the historical development of the modern state could quite easily skip this chapter, but these arguments and historical processes are integral to any coherent account of terrorism, violence and the state.

Chapter 2 provides an account of the modern state, the various theoretical approaches to it, and an examination of the varied forms it can take. The chapter focuses attention on the theoretical accounts of the modern state. This is important, because social objects such as the state are not simply things, but are, in part, constituted by the ideas we have of them. States have a history, but that history is not necessarily contiguous with the ideas people have of the state. Moreover, ideas about the value of the state are contested, and in part, protest against the state is an expression of that contestation. Again, the aim is not to provide a comprehensive account of state theory, but to provide a description of the varied approaches to the modern state. It is only if we have an understanding of the differences between these competing accounts that we can grasp the ethical and moral arguments surrounding various forms of action orientated against the state.

In Chapter 3, I address the issue of both violent and non-violent protest against the state, concentrating on 'civil disobedience', but situating this in the context of 'legal protest' and more radical and violent forms of political action. One important aspect of theories of civil disobedience, when compared to theories of the state, is that they largely emerge out of political practice, as well as academic study. Hence, key figures to consider in this chapter will be David Henry Thoreau, Mahatma Gandhi, Martin Luther King and John Rawls. Issues to be addressed in this chapter will include: What responsibilities do citizens owe the state, and why? Should we always obey the laws of the state? If not, who decides when it is right to challenge a law? Which laws can we challenge and which can we not? What is the legitimate scope and form of civil disobedience? Is violent civil disobedience ever legitimate? In what circumstances does non-violent civil disobedience lead to revolution? Through a discussion of these and other related issues the chapter aims to examine the limits and scope of civil disobedience and situate it as a genuine alternative to more extreme forms of political violence. A crucial dimension of this discussion will be to link the analysis of civil disobedience to the analysis of the state contained in previous chapters. Here the aim is to explore the relationship between forms of state, the failure of civil disobedience and associated form of political protest, and the resort to violence.

Chapter 4 provides an introduction to the issue of terrorism, the main areas of debate surrounding it and other forms of political violence. The main focus of the chapter is to place terrorism in the context of alternative forms of political violence. An important issue in this chapter is to examine the difficulty we face in defining terrorism. The chapter argues that any coherent definition must be able to achieve three things. First, be consistent with how actors themselves define the term. Second, provide a means of differentiating terrorism from alternative forms of political violence. Third, through the process of differentiation, provide a deflationary definition of terrorism that allows us to situate the threat from it in a realistic context. There is no general theory of political violence, and hence it must be examined through its practices. Thus theories of violence must be as varied as the practices and contexts within which it emerges. To flatten out these differences and attempt to deal with differing modes of violence under the one descriptive term is a serious error. It is an error that is compounded when there is little, or no, consensus on that term. In order to make sense of the context of terrorism, we need a clear sense of what it is, and what it is not. As such, the definitional problem will not go away.

Chapter 5 tackles the issue of state terrorism head-on. State terrorism has always been one of the most contested areas of research into terrorism. I argue that that concept of state terrorism, although it makes intuitive sense, provides no additional purchase on a critique of unacceptable state practices beyond that already covered by international law. Indeed, since there is no agreed international definition of terrorism, then to move certain state practices into the realm of state terrorism effectively leaves those practices outside legal redress. Nothing is gained, and much lost, by talking of state terrorism.

Chapter 6 focuses on issues concerning the justification and explanation of terrorism as a form of political practice. Is terrorism ever justified? Does the particular form of the state within which violent acts are conducted make a difference to how we approach the morality of terrorist acts? Is it possible to differentiate between combatants and non-combatants in complex, highly structured societies? The chapter also explores some of the dominant explanations for the emergence of terrorism, and argues that psychological explanations have a limited role to play in terms of our understanding, and that where they do play a role they always require supplementing with structural complexes. The causes of terrorism are multifaceted and we have to be attentive to the complex interplay of social, political, economic, religious, ideological and psychological factors when attempting to address the issue. There are no 'root causes' as such that explain all manifestations of this particular form of political violence. There are only 'assemblages' of interacting and dynamic forces that change over place and time and which lead to the emergence of differing responses to political configurations. Some of these responses we call terrorism, but there is not one explanation of why such responses emerge.

In Chapter 7 I deal with the structure and organization of groups using terrorism and examine the tactics they employ to achieve their political ends. The chapter begins by introducing the concept of 'self-organizing' systems and develops this to situate groups that use terrorism as existing on a continuum structured around varied degrees of self-organization. Groups using terrorism prior to the emergence of al-Qaeda varied in configuration, but various forms of cell-type structures were common. Nonetheless all still displayed, by necessity, elements of self-organization. Al-Qaeda marks a significant difference, however, and is almost completely self-organizing. The chapter also examines the various types of terrorism and deals with the vexed issues of whether religious terrorism constitutes a distinctive form.

Chapter 8 turns its attention to the nature of contemporary international terrorism and the war on terror. In a globalized world international terrorism poses unique challenges. New forms of self-organizing groups that deploy terrorism thrive in a world where time and space have been compressed and where new technologies offer new opportunities for conveying political messages. Images of decapitated hostages published on the internet are clearly highly efficient forms of political communication. Whilst the chapter will focus on contemporary forms, it will also include analyses of the historical development of various modes of international terrorism and state-sponsored terrorism.

1

Owning Violence: A History of the Modern Nation State

'Political power grows out of the barrel of a gun.'

Mao Zedong

The development of the modern state can be understood as a series of struggles over the use and ownership of violence. Weber's influential definition of the state endures because it captures something essential about the nature of the state. No other entity, organization, individual or institutional form is legitimately allowed to exercise violence in the modern state system. Where other actors do use violence, it is either explicitly sanctioned by the state, or viewed as an illegitimate form of violence. How did the state come to control the ownership of violence, and why does this matter for understanding terrorism and other forms of protest against the state?

State control and ownership of violence primarily came about through the use of violence. Throughout history, groups and communities have competed with each other in order to claim the exclusive right to use violence in a given terrain. Over the course of that history they have configured their political relations in specific ways to deal with the problem of violence by claiming ownership of it. This has not been an easy process, and attempts to monopolize the use of violence have not gone unchallenged. The modern state is a reflection of those struggles. Political configurations have varied over time, but the modern state form is simply the instantiation of the conflict over the ownership of violence in a form of politics we take to be natural, but which is anything but.

Through this historical process there have been winners and losers. The losers have not only lost territory, resources, and in some instances their identities, but they have also been denied the right to use violence to redress their situations. This matters because generally the winners have not reached their elevated position because of the 'rightness' of their cause, but how much 'might' they we able to exercise. Yet the fact that the legitimacy of the claim to exercise ownership over the use of violence is predicated on 'might' and not 'right' has become obscured over historical time. We now view states as the legitimate source of order and authority in the international system. In addition, in democratic states we assume that this legitimacy is derived from the people. Viewed ahistorically, this assumption is correct. But viewed from the perspective of history, on the other hand, we can see that modern liberal-democratic states are also founded on violence.

This historical forgetting of the role, and place, of violence in the modern state allows the easy assumption that non-state violence is almost always, by definition, deemed to be illegitimate. Yet, much as we might abhor the use of violence, this assumption is incorrect. If violence has historically played a role in founding the state, why should groups that object to the outcomes of that process be denied the use of violence to correct those outcomes? Only a pacifist could deny the validity of violence in the structural constitution of the state and political order. Equally, in accepting the legitimacy of the rule of democracy – a legitimacy itself founded on violence – it also becomes easy to think that violence against non-democratic states might be more justified than violence against democratic states. Thus there is a tendency to think that terrorism is largely a problem that affects democracies, whereas authoritarian states confront 'freedom fighters' (Wilkinson, 1986, 2011). Again, this is an error: fighting for freedom is an end, terrorism a means. Violence, politics, protest and the state are structurally inscribed in the modern state system.

The history of how this came to be is essential to understanding any account of terrorism. In many respects, the idea that the state exercises a legitimate monopoly on the use of violence is universally accepted today. Even those who use violence against the state are not challenging the right of the state to monopolize the use of violence but rather, they merely want to gain control of the state so that they may control it and the ownership of violence that accompanies it. Understanding the relationship between violence and the state, and how this relationship has been constituted throughout history, allows us to situate a form of protest against the state, some violent, some not, as legitimate attempts to address past grievances and challenge the ownership of violence thesis.

Thus, this chapter explores the history of the state, placing violence at the centre of this analysis. Focusing on political violence in this way is obviously a gross oversimplification of what is a complex and contested historical process. Nonetheless, foregrounding the role of violence in the constitution of the state opens up the vexed question of contemporary discourse surrounding state legitimacy. In this respect, even the legitimacy of contemporary liberal-democratic states cannot be taken for granted. This means that states differ depending on the context in which the violence they use is mobilized and deployed. However, my concern is not with individual states, but with the state itself. This means that some of the differences are necessarily flattened out, and detail has been sacrificed for explanatory purchase.

A Brief History of the Nation State

Much like terrorism, the concept of the state is deeply contested (Mann, 1984), yet despite this there is probably a minimum of agreement that the modern state has four main features: fixed territorial boundaries; a monopoly on force and the means of coercion; a sovereign political order embedded in well-understood and structured hierarchical relationships; and the legitimacy to represent the needs and interests of its citizens. Beyond this, however, there is little agreement as to how to conceptualize the state. According to Robert Berki, 'the modern state … is a rather baffling phenomenon' (Berki, 1989: 12), or as Michael Mann has put it, 'the state is an undeniably messy concept' (Mann, 1984: 333). Yet no matter how baffling or messy the concept is, states confront us all of our lives. They are there at our birth, providing the procedures that give us our names, existence and national identity, and they legitimate when we die. Thus, in one very real sense, we are children of the state before we are children of our parents. Without state recognition, it is fair to say, individuals do not exist, at least not in a social sense. Or as Pierre-Joseph Proudhon put it, to be governed is to be 'noted, registered, enrolled, taxed, stamped, measured, numbered, assessed, licensed, authorised, admonished, forbidden, reformed, corrected, punished' (Proudhon, 1989: 294).

States also set the conditions for all other institutional orders within society, and often intervene directly in them when crises emerge that might threaten the ability of the state to function; the global banking and financial crisis of 2008/09 being a perfect example of this state intervention (Lewis, 2010). All forms of contemporary social life are dependent, to some extent, on state practices, rules, norms and laws. Moreover, apart from some rare instances of state failure, modern nation states exercise control over the whole of the globe. Admittedly, the extent to which this control is enacted varies from place to place, but nonetheless, in theory, states claim territorial sovereignty over every part of the planet. States exercise this control in various ways, but it can be usefully discussed under the dual notions of force and consent (Hall, 1994).

There is no doubt that the state is an apparatus of coercion. That is, it is a particular set of institutions, which carry out the functions of rule-making and rule enforcement within a given territory. Moreover, and as a result of the principle of sovereignty, the state claims to be the sole source of this authority within a given territory, and challenges to this claim, either from domestic or international sources, are likely to be met with a violent reaction. Yet coercion is not the only dimension of state power, and states also rule, to varying degrees, through the consent of the people; a population, that is, who view state claims to sovereignty as being largely legitimate (Hall, 1994: 99–124). In fact, the coercive aspects of the state tend to remain hidden from most citizens, as long as they obey its rules. Individuals and groups who step out of line, however, and protest against the state, or challenge its authority, can find that they are 'repressed, fined, despised, harassed, tracked, abused, clubbed, disarmed, choked, imprisoned, judged, condemned, shot, deported, sacrificed, sold, betrayed; and, to crown all, mocked, ridiculed, outraged, dishonoured' (Proudhon, 1989: 24). What this list highlights is that although consent and legitimacy are perhaps the dominant forms of social control within the modern state, the ultimate source still rests with violence (Mann, 2012). For it is exactly at the moment when legitimacy and consent fail that violence and force re-emerge. In fact, when the history of the state is considered, what we see is a project of state construction enacted through the violent appropriation of peoples, territory and resources, allied to the attempt to claim the sole right to the use of violence for itself. So it is not just the case that ownership of territory, people and resources was the aim of the state project, but it was also the ownership of violence.

In contemporary modern nation states, however, particularly those of the liberal democratic form, the place of violence in the state has largely been forgotten (Mann, 2005: 70–110).

Equally, although the state is a universal social form encompassing the globe, the balance between force and consent varies from state to state. This illustrates the fact that although we talk about the state in the abstract, and as a generic form of social and political control, empirically at least states are differentiated and take many forms. One explanation of this variation resides in the fact that populations, territories and communities throughout the world did not embark on the journey towards statehood at the same time, and the importation, and often imposition, of the modern state to large parts of the globe is a fairly recent phenomenon, at least in historical terms. Equally, the modern state project began in Europe and has subsequently been imposed, exported, adopted and copied across the world (Giddens, 1985).Yet the modern state also embodies a particular account of politics and of sovereign authority that is itself a reflection of a particular European, and largely secular, way of thinking about political order. Given this, it is not difficult to see contemporary international terrorism, particularly in its Islamic form, not as an expression of religious fanaticism, but of a competing vision of what politics is and should be (Esposito, 1998; Kepel, 2006). Thus contemporary international terrorism represents a challenge not just to particular states, but also to our very understanding of politics itself; as such, it is also a challenge to the very idea of the modern state. This follows logically from Carl Schmitt's assertion that '[t]he concept of the state presupposes the concept of the political' (Schmitt, 1996: 19). Understanding why this is so requires us to look at the historical development of the modern nation state, since the emergence of such a state is also the expression of a particular form of politics, and not one that can necessarily be generalized across the globe without the use of violence to enforce that account of politics on peoples with a different concept of what the political might involve.

It is normal to think of state development in terms of phases. Some authors, such as Gianfranco Poggi, identify four phases. For Poggi, these are the feudal state, the polity of estates, the absolutist state and the modern nation state (Poggi, 1990). Others, such as David Held, identify five phases; Held add to Poggi's four phases a prior phase, that of Empire (Held, 1992). Shmuel Eisenstadt, on the other hand, includes in his list city states, feudal systems, patrimonial empires, nomad or conquest empires and centralized historical bureaucratic empires (Eisenstadt, 1963: 10). Although these differences are not unimportant, my preference is to go with Poggi's four-phase scheme, since most analysts agree that these were at least a minimal set of phases integral to the development of the modern state. Although this is a valid framework for looking at the development of the modern nation state, it is not without its problems. First, like all synoptic devices, it oversimplifies what is a very complex story. Yet to tell the complex development of the nation state in full detail would be well beyond the task of any book. Equally, although I will largely base my account on that of Poggi, I will be concentrating my attention on the manner in which violence and force become embedded within state institutions, but remain largely hidden from view until state authority is challenged. In this sense the claim to monopolize the use of violence did not just happen but had to be fought for. The ownership of violence was achieved through violence.

A second problem with all such historical periodizations is that they can give the illusion that when one period stops the other begins. But history is not like this; it is not a series of discrete moments in time, and historical periods always overlap to some extent. Indeed, there is a sense in which the early periods of state development are present in all of the later stages. We can represent this process in diagrammatic form (see Figure 1.1).

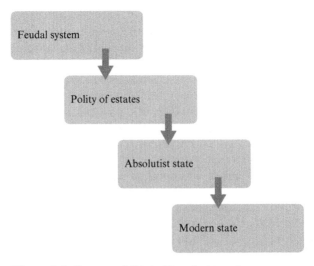

Figure 1.1 Stages of State Development

The Feudal State

It might, of course, be anachronistic to talk of prior political forms as states. Indeed, there is a large body of opinion that considers the modern state to have only emerged in the aftermath of the treaties of Westphalia (Gross, 1948; Holsti, 1991: 25). It was these treaties, signed to end the wars of religion that had dominated European politics for over thirty years, that essentially set in place the necessary conditions for the emergence of contemporary sovereignty. There is something to this argument, but it rests on an over-essentialized view of what the state is or can be (for examples of this see Krasner, 1993; Teschke, 2003). When we use the term state to refer to prior historical political forms of social organization, what we are really highlighting is the fact that this is where political authority and control are centralized. Or as Charles Tilly puts it, states are 'coercion-wielding organisations that are distinct from households and kinship groups and exercise clear priority in some respects over all other organisations within substantial territories' (Tilly, 1990: 1). It is clear that historically, the form this centralization and priority has taken differs markedly from how we would define states today. However, although some of the fundamental features of pre-Westphalian states are clearly very different from how we understand the state, when we refer to them as states, what we are really getting at is the ability of some organization or group to exercise force and political control over some demarcated territorial domain or political community. Yet the ability of pre-Westphalian states to exercise control over their territory varied enormously, and in some respects it is perhaps territorial integrity or the lack of it that clearly demarcate the modern nation state from its pre-Westphalian forms. As Anthony Giddens has argued, pre-Westphalian states did not possess clear and well-defined borders, so much as fuzzy, disputed and ill-defined frontier areas (Giddens, 1985: 49–50).

This is very different from the modern state, which perhaps has territorial integrity as one of its defining elements. What this means is that although pre-Westphalian states might have attempted to exercise rule in a particular territory, they generally lacked the capacity to enforce that rule. In essence, that lacked control over the ownership of violence. Another key difference between the modern and the pre-Westphalian state is that although control of resources was an important aspect of pre-Westphalian states, this was achieved largely through extortion or force, rather than the formalized taxation systems deployed by modern states to generate revenues. In this respect, the use of violence to appropriate territory and resources was a key aspect of the pre-Westphalian state, and in some respects, until very recently, even played a major role for the modern state. However, although there are clear differences between the pre-Westphalian and the modern state, it is out of these prior historical forms that the contemporary state emerges. Moreover, given the processual nature of social life, then, state construction is an ongoing accomplishment; hence understanding the contemporary state requires us to examine prior forms of political organization, out of which the contemporary state has emerged.

According to Poggi, the first phase of modern state development was that of the feudal period, which can be dated to sometime between the twelfth and fourteenth centuries (Poggi, 1990: 35). An important aspect of political control in this era was a close set of personal relationships that served to bind political configurations together, but which also ensured that the resort to violence was always personally mediated through the ruler. Likewise, the dignitaries that ran the kingdom at the provincial and local levels were composed of privileged families that had close, often family, ties to the ruler. This made the feudal state a collection of separate political entities that, in theory, owed allegiance to a common monarch. Thus, political organization in the feudal era was dependent on the relationship between the ruler and his/her warriors, as indeed was the access to formalized political violence. These relationships were largely forged through the deployment of violence, and maintained through the use of violence. Thus these relationships were, in effect, little more than a de facto military organization, which, in virtue of its capacity to impose its will, exercised political control through the use, or threat of, violence. Thus in a feudal system, war, violence and political arrangements were mutually implicated (Poggi, 1990: 35).

In this period, however, there were no standing military organizations, and when armies formed they were constituted for the sole purpose, and duration, of dealing with a specific issue. A key aspect of this political control was the manner in which the ruler would subcontract control over particular territorial domains to other nobles and lesser dignitaries, often called vassals. These vassals formed an elite group within the social and political order and formed close bonds with the ruler. At the bottom of the social order were the masses; the vast majority of the populace, who although important to the functioning of the system, since they were the means through which economic surplus was generated, were exempted from political influence, and who were seen, according to Poggi, 'as the objects of rule ... never the subjects of a political relationship' (Poggi, 1990: 23).

The lesser dignitaries (vassals), on the other hand, were always expected to have a relationship of obedience to the ruler, yet not in the tightly defined sense that we understand political authority today. Completely absent from this period were notions of sovereignty, monopolistic authority, nationality or the idea that mutual reciprocity governs relations between states. This period of state development can be characterized as a system of loosely structured personal, or familial, relationships, which, taken together, formed a social and political hierarchy with high levels of instability. Authority among these relationships was overlapping, and there was no source of sovereignty as we might understand it today. Indeed, divided authority might be a better way to think of this political structure (Anderson, 1974: 149; Bull, 1977: 254). Such a political structure was inherently unstable and the relationship between rulers and vassals was prone to regular periods of collapse in which the vassals were able to deploy their own resources against the established feudal authority (Pierson, 1996: 43).

Hence this was an exceptionally fragile political system, always susceptible to the emergence of open dissent, revolt and warfare; not only among those within the relationships, but there was also the continual possibility of conflict with neighbouring feudal regimes. Many disputes that did emerge in this period revolved around competing claims to exercise political rule over areas of territory on the fringes of the embryonic state (Tilly, 1990: 4–5, also Ch. 2). The fragmentation of the feudal political order was also heightened by the claim to authority emanating from the Church, which represented a major challenge to the political rule of the feudal lords (Pierson, 1996: 43).

Such a fragile political system was always prone to collapse. In particular, the relationship between the ruler and the vassals had a structural tendency to create political conflict. Rulers simply did not possess, or have the means to acquire, enough resources to control large expanses of territory. As a result the rulers had no other choice but to relinquish territory to the vassals in return for their support in military campaigns and the maintenance of order. Moreover, low levels of technological development and poor communications systems also meant command and control procedures were difficult to implement. In addition, vassals were required to equip and train their own followers for the practice of war, the defending and policing of the territory, the administration of justice and local implementation of the ruler's policies. But whilst each vassal was meant to perform these activities on the ruler's behalf, the vassals' possession of their own resources, such as territory and military potential, ensured that they enjoyed a considerable amount of autonomy themselves. And these fragmented relationships went all the way down, with many other vassals themselves unable to control the territory they had been awarded and hence themselves, rewarding those below them with the same privileges.

This multi-tiered and fragmented political structure was reliant on the vassals meeting their obligations to the ruler, and vice versa. If an individual failed to meet their obligations, the ruler would need to possess the means to act against them, and in general, this could only be achieved through the use of, or threat of, violence. Often rulers would punish delinquent vassals by forcibly reclaiming the territory that had been granted to them and often passing the territory on to another, perhaps more trusted, vassal. In many cases this was often a close family member of the miscreant vassal. This meant that structurally, even familial relationships were filled with distrust (Bloch, 1989: 134–44).

Structurally, then, the feudal system was filled with potential problems. The reliance of the ruler on the vassals to exercise control over large parts of the ruler's territory effectively meant that they did not control such territory themselves. Indeed, although each vassal was expected to maintain an autonomous military capability in order to fulfil their obligations to the ruler, in effect, this meant that they could use such capability against the ruler, if they so desired. The fragmented and multi-levelled structure was also prone to competing rivalries amongst the vassals as they tried to gain favour with the ruler. Moreover, communication in such a system was extremely difficult; roads and transport links were very poor and literacy levels very low. In addition, the economy was heavily reliant on agriculture, which is itself, of course, reliant on the possession of land. Thus territory was the primary source of economic wealth, since no vassal could afford to be deprived of his land, given the way it was inextricably linked to his military power, and hence, when given the opportunity, each vassal would grab extra land in order to increase his economic wealth and therefore military power. This ensured that there were large incentives for all vassals to be constantly vigilant for opportunities to appropriate adjoining territory. Finally, the strong personal bonds that had existed between ruler and vassals disintegrated over time, particularly given the short life expectancy and the manner in which control of territory was passed down through families; the heirs of the original vassals often felt little or no allegiance to the rulers. An added structural problem was that of religious interference. Church institutions crossed territorial boundaries and provided a sense of commonality and shared purpose that was a direct threat to the ruler's authority. In fact, church interference in political affairs was to remain a constant problem for all political leaders until the treaties of Westphalia in 1648 formally enforced a clear distinction between affairs of state and religious matters (Bloch, 1989).

In the final analysis, such a system could only survive as long as ambitious and ruthless rulers could prevail and overcome the vested interests that ran contrary to their own ambitions, and insofar as they could inflict decisive defeats against other rulers with whom they were in competition. That is why the feudal system might best be characterized as a military/political institution, not a political institution with a military capacity. The structural logic concerning the relationship between territorial control and power at the heart of the feudal system inevitably resulted in an ever-increasing attempt to exercise control over a larger and larger territories; but this very attempt was to be constitutive of the systems' failure. At the level of ideas, the shared understandings necessary for the maintenance of any social system were not well developed in the feudal era, and there was certainly no body of formalized or codified rules in any consistent form. Equally, specific material developments, such as increasing urbanization, the building of roads and increased transport and communication links would eventually lead to the emergence of new forms of political organization.

But perhaps most important in terms of understanding the failure of the feudal system was the fragmented nature of the ownership of violence. As long as violence was controlled by many different political entities, it was an inevitable that violence would be used to settle disputes and/or attempt to stop any political leader gaining preponderance in terms of their ability to exercise violence.

The Polity of Estates

The next phase in Poggi's account is that of the 'polity of estates'. Increasing urbanization and changing patterns of trade had led to new relationships focused on towns and cities. New power centres emerged, many concentrated on commercial interests, rather than the ruler/vassal relationship. Interestingly, although these new sites of power did not control violence themselves, they controlled the access to it. The increasing economic requirements of trade necessitated greater territorial reach and this, in turn, required that political and military control be exercised over larger territorial areas in order to secure economic transactions. These newly emerging commercial sites of power inevitably sought political representation of their collective or corporate interests, and they rejected the personal ties that had underpinned the feudal system. In theory, and in practice, these 'estates', as they were known, effectively existed as alternative centres of power to that of the rulers. Indeed, as Poggi puts it, structurally this was a dualistic political system which fundamentally differed from the feudal system in that it was more institutionalized in terms of clear sets of rules governing political relationships and decision making, and in terms of having a more explicit territorial reference (Poggi, 1990: 40–1). In effect, this now meant that the political rulers had to reach accommodations with the new centres of power, and this in turn led to the emergence of differing understandings of political authority and new arrangements to govern political decision making. In particular, a political leader wishing to use violence was largely dependent upon the 'estates' to provide the resources needed to fund violence.

A key aspect of these new centres of power was that they did not represent individual challenges to the ruler, but rather were collections of interests. Each of these collectivities (estates) represented the interests of groups that shared things in common. These might be the noblemen of a particular rank, the residents of a town, the members of a parish, or those bound together through engagement in a particular trade. Collectively, the estates represented a more abstract and wider territorial entity than that governed by the ruler, and he/she was entitled to rule only insofar as they upheld the customs and interests of this wider body.

In practice, this meant that the ruler was forced at regular intervals to convene the estates of a given territory into a public gathering, since only by appealing to such a gathering and becoming involved in its deliberations could the ruler jointly, with the estates, determine policy. Such gatherings were always governed by an explicit, and often sophisticated, body of rules. The outcome of such gatherings represented the struggle for the power between the estates and the ruler. This was a fundamentally different kind of political structure than that of the feudal era. Under a feudal system, the ruler was under no obligation to explain his policy demands to anyone, let alone seek prior approval of them; under the polity of estates, on the other hand, the ruler was compelled to justify and articulate the grounds of his claims.

Again, however, at the heart of the 'polity of estates' are war and violence. The main rationale for any ruler to convene the estates was to raise resources for the purpose of waging war. Yet there were no guarantees that his/her demands would be met, and the ruler needed to justify their requests in terms of the publicly recognized interests of the estates. Thus the appeal for resources to wage war had to be based on more than the interests of the ruling dynasty and needed, in some way, to represent those of the land itself and its people; as represented, of course, by the estates. The structure of power in such a system is dualistic, with both rulers and estates duplicating, in many instances, the apparatus of power, officials, courts, finances, and in some cases even their own armies.

This dualistic power structure came under increasing challenge as levels of literacy and increased learning led to questioning and public debate over the contrasting claims of rulers and estates. Although force would be the ultimate arbiter of such disputes, each party had an interest in articulating its own claims as convincingly as possible in order to operate as a collective body of like-minded individuals. The later phases of the 'polity of estates' were a protracted and sophisticated series of intellectual arguments over the proper arrangements for political rule, which would eventually lead to the modern articulation of sovereignty. The key principle of sovereignty is that law and order can only be maintained within each given territorial domain, and that one source of power alone possesses the distinct prerogative to make and unmake law and exercise exclusive control over coercive force. What brought matters to a head over this issue were the religious wars on continental Europe and revolutions in England and France. These events brought into focus the potential costs of a country not possessing a centre of unchallengeable, ultimate power before which all others must submit; an idea, of course, that was brilliantly articulated in Thomas Hobbes's *Leviathan* (Hobbes, 1946). At the core of this belief is the view that such a centre of power must represent a distinctive set of interests of a political nature and not be embedded within familial or commercial relationships.

One important aspect of this argument for the purposes of this book is the manner in which the pursuit of specifically political interests, or the interests of state, slowly began to be acknowledged as existing outside understandings and constraints of morality and law; and hence the source of such political power can lay claim to legitimately use unrestrained force and premeditated violence. As Hobbes was to put it, the legitimate scope for dissent against the state was extremely limited. In this respect, the sovereign state emerges not as a guarantor of specific rights and moral claims, but as the origin of order; order was a necessary condition for moral universes and forms of community to emerge; and order could only emerge if violence was controlled and concentrated in one institution (Hobbes, 1946).

From the Absolutist State to the Modern State

There are many reasons as to why the estates eventually acceded to the demands of the sovereign, which led to the emergence of what is known as the absolutist state. David Held provides a lengthy list, including peasant rebellions against taxation; the spread of trade, and market relations; changes in technology, particularly military; the consolidation of national monarchies; religious strife; and the struggle between Church and State. In the face of all of these problems, and the social upheaval that emerged as a result of these problems, the notion of absolute sovereignty became increasingly attractive (Held, 1992: 83). Poggi refers to this as the era of the absolutist state and argues that it is the first major institutional embodiment of the modern state

(Poggi, 1990: 42). This argument is not universally accepted. Indeed, in his influential study Giddens argues that for all the changes that emerge with the absolutist state, it is still best characterized as a traditional state, not a modern one (Giddens, 1985: 93). Thankfully we do not have to settle this argument here, and following Christopher Pierson, I think it safe to say that the absolutist state is a transitional form (Pierson, 1996: 45). However, this issue does demonstrate the importance of rejecting the idea that historical periods are discrete.

If anything, what clearly differentiates the absolutist state from the polity of estates is that power, and the use of violence in the absolutist state, was now becoming concentrated and centralized in one source. Perry Anderson argues that absolutism was a redeployed apparatus of feudal domination (Anderson, 1974: 18). Whilst there is something to this argument, it misses some fundamental differences between feudal political systems and the absolutist state. In particular, the absolutist state, by definition, only allows one locus of power and authority. In the absolutist period the monarch and his/her court became established as the sole centre of policy formation, and alongside this development a new administrative system was constructed, which bypassed the state-based system and connected the centre of political rule with the country at large. In France, in particular, this became the dominant political form. This is best articulated through the words of Louis XV in a document of 1766, in which he forthrightly rebutted the claim to autonomous power of the courts:

> In my person alone resides the sovereign power, and it is from me alone that the courts hold their existence and their authority ... authority can only be exercised in my name ... For it is to me exclusively that the legislative power belongs ... the whole public order emanates from me since I am its supreme guardian ... The rights and interests of the nation ... Are necessarily united with my own and can only rest in my hands. (quoted in Held, 1989: 104)

Given such a declaration, it is little wonder that eventually, the French state would take over effective control of its armed forces; a process that had begun, but was not completed, during the reign of Louis XVI. Another aspect of the centralization of power in the absolutist state was the role of the royal court. The court functioned as a symbolic centre of power and the construction of opulent palaces was a symbolic manifestation of this power. The 'court' also as served as a site of political power to nobles drawn towards the status and economic rewards court attendance could bring; to be excluded from court was to be excluded from the exercise of power, both political and economic. Conversely, of course, attendance at court tended to loosen the ties between noblemen, and the subjects of their particular regions. Attendance at court, moreover, tended to introduce heightened senses of competition amongst the noblemen as they competed for the king's attention and favour.

With the emergence of the absolutist state also came other social and political changes that were to form the basis of the modern state. Anderson identifies five: a standing army, a centralized bureaucracy, a systematic and statewide taxation regime, a formal diplomatic service, and state regulation of commerce and economic development. These institutional developments clearly become important elements, albeit in drastically enlarged forms, of the modern nation state. Yet, as a transitional state form, Anderson is right to highlight the ways in which these institutional arrangements were also deeply embedded in residues of the feudal system, even if they differed from that era in important ways. In particular, although standing armies were to become the norm, they were not of the form we would understand them today, and were largely dependent on foreign mercenaries as opposed to conscription or volunteers (Percy, 2007). In absolutist states, standing armies did not resemble the highly professional standing armies of the modern state. Equally, positions within the bureaucracy could still be based on family ties and taxation was largely seen as a source of funding for wars, when necessary. Nonetheless, the apparatus of state that began to emerge in the absolutist era was orientated towards controlling the means of violence, and ensuring that the resources needed to engage in violence were available.

With the centralization of power that the absolutist state embodied came increased demands for territorial integrity that could only be met if states could agree on territorial boundaries, and on where judicial competence and control ended and began. In short, it was becoming increasingly apparent that individual states existed as part of an international system of states that had as its core principle the notion of sovereignty; understood now as the universalized acceptance of the legitimacy of all states and the belief that all states could exercise control over their own territory and populations, and that no one state has the right to universalize its own administration or law at the expense of other states.

The importance of the emergence of sovereignty cannot be overstated, and whilst it is certainly true that there had been expressions of the principle prior to the absolutist era, it is really in the writing of Hobbes that we find the first fully articulated statement of the necessity of the absolute power of the sovereign. In terms of IR this newly emerging international order displayed many important features. Crucial among these was the principle of non-intervention and the possibility of a resort to war if sovereignty was violated. Indeed, for Anderson, the permanence of international armed conflict was one of the essential features of absolutism (Anderson, 1974: 428–31). War and interstate violence were structurally necessary components of a system that was rapidly attempting to come to terms with a new political order. War between absolutist states was often fought between standing armies that grew increasingly larger in size. And as armies expanded war became big business (Porter, 1994: 11–15). And big business required ever-larger states. Hence the demands to wage large-scale war required that states took over ever-increasing elements of social life. Thus what we see in the modern state system is the outcome of a state-making contest, with the winners reigning supreme and the losers largely forgotten.

Another global aspect of the absolutist state was the manner in which territorial entities outside the European heartland of the sovereign state were forced to engage with it. Rulers of absolutist states recognized that they existed within a system of states, yet this system was not truly global. When confronted with absolutist states, political communities outside this system were forced to confront it on its own terms (Anderson, 1974: 397–431), often being forced to adopt its norms and procedures, and often becoming, quite literally, subjects of its will. Eventually, and more often than not through the use of force, these political communities began to take on the European state form. This is an important point in terms of understanding contemporary international terrorism. The forced imposition of the Western state form onto communities not embedded within Western norms and understandings of politics has left a global residue of resentment that is now emerging as a distinctive political challenge to the form of secular politics at the heart of the modern state. Nowhere is this potential conflict clearer than in the issue of the role of religion in the state.

The absolutist state set in place a movement that would lead to a strong separation of politics and religion. Up until the treaties of Westphalia the Church had always effectively functioned as an alternative source of power, identity and loyalty in political life. The accommodations reached in the 1648 treaties explicitly set out to ensure that this religious interference in political affairs was to end. Of course, it did not happen overnight, and the success of secularism has been varied. Nonetheless, and despite the close relationship that still exists between Church and State in many societies, there has been a widespread acceptance of the norm that official church interference into affairs of state was no longer admissible (Smith, 2008).

There is some disagreement as to the extent to which absolutism functioned effectively in Europe. Anderson (1974), for example, argues that quite a few monarchs achieved high levels of control over their territory and populations, while Roger Mettam (1988), on the other hand, disputes the validity of the concept. According to Mettam, most of those rulers labelled absolutist exerted no greater power over their subjects than any other rulers; in short, the rhetoric of absolutism was not matched by the reality. Whether the absolutist state was ever effectively able to rule all aspects of social and political life is, in many respects, beside the point. What is undeniable is that the move to absolutism was to radically alter the power configurations within and between states (Kimmel, 1988; Wilson, 2000).

Nowhere is this more evident than in the relationship between the state and its own citizens. Absolutism essentially revolved around the claim that jurisdiction within a given territory was absolute and that no external interference in the internal affairs of any state would be tolerated (Kimmel, 1988: 13–16; Wilson, 2000). Of course, in practice, this principle was, and is, regularly violated, particularly by the more powerful states, who have regularly interfered in the internal affairs of other states under the guise of acting in defence of the interests of their citizens. Moreover, the principle of non-intervention was not universally extended to those political communities outside Europe which were simply denied political community status as European powers sought to colonize the globe.

In this context, another important issue to keep in mind is the distinction between legal sovereignty and empirical sovereignty; or the difference between the claim to be sovereign and the capacity to act in a sovereign manner (Krasner, 1999). States might be sovereign and might be recognized as sovereign, but without the means to carry out their programmes, the actual exercise of power might be quite feeble. Yet even if the ability of absolutist states to act in a sovereign manner varied widely, one of the most important aspects of absolutism was the manner in which it clearly represented an attempt to increase the capacities of the sovereign. Some of the structural changes that began with the rise of absolutism and which are now integral to the modern state were new forms of bureaucratic organization, increased modes of communication, and a developing apparatus of surveillance and control. All of these constituted a set of overlapping technologies of social control that effectively increased the structural power of the state and allowed for greater control of populations (Foucault, 1977). In many respects, this was a process of the state gaining ever more control over its own subjects. Under previous political configurations individuals might have had much to fear from the random violence of a despotic ruler, but in general, the individual was invisible to the state and would not routinely be the object of the state's attention. These powers of control and surveillance that began to emerge in the absolutist era became a routine, perhaps even essential, part of the modern state, where every aspect of an individual's life is subject to some form of state interference and control.

This control over populations, however, required resources. All forms of political organization require resources to function, and the need to solve the resource problem has been a central determinant in state development. A major means of increasing resource capacity has always been war. Yet waging war had become increasingly expensive. War requires both men and money, and as technology made war an ever-larger experience states needed to find creative ways to increase the resource base of their economies. Often this was achieved through the appropriation of resources through war, and there is no doubt that this requirement was a major factor in the European colonization process. But the lessons of the 'era of estates' had also been learnt and state leaders began to search for new ways to increase their resource base that was not reliant on the whim of social interests beyond the state. What was needed was a material base that states could draw on independently of the interests of groups within society. To achieve this, states thus began to develop large wealth-generating economies and sustainable systems of taxation (Porter, 1994). To complement this resource base, and at the level of ideas, what was needed was a discourse orientated around the concept of state interests; hence the notion of national interest; itself reliant on the notion of the nation (Anderson, 1974). As such, the most successful states tended to be those in which capitalism was most fully developed alongside well-embedded notions of the national community.

The relationship between war, capitalism and state-making is brilliantly articulated in Tilly's account of state development (Tilly, 1990). According to Tilly, the process of 'state making' consists of three elements; eliminating external rivals, neutralizing internal opposition and extracting resources from the population. War plays a fundamental role in this process, tying the three elements together. In essence, Tilly's argument is that war making helped create strong states because it increased the extractive capabilities of states. In order to fight large-scale wars in Europe states needed to demand greater taxation from their populations. Moreover, because the protection that the state provides is afforded to all people within a state, war created a justification for the extracting of resources from all the populace; if protection was to be afforded to all then all could contribute. Thus, war helped to expand the scope of the state and the burgeoning state apparatus needed for it to operate. War making and tax collection also required increases in the size and form of bureaucratic structures needed for states to function (Porter, 1994; Tilly, 1990). Alongside these developments were also increases in the strength and size of the political, judicial and economic systems within the state. Thus the imperatives of war and the existence of external threats created an ever-expanding apparatus of the state. War and external threat also helped to create social cohesion within states. The threat of an 'other' outside the state had the effect of creating unity within the borders and strengthened the legitimacy of the state. People began to think of themselves in terms of national identity, and loyalty began to lie in the concept of the nation state. As Émile Durkheim argues, 'great popular wars rouse collective sentiments, stimulate partisan spirit and patriotism, political and national faith ... As they force men to close ranks and confront a common danger, the individual thinks less of himself and more of the common cause' (Durkheim, Thompson and Thompson, 1985: 76).

Thus, out of the absolutist state system came many features characteristic of the modern state. In brief these were: control over the means of violence, control over a well-defined territory, acceptance of sovereignty, a large bureaucracy, an expansive and ever-increasing taxation system and an increased ability to wage large-scale war. One other major characteristic of the modern state that also emerged during the absolutist system is the idea that the state is something that goes beyond any person or individual in whom it is embodied. Governments, presidents and prime ministers may come and go, but the state persists. This seems ironic when one thinks of absolutism, which in some respects seems to epitomize the idea of personalized rule. Yet despite the oft-cited claim of Louis XIV: '*L'État, c'est moi*' ('I am the State'), a more accurate account of the state/monarch relationship comes from that articulated by Louis on his deathbed: '*Je m'en vais, mais l'État demeurera toujours*' ('I depart, but the State shall always remain'). Thus, even in absolutism it was clear that the monarch was in a singular position at the apex of a particular form of political organization that no longer represented his/her own personal or familial interests, but those of a larger and more abstract entity, the state.

Another aspect of the modern state already anticipated in the absolutist period is the commitment to constitutionalism, and the belief that government should be conducted according to clearly established laws and that all participants should respect certain rules of the game. Obviously there is some tension between the idea of absolutism defined in terms of absolute sovereignty and the absence of external interference and the constitutional principle of limited government. Yet even in the European centre of absolutism some states had already embraced a limited form of constitutionalism; Holland and the UK, for example (van Gelderen and Skinner, 2002). But equally, forms of strong absolutism also persisted in Eastern Europe after it had ceded to a much more constitutionalist set of procedures throughout most of Western Europe; which only goes to highlight again the warnings about the problems of historical periodization made earlier.

One other key aspect of the modern state when compared to prior state forms is its sheer size. States used to be many and small; now they are few and enormous. The twentieth century, in particular, saw a rapid increase in the size and scope of the state. Mobilization for total war had a dramatic and lasting impact on the size of states and their capacity for extraction. Robert Higgs refers to a 'ratchet effect' in which the high levels of extraction required by mass warfare are never quite abandoned once the immediate military necessity has passed (Higgs, 1987). The twentieth century also saw a transformation in the deployment of this public expenditure, with ever-increasing sums of money spent on those areas of social provision that have come to be identified with the welfare state. Much of the remarkable overall growth in state expenditure in the twentieth century can be attributed to the growth of this social budget. As recently as a hundred years ago, states consumed little more than 10 per cent of their gross national product. Today, in some states, more than half of the national economic product is consumed by the requirements of government. Patterns of employment have also been transformed, and public servants came to be numbered in their millions and governments became major employers in most countries as the state took an increasingly active part in the management and sometimes ownership of the national economy. Even where such intervention was limited, the role of the state as a large employer, big spender and guarantor of the national currency gave it a preponderant economic role. Thus the modern state is increasingly managing and shaping its constituent population across all sectors of their existence. The modern state involves itself in the most intimate details of its citizens' day-to-day lives in a way that would be unrecognizable to the subjects of prior forms of state.

Yet the growing relationship between state and society has not all been one-way, and in modern liberal-democratic states citizens are afforded opportunities, and even the right, to protest. Citizens also have resources that enable them to negotiate, albeit on very unequal terms, with the state. The most benign account of the state–society relationship stresses the increasing accountability of the modern state to an empowered citizenry. In its most positive version the argument suggests that what is distinctive about the modern state is that it is democratic. What justifies, indeed mandates, its greater social intervention is the fact that it is the expression of the will of its people. Upon such an account, the state is subject to the collectively expressed will of society; in fact, according to the theory of democracy, the state is the expression of the will of the people (Conkin, 1974; Mostov, 1992). Although this argument is perhaps a little naïve, and neglects the violent history of the state, it is a fact that modern states in the developed world have taken a broadly representative democratic form based on nations of popular sovereignty.

This cannot be claimed for most modern states elsewhere in the world, however.

Conclusion

The modern state, then, has a distinctive form that marks it out as clearly different from prior forms of state. It has emerged as a specialized apparatus of power and a set of institutions of domination distinguishable and separate from the particular person or group who happens to control the state at any one time. The state, then, is not the government. The state is a sovereign body, in the sense of a set of complex institutions, superior to and different from the mass of citizens, hence it is a set of institutions above society. These institutions have a specialized set of functions, and claim a monopoly of those functions, laying down the rules for the wider society. Thus the modern state aspires to set the terms on which it deals with all other associations and subordinate groupings.

Although the state is an apparatus of domination it is important to realize that this apparatus has different branches or sections. Most states have a representative assembly, a government or political executive, a bureaucracy, the military, police and the judiciary. Thus the state is best understood as a differentiated set of institutions; differentiated both internally and externally and separated from society. The state is the supreme sovereign power deciding the rules of social life and the terms on which other groups and institutions in society can compete and exercise their own power. Different theories of politics give contrasting answers to this issue, but there can be no doubting the significance of the power possessed by the state elite; in effect, those who control the modern state. The concern to limit state power has led to attempts to introduce checks and balances on state power. Of course, for Hobbes, there could be no checks on the power of the state, for the very significance and meaning of 'sovereign power' resides in the fact that it is supreme and uncontrolled; since nothing less will suffice to maintain order and prevent a war of all against all.

Another key aspect of the modern state has been the link with nationalism. The term nation state is often considered to be synonymous with the modern state. Most nationalist movements hold the idea that the state and nation should coincide. Each nation, however that term is defined, should have its own state and, by the same token, the state should rule over and express the common interests of the members of a relatively united nation. Thus the modern nation state involves an apparatus of coercion (the state) and a group of people having certain historical and cultural features in common. In practice, of course, very few states have met this norm, and it is often minority groups within nation states that have formed a breeding ground for protest, and sometimes even terrorism against the state. For if the state is not seen to represent the interests of all of the groups within society then it is clear that some would want to challenge its legitimacy. For the modern state is not merely a territorial association, it is also a membership organization, and if people do not wish to be members of that association and perhaps set up their own state to represent their own interests, then the state might be subject to challenge. By the same token, the modern nation state not only brings together citizens but also excludes others from becoming citizens. The modern state, then, bases itself on the idea of a national group and a nation ruling itself and it is the institution or set of institutions appropriate to the task of national security and national defence.

As a set of institutions orientated around coercion and control we can talk about state power as being exercised by human beings. But the state itself does not exercise power. The modern state, as an apparatus of power, requires a body of people whose sole task is the exercise of state power carried out in accordance with certain rules. Weber, among others, concentrated on the bureaucracy in this respect but it is fair to say that state power also manifests itself in the military, security and judiciary. The modern state has also assumed an ever-wider range of tasks and functions. The expansion of the role of state went hand in hand with a growth in the administrative apparatus necessary to achieve state aims. Thus Marx could write: 'the executive power possesses an immense bureaucratic and military organisation, an ingenious and broadly based state machinery, and an army of half a million officials alongside the actual army' (Marx and Fernbach, 1973: 237).

The modern state has expanded its functions and increased the number and also the powers of the state elite, and thus has to be understood in terms of a vast and differentiated administrative structure. This raises a question concerning this vast machinery of state domination: is the state a body that is over and above society and independent of social pressures, or does it represent the interests of some groups within society over and above others? Obviously, views about this question will vary depending on particular circumstances of individual states, but there are a range of theoretical positions that attempt a generic understanding of the relationship between the state and its people.

What is clear, however, is that the state was born out of violence and developed its distinctive capacities through the use of violence. States are not neutral mediation mechanisms through which the conflicts in society flow, but rather, are historically configured responses to past conflicts that represent the outcome of those struggles. As such, if they do mediate conflicts in society they do so in ways that reflect the history of those struggles. That we in the supposedly 'developed' world seem to have reached a broad consensus on the legitimacy of this process, and its outcomes, should not lead us to assume that others must accept our view. Moreover, the fact that the European state model was largely violently imposed on the rest of the world through imperialism and colonization should be evidence enough that others might find the outcome of these processes unacceptable. There are many ways such views can be expressed, but in some circumstances those objecting might decide that violence is their only option. Given the place of state violence in constituting and maintaining this order, states have no legitimate right to deny others a recourse to violence in order to redress perceived wrongs. What we can object to, however, is the form that violence takes. And when it turns to terrorism – the deliberate targeting of non-state actors – we should reject it completely.

2
The Modern State

In this chapter, I examine the modern state; its form, modes of operation, functions and processes. The aim is to provide an account of the modern state that is broad enough to be meaningful across the vast terrain of global politics today, but one that is also sensitive to the particularities of different states in different places and that can situate differing forms of protest against it. It may be the case that no such overarching account of the modern state is possible. After all, the diversity of state forms across the globe would suggest that such a description of the state could only be constructed on the basis of downplaying, or denying, the differences between states. Even if we can talk about such a thing as the modern state, the different forms that the state has taken throughout the world demand that we approach its theorization with a degree of humility. Notwithstanding these caveats, however, there is no doubt that although having emerged in Europe, the modern state form has now been universalized throughout the world (Spruyt, 2002). Moreover, an understanding of state theory helps locate those sites of contestation around which protest against the state coheres. Any political moral or ethical judgement against, or for, any kind of protest in opposition to the state must rest on some account, or theory, of what the prevailing dynamics of that state are, as well as some account of how alternative forms of political organization might be structured. Hence, in order to situate protest against the state we need a clear account of what it is that is the subject of such protest.

Which account/theory of the state we adopt, then, has a crucial bearing on how we assess the validity of forms of protest against it. Given the deeply charged political nature of the modern state itself there are a range of theories that attempt to explain how state power, both in its coercive and consensual forms, is operationalized. These different theories play a crucial role in determining whether protest against the state is deemed to be legitimate or illegitimate. Hence, political protest, in any form that is waged against a repressive state, is often viewed in a positive light, whereas protest against a state that is largely deemed to rest on democratic principles is largely deemed to be unacceptable. Nothing illustrates this relationship better than the events in Egypt in 2013 that led to the overthrow of the Mohamed Morsi regime (30 June 2012–3 July 2013). The debate immediately following military intervention was structured around whether we had witnessed a 'revolution' or a 'military coup' (Al Jazeera, 2013). This was a judgement that could only be made on the basis of some account of the legitimacy of the Morsi regime. Those that supported the regime claimed that the action of the army was a 'military coup', whereas those who did not support the regime saw it as part of a legitimate peoples' revolution.

Hence, the legitimacy of the state is integral to any judgement of the legitimacy of the protest; and this is a judgement that requires a historical framework. The chapter begins with an examination of the role that violence, and in particular war making, has played in the development of the modern state. I then outline the three main theories of the modern state before providing a sketch of my own account of the state embedded within the critical realist assumptions detailed in the introduction. In short, a comprehensive analysis of the state must take into account all five levels of social activity (the material, intersubjective understandings, social relations, positioned practices and the level of individual subjectivity).

Violence and the Modern State

In this section, I briefly discuss the specific role that violence has played, and continues to play, in the modern state. As argued in the previous chapter, the development of the state was a process that led to larger, yet functionally diverse, units of political, economic, fiscal, judicial and legal institutional forms. These institutional forms play a functional role in the maintenance of the state; security, legal, administrative, juridical, and so on. It is in this sense that we can talk of the state as a 'complex institutional ensemble' (Jessop, 1990: 366). The growth of this institutional ensemble was largely, although not exclusively, achieved through the use of violence, and it developed out of the need to deploy that violence in the domestic and international arenas. Of course, this is not to suggest that only violence, and in particular war, was the only factor in state development. Economic production, the influence of the global system, internal political dynamics, and cultural forces, as well as other factors, have all played a role in state growth and development. Nonetheless, this book is concerned with the violent aspects of the state. Moreover, the importance of violence to the process of state development is underscored, given that the claim to be the legitimate source of violence is often considered to be intrinsic to any definition of the modern state (Weber, 1965).

There is no doubt that as the state grew ever larger its capacity to engage in violence also grew (Porter, 1994). Or to put this another way: as competition at the international level necessitated ever-increasing levels of violence, even if only as a potentiality, the state was forced to expand its remit into all aspects of social life (Porter, 1994: 11–22). The state was forced to encroach on ever-increasing areas of domestic political and social life in order to monitor and control its population, but also to extract the resources needed to prepare for, or engage in, war.

Technological advances and changing political configurations enabled violence to be used more effectively, more efficiently and with the explicit support of subject populations; a process that was accelerated with the advent of nationalism and notions of popular sovereignty (Gellner, 2006; Hobsbawm, 1990; Smith, 2001). Moreover, with the advent of democracy the use of such violence was deemed to be legitimate insofar as it rested on the support of the people. Over time only state violence was deemed to be legitimate. But this was not always the case, and throughout the history of state development many groups claimed the right to use violence (Tilly, 1985: 173). In the modern state, however, only one source of violence is deemed to be legitimate, although the privatization of security, and the increasing use of private security organizations in conflict zones, are interesting developments and perhaps can be said to represent a return to a more medieval framework of political control over the use of violence

(Percy, 2007). However, these groups only operate insofar as they receive explicit recognition from states, hence states still ultimately decide how the non-state security firms can function and where (Tonkin, 2011).

Charles Tilly identifies four activities that come under the heading of state violence:

1. War making: Eliminating or neutralizing their own rivals outside the territories in which they have clear and continuous priority as wielders of force.
2. State making: Eliminating or neutralizing their rivals inside those territories.
3. Protection: Eliminating or neutralizing the enemies of their clients.
4. Extraction: Acquiring the means of carrying out the first three activities – war making, state making, and protection. (Tilly, 1985: 181)

Tilly argues that it is important to see that these four functions overlap to varying degrees. In particular, the relationship between state making and protection is complex insofar as a population might be divided into competing classes, and the state, potentially at least, may partially favour one class over another. In such cases, state making can involve reducing the protection given to some groups within the state at the expense of other groups. In this sense, for Tilly, the state is not neutral in terms of its standing across parts of its population; internally the state provides more protection to some groups than others. All four state functions depend on the state's ability to monopolize the means of coercion, and they are linked and often mutually reinforcing; an increased ability in one area reinforces state capacity in others. Thus, for example, a state that is able to maintain high levels of domestic control through the elimination of internal competition increases its capacity to extract resources and wage war.

The use of violence to serve these state functions has produced differentiated forms of political organization and modes of control. War making, for example, has required armies, navies and supporting services, and instruments of surveillance and control within state territory. Protection, on the other hand, relied on the organization of war making and state making, but with the advent of democracy has added to it an array of mechanisms through which the protected could hold to account the institutions providing the protection; notably through the media, elections, courts and representative forms of government. Resource extraction from populations to fund war also brought increasingly complex fiscal and accounting structures into being. To the extent, for example, that a government invested in large standing armies, then the bureaucracy created to service the army was also likely to become bulky (Porter, 1994: 58–61).

Finally, the cost of providing protection for populations grew exponentially with the range over which that protection extended. The size of government varied directly with the effort devoted to extraction, state making, protection, and, especially, war making. Clearly, war making, extraction, state making and protection represented differing aspect of state development; nonetheless they were interdependent in important ways. Hence, the organization and deployment of violence accounts for much of the characteristic structure of the modern state (Giddens, 1985; Porter, 1994).

Warfare, and violence, then, both internationally and domestically, would appear to be central to the development of the modern state; both in terms of efforts by the state to preserve (and at times increase) its territorial integrity, and its domestic legitimacy and control. Internationally, competition among states was largely driven by insecurity and vast amounts of capital and resources were, and still are, needed to enable a state to be secure. All states needed at the very least to prepare for the possibility of war to secure their territorial boundaries, even if such preparation was only intended to act as a deterrent. In turn neighbouring states, feeling insecure at their neighbours' war preparation, would also need to arm; a vicious circle of insecurity often referred to as the 'security dilemma' (Booth and Wheeler, 2008).

Another reason for states to maintain fully equipped armies was the potential leverage this could give them in negotiations with other states. The ability of a state to secure and/or extend its boundaries was dependent upon the resources available to it and its ability to extract these resources from the citizens of that state; manpower, weaponry, foodstuffs or finance. As the state got larger the need for resources became greater. Hence, boundaries needed to be extended in order to increase resources. These structural forces driving state growth in Europe led inevitably to colonialism, in most cases itself imposed and sustained through the use of force and violence (Doyle, 1986). However, citizens within states were often unwilling to suffer the loss of life or resources required to engage in interstate conflict without gaining some acknowledgement of their sacrifice, and there were many conflicts and rebellions against state demands that the people should sacrifice both themselves, and their economic prosperity, in order to advance the cause of the state – particularly when any given state might seem to be aligned with certain parts of a society and not others. Accordingly, the state required the building of 'administrative, bureaucratic and coercive structures' to control and coordinate their populations. This administrative infrastructure was a major development of the modern state (Weber, Alexander and Parsons, 1964). States' finances and access to resources were dominated by wars, and the development and maintenance of a military capability was fundamental to the development of the state. The objectives of war became more economic and often the need for conquest was closely connected to economic advantages (Croucher and Weiss, 2011; Hobson, 1965).

Industrialization and technological change also played a major role in the development of the modern state. The ability to build ships to transport armies and their equipment around the world gave states the opportunity to colonize mainly non-European countries, in many cases exploiting these countries through the extraction of resources for their own gain (Lenin, 2010; Wallerstein, 2004). As the European states expanded and their capacity to extract the resources necessary for warfare grew, so their ability to organize and finance military power also increased. States that we able to assemble and support standing armies clearly gained an advantage in terms of their ability to undertake and wage war, and hence 'States that had access to large rural populations, capitalists and relatively commercialized economies won out' (Tilly, 1990: 58).

One of the key features of capitalism is its distinctive set of class relations. Industrialization gave rise to the growth of the working classes as many people left the land to live in urban areas and some women joined the workforce. The capitalist economy also created a worldwide division of labour and a global economy in which it became necessary for political structures and states to enter into trade and production relationships on a global scale. The state gradually became increasingly involved in civil society in order to control fiscal policy and secure the income it required to pursue their policies, often of a military nature. The more successful the economic activities of their regions, the more money could be claimed in tax, sufficient to maintain their own interests. There was also a need to regulate the developing capitalist economy if the state was to be protected; hence banking and other financial institutions were established. However, at the same time, civil society was becoming involved in the state, and powerful groups of capitalists and the upper classes hoped to influence the state to act in their interests. These elite groups in society had long had political representation, often denied to others – women, for example – but the needs of the capitalist world created new demands.

Democratization is another major factor in the development of the modern state and would appear to be a direct consequence of war making. In many ways it was the price the state had to pay to maintain its ability to wage war. Men [*sic*] were no longer prepared to go to war, leave their families, pay taxes, even lose their lives without some concessions. More demands were made on the people to meet the ever-increasing costs of war and they believed they had a right to have some input into government, or at least be entitled to the franchise, which up until that time had been restricted to the upper echelons of society. State populations began to feel part of a political community, and in these conditions representative democracy became established in many countries. This resulted in the public legitimatization of the modern state. As its military, organizational and coordinating functions grew and it relied increasingly on the cooperation and support of the people, it was able to claim that its actions were popular and/or democratic, and thus it became possible to align the state with the people. This was an important symbolic move as it fostered a belief in state constituencies that this was their state, and not something alien to them, or a political structure that served the interests of some of the population at the expense of others. However, not all states became democracies because of their war-making activities; some became democracies against their will, because they were defeated in war.

In conclusion, there would appear to be no monocausal explanation for the development of the modern state. However, the requirements of warfare appear paramount. The need for states to secure their boundaries and maintain and equip a standing military capability appears to be one of the main reasons for establishing the administrative, bureaucratic and coercive infrastructure that was a major development of the modern state. Capitalism also developed, in part, because of the growing financial requirements of the state and its needs to strengthen and increase its boundaries. However, the development of capitalism may not have been possible without industrialization and technological advances. Capitalism brought in its wake the state's involvement in civil society, and in order that it could control and secure the finances it required to maintain its own interests, often of a military nature, it established financial institutions. This in turn led to civil society becoming involved in the state, with the people wishing to have a greater say in how they were governed in return for giving up their resources, food, taxes and even their lives. The franchise was extended and representative democracy became established in many countries. Thus although there is little doubt that the modern state was formed to a large extent by the requirements of warfare, capitalism and democratization also played a considerable part, and it would appear that these three elements are closely interlinked (Weber, 1978).

In addition to the role of war in making the state, it is also important to recognize that violence, or the threat of it, was intrinsic to the control of the domestic sphere. The violent capacity of states could be turned outwards against external threats, but was also often brutally deployed to ensure domestic order was maintained. These two processes went hand in hand. A state preparing for, or engaging in, warfare had to ensure that domestic constituencies did nothing to jeopardize the war effort. It is normal in modern Western states to assume that the violent aspect of state control of the domestic political sphere plays a minor role. Typically it is often thought that modern liberal democratic states operate through consent rather than coercion (La Boétie and Kurz, 1975). Whilst there is clearly a germ of truth to this argument, it needs to be placed in a wider context that situates the possibility of consent within a coercive horizon of possibility. Modern states do, to a large extent, maintain control over large parts of their populations because those populations consent to state rule. However, states still maintain an apparatus of control that relies on violence, or the threat of it, as an instrument of last resort. Thus, whilst consent may be the overriding dynamic in most situations concerning state control of domestic populations, when consent fails, coercion will follow. Criminals, violent protesters, and those engaging in peaceful civil disobedience are often those who confront this violent aspect of the state in the most direct manner, but the potential of the state to unleash violence remains behind every act of consent. Coercion and consent, then, are mutually reinforcing, but it is state violence that will be deployed in the last instance, if all else fails. Police forces, security agencies, legal systems and penal organizations, all to a varying degree, rely on populations being aware of this aspect of state control.

Liberalism and the Neutral State

Although the modern state was born, developed and became sedimented in the social field primarily through the use of violence, its violent history (and potentially violent present) are largely subordinated in contemporary theories of the state. State violence, although an ever-present threat and structurally written into the very nature of the state itself, is not, primarily at least, the dominant form of control in the modern state. State elites, political leaders and groups in power seek to secure their relative positions through a process of legitimation. Social and political power in most modern social systems is effective because the majority of those subject to the wielding of power feel that it is right for them to obey. For this reason, all power holders seek to secure the legitimation of their power; if only because this enables them to continue to govern with limited use of the apparatus of physical coercion.

The more consent that can be manufactured the less coercion is required. In most liberal democratic states, people obey the law not because they think they will be put in prison if they refuse to obey, but because they are committed to the laws of the state. This does not mean that they are committed to every law and every application of it, but they are committed to the 'rule of law' itself; a rule ultimately backed up by the potential use of force by the state. But from where does this commitment come? Generally, citizens within a state embrace the rule of law because they accept that those in power have a right to command; and that the government has a right to command because it has achieved a position of power through the application of, and adherence to, certain agreed procedures. The power of political elites is embedded in rules that give them a legitimacy that would be lacking had power had been obtained through force or other forms of violence; a military coup, perhaps. In the modern state this legitimacy is derived from the belief that those in positions of authority derive their power from the people (Ochoa-Espejo, 2011). In the modern state, on the other hand, political power does not depend purely or exclusively on coercion or consent but also on processes of legitimation; there is no consent unless there is legitimation. Political elites attempt to achieve the consent of the governed generated through elections and other mechanisms that serve to symbolize and reinforce their legitimacy. These can range from the outright exercise of power, a belief in the divine right of kings, or, as in the modern state, beliefs about democracy. Absolutist systems sought to ground this legitimation in the divine right of kings (Figgis, 1914). In the modern state, on the other hand, most political units have come to seek legitimation in terms of the idea of popular sovereignty. Of course, there are various ways in which this can be achieved, and who the people are is a question that can be given various answers (Ochoa-Espejo, 2011: 58–83).

Fascist systems that emerged in Europe claimed that the people meant only those of a particular race, or ethnic purity (Eatwell, 1995; Griffin and Feldman, 2004). Communist systems, on the other hand, were dominated by the leading role of the party, which also sought legitimation on the basis of ideas of popular sovereignty (Kase, 1968; Triska, 1969). In communist states the people are the workers and the party is composed of workers in a supposedly classless society. Running the sole political party, however, was a political elite drawn from the working class, often known as the vanguard (Lenin, 1960: 347–530). This vanguard was to keep in touch with the people through a variety of forms of participation that were controlled and structured from above. The communist party claimed that its power was derived from the people who were the workers (Farber, 1990; Fischer, 2012). Liberal democratic states, on the other hand, claim to have a superior system by claiming that political participation is unrestricted by exclusions on the basis of race, class and gender; in effect, universal political participation. However, even in democracies this 'universal suffrage' was often the result of reform processes aimed at holding back revolutionary forces (Przeworski, 2009). Nonetheless, exclusions re-emerge in liberal democracies in terms of citizenship; those denied citizenship are denied political participation (Faulks, 2000: 29–54).

Liberals, and pluralist approaches, tend to adopt what I will call a 'neutral view' of the state. According to this approach the state is conceptualized as an arena in which political conflicts are mediated. The state, for liberals, is in essence a neutral arena that facilitates, monitors and controls political discourse; as such it has no political stake in that discourse. It is in this sense that the state itself can be said to be 'neutral'; which particular political party controls the state is simply the outcome of the democratic process (Galston, 1991: 79–97). Of course, in specific circumstances particular liberals can hold either negative or positive views of the state (Giddens, 1998; Nozick, 1974). On the negative side, liberals have always worried about a monolithic and overbearing state sovereignty that infringes on the rights of the individual (Nozick, 1974). For these liberals the fear was a society in which the state functioned as the sole centre of power exercised over individuals. Taken to extremes, liberal fears about a strong state can lead to anarchism, where the idea of a state is rejected outright (Bakunin, 1971; Kropotkin, 2002).

To guard against too many incursions of the state into the private lives of individuals, liberalism generally holds that within the state there should be a separation or division of powers so that the state does not constitute a monolithic bloc exercising power in an unrestrained manner (Campbell, 2004). State power must be divided and subject to checks and balances. Furthermore, state power must be responsive to pressures from the various interest groups of the wider society, and in some respects the state, for liberals, can be seen as an organization that answers to the pressures expressed by certain groups of various kinds. As such, the state is a neutral arena where political conflicts are worked out. According to this theory, the state is that body which takes and implements key decisions but its agenda is set by the demands emerging from the wider society. Citizens organize and mobilize through parties and pressure groups and seek responses from the state. They also seek to affect the allocation of resources, gain access to policy decisions, and in general, influence the policy-making process in ways that ensure their interests are taken into account. The state itself, however, has no interests of its own beyond mediating the conflicts, according to a well-defined set of rules and procedures that arise from the competition among groups within the state. State elites and managers are meant to act in a responsive mode according to the strength and intensity of demands emerging from the society, and not in terms of the vested interests of any one group.

This theory presents the state in a relatively passive light. The state is thought to be a relatively neutral and impartial arbiter that allocates resources in response to the pressures from competing groups within society. Many liberals (and conservatives) aim to cut the state down to size and prevent the emergence of a strong state that corrodes the economy, society and personal freedoms. In many respects this view of a minimal state (Nozick, 1974) is representative of American political culture, where there is a long history of distrust towards Federal state interference in local affairs. In Europe, on the other hand, the tendency, particularly since the Second World War, has been to embrace a more comprehensive and social democratic view of the state, one that provides more resources for individual citizens, but which, in exchange, also implies more interference in and control of their private lives. One the key problem for any liberal account of the state is how it deals with diversity while maintaining a degree of unity, and at the same time ensuring that society is prevented from fragmenting into a situation in which there is no representative or common interest. The state plays a key role here and is invested with the function of maintaining the consensus, of keeping unity and enforcing certain rules of the game. The state is also responsible for the task of deciding which interests are legitimate and which should be responded to; which should be ignored and which suppressed. In this sense the state remains the supreme judge and a neutral arbiter of the validity of different interests that clamour for recognition (Macpherson, 1977: 93–114).

This idealized view of democracy has some serious flaws. In a liberal democratic political system, governments are formed by one or more political parties who have particular programmes and particular policies developed in accordance with their stated ideology or worldview. In other words, given that a particular party forms a government and hence controls the state then the state apparatus is not necessarily a neutral one. Some interests may well be responded to more positively than others; some will be ignored. In this way the state, once captured, is anything but neutral; it is a machine for enforcing particular interests. Liberals would respond to this problem by suggesting that, while the neutrality of the state is compromised to the extent that a particular group forms the government and steers state power in particular directions, the partiality of the state is minimized because of the very nature of contemporary liberal democratic political systems. Equally, the neutrality of the state is enhanced by the fact that the state is not a single institution. There are various dimensions of the state apparatus and checks and balances control the powers of the ruling party. Secondly, liberal systems involve competition between ruling parties and an opposition that challenge those in power to justify their policies in representative assemblies. Thus, the liberal democratic state is said to allow elements of an opposition to challenge the policies of the government.

Elite Theory

An alternative view of the state has often been referred to as elite theory (Mills, 1957). Elite theories of the state can be contrasted with the liberal view. Elite theory emerged towards the end of the nineteenth century, as a challenge to the progress and claims of both democracy and socialism (Pareto, 1963: Ch. XI; Pareto, 1968). In its broadest sense elite theory can be put very simply: it asserts that in all societies, past, present and future, the few will always rule the many. Elitism maintains the inevitability of minority rule and hence it effectively denies the possibility of popular sovereignty. There are, of course, differences in how specific theorists conceived of this form of rule. Gaetano Mosca, one of the original theorists of this approach, emphasized the ways in which minorities gain an organizational advantage and are hence able to outwit majorities, and argued that political elites usually have a certain 'material intellectual or even moral superiority over those they govern' (Mosca, 1939: 51). For Wilfredo Pareto, on the other hand, in a society with truly unrestricted social mobility, an elite would emerge among the most talented and deserving individuals. However, this was only a theoretical possibility; in actual societies, the elite would not emerge out of talent, but political acumen, power and cunning. Thus, for Pareto, elites would be those most adept at using the two modes of political rule, force and persuasion. In general, these would be those that also enjoy important advantages such as inherited wealth and family connections (Pareto, 1963: 2031–4). Robert Michels believed that elites were rooted in the functional requirement of organizations for leaders and experts in order to operate efficiently; as these individuals gain control of funds, information flows, promotions and other aspects of organizational functions, power becomes concentrated in their hands (Michels, 1966). Weber, on the other hand, believed political action is always determined by 'the principle of small numbers, that means, the superior political manoeuvrability of small leading groups' and that in 'mass states, this Caesarist element is eradicable' (Weber, 1978: 1414).

Democracy in its pristine form can never be achieved, according to elitist state theory. Popular aspirations to power could never be fully realized and state control and access to state resource was always going to be only accessible to a few. People might think they lived in a democracy, but they were fooling themselves. According to elite state theory, a minority group would always monopolize the effective exercise of power (Michels, 1966). Elite theory asserts that beneath the surface appearance of democratic diversity there is a single power elite that exercises effective political control. For the elitists there is a basic division in all societies between the elites and the masses, and it is a theory that sees the power structure of society as dichotomous. At the top is a ruling group, who can be considered a governing elite, a ruling class or political elite (Mills, 1957: 3–29, 269–7). Elite theory stresses the different capacities of individuals and insists that in every field of human activity, including politics, some will be more skilled than others. In politics, as in any other activity, there will be elites who exhibit particular abilities in the skills and capacities needed to gain and hold on to political power. In any political system, whatever the justification for their position, the political elites will have a grip on power. This elite group is to be distinguished from the non-governing elite, the minority or minorities of those who excel in other non-political dimension.

Thus for elitist state theorists, democracy is a façade or sham. The idea of democracy is a means by which the elite group seek to hide from the masses. Democracy is something unattainable, or a justification for rationalization that serves to mask the true facts of the situation (Mills, 1957: 18, 298–324). Thus in the elitist perspective the emergence of a political leadership group is inevitable because of the inescapable differences in human capacities, or the ability of minorities to manipulate circumstances to their own advantage. The gap between the elite and the masses is a constant factor of all social and political formations. Since democracy can never be realized, the flow of power goes from the top to the bottom as the controlling elite are able to control the agenda of politics and take the initiative in decisions. C. Wright Mills (Mills, 1957) refers to what he calls the 'power elite', a minority of people occupying top positions in the state apparatus and outside it, linked by a common consciousness of shared interests and power positions. Some sections of this power elite may be elected; others, like top civil servants and military leaders, are appointed.

Elite theory does not suggest that the masses are always without power. In a representative system, for example, their wishes may to some extent be taken into account by the political elite, and indeed a stable political system will be one where elite groups do precisely that, if only for their own self-interest and preservation. Nevertheless, the masses are spectators rather than players in the political game and the initiative flows from top to bottom, even if those at the bottom, to some degree at least in a representative system, have their wishes responded to. One major problem of elitist theory is that it provides no real account of how elites emerge. Recourse to a natural division of labour embedded in human capacities is unsatisfactory. Moreover, the overarching image of this theory is that of an elite group of political actors manipulating and controlling the political system, hence it places far too much stress on individual capacities rather than structural imperatives. Robert Putnam's work can be considered as an attempt to get around these concerns, by moving the focus away from a political elite to a technological and/or administrative elite that exercises power. According to Putnam, 'If the dominant figures of the past hundred years have been the entrepreneur, the businessman, and the industrial executive, the "new men" are the scientists, the mathematicians, the economists, and the engineers of the new intellectual technology' (Putnam, 1976: 384).

Marxist Views of the State

An alternative, although related, view of the state comes from Marxism, which highlights the deeper structural patterns that produce political systems. Marxists generally adopt a negative attitude towards the state. Although in practice communist states such as the Soviet Union and China did seem to grow ever larger and control all aspects of society, Marx and Engels ultimately envisaged the achievement of a society free from what Marx saw as the redundant nature of the state; 'the communist revolution, which removes the division of labour, ultimately abolishes [*beseitigt*, removes] political institutions' (Marx and Engels, 1964: 414). For Marx the state is seen as an instrument of class rule – an apparatus of class domination – and in a classless society there would be no need for the state. The modern state is viewed by Marxists as a centralized and complicated apparatus growing ever more stifling and interfering. This is nicely encapsulated by Marx, who stated: 'the centralised state machinery which, with its ubiquitous and complicated military, bureaucratic, clerical and judiciary organs, enmeshes the living civil society like a boa constrictor' (Marx, 1870: 1). It is also a capitalist state (Jessop, 1990).

The state is, therefore, certainly not viewed as a class-neutral agency performing tasks of common social interest. Marxists recognize that societies have some common tasks that need to be fulfilled, and these are realized through an institution (the state) which is superimposed on society, and exists to maintain a system of class power. The common social tasks required for the maintenance of the workers are taken out of the hands of society and carried out by the state. This organization is not class-neutral or impartial but exists in the context of class power that it is the state's purpose to maintain. The Marxist view of the state is thus in sharp contrast to the liberal view. Liberals tend to view the state as a necessary evil whose purpose is to secure individual rights, including notably property rights, and whose power has to be restricted. The Marxist view, on the other hand, sees the state as the guardian of property rights, of class property, but also as a necessity only in class-divided societies. Marxists deny that the state is a neutral agency for policy formation, and its primary function is to secure the interests of one class and repress those of another. Hence, the state is an apparatus that maintains class rule through repression and coercion, against those who challenge the power of the ruling class. This does not mean, however, that force is the only means through which the state power operates. We also have to consider the power of ideology. For example, the ideology of the liberal democratic state disseminates the belief that all citizens counts for one, and no more than one. Of course, from the point of view of universal suffrage this might be right, but the control of the state is not only achieved through the electoral process.

The state is superimposed on society as an apparatus that is separate from society and relatively autonomous from civil society. Hence Marx was critical of the view that the state represented a universal common interest over and above the antagonisms of civil society. In a Marxist view the state could never entertain this universality despite its autonomy from society, because it was still a representative of class interests and not of a common or general interest (Barrow, 1993). However, some Marxists, such as Nicos Poulantzas, reacted against this supposed simplistic understanding of the state within Marxism (Poulantzas, 1978). Most Marxists believed that the state was essentially an instrument to be used in the service of the ruling and property-owning class. Poulantzas, on the other hand, argued that the capitalist class was simply too focused on the short-term pursuit of profit, and hence the idea that the ruling class deliberately orientated themselves towards the controlling of state power was fanciful (Poulantzas, 1969: 70). However, Poulantzas did not reject outright all elements of the Marxist account of the state. His argument was that the state was 'relatively autonomous' from the capitalist class, but that its primary function was still to oversee the efficient operation of the capitalist order (Poulantzas, 1973: 143). As such, even on Poulantzas's modified view the state still benefits the capitalist class over other groups in society. Hence, for Poulantzas, a divisive system such as capitalism could produce social stability and continue to reproduce itself over the long term (Poulantzas, 1978: 73). Moreover, capitalism was enabled in this process by the emergence of nationalism, which enabled the system to obscure, or even overcome, the class divisions generated by inequality (Poulantzas, 1978: 26).

Hence, even if relatively autonomous from society, there remains a crucial link between state power and class power; the two are not the same, but the former is the means of ensuring that the latter endures over time. Those individuals who hold and exercise state power may indeed have a certain independence from the dominant ruling class, but this relative independence is still inhibited by the class structure and the economic power of the ruling class. The concept of relative autonomy is useful to help understand the way in which the holders of state power are not simply puppets of the ruling class, but also to demonstrate that the state is not just directly controlled by them either. In this respect, state leaders are still constrained by the structure of economic class power, even if they are not themselves part of that class. It is for this reason, according to Poulantzas, that even if political parties seemingly aligned with the workers gain control of the state, they are nonetheless determined to end up reproducing the system rather than fundamentally challenging it (Poulantzas, 1978: 56, 233, 238).

Marxists also recognize that states can have differing forms, and hence the liberal democratic state is simply one of the many forms the modern state could potentially take. Often referred to by Marxists as a form of bourgeois democracy, the liberal democratic state is differentiated from authoritarian forms of state such as fascism or military dictatorships. Likewise, Marxist state theory does not deny the significance of the rights and liberties that are so fundamental to liberal versions of the modern state, and there is no doubt that, forced to choose, most Marxists would prefer liberal democratic states to authoritarian forms of state. Thus, just because all states are constructed along class dynamics, it does not mean that the distinctions between differing forms of capitalist states are of no importance.

These theories of the state form an important starting point in understanding how protest against the state emerges. There are others, of course, that I have not considered – feminist theories, for example. But these can usefully be incorporated to a varying degree under the frameworks already developed here. The crucial point is that the theory of the state that is embraced can radically alter the perspective on the forms of protest that are deemed admissible.

A Realist Institutional Theory of the State

Setting aside for the moment questions of whether we can view the state as an instrument of class control, a neutral arena for the resolution of political differences, or a space in which differences can be aired, we might first ask: what is the state? Indeed, is there such a thing as the state? This is a question that has troubled political philosophers (Bosanquet, 1899; Willoughby, 1896) for some time, but which international rlations scholars, apart from some notable exceptions, seemed to have collectively resolved not to address (Hobson, 2000). The reasons for this neglect are embedded within the positivist assumptions that have dominated the discipline until recently. There are two main aspects to how the state is treated in IR. First, it is often considered to be a totality defined in territorial terms and encompassing everything within that territory. Hence states, on this reading, are synonymous with the entities pictured on a map. Typically included in this account of the state are a well-defined territory, a population, military/ security forces, a structure of governance/administration and a bound economy. In effect, this account of the state treats it as a black box, or a container that encompasses everything contained within it. In addition, this unitary state is also considered to be an actor with a well-defined set of interests. This is a very simplistic account of what the state is, but it does have the benefit of allowing the discipline to identify its key unit of analysis. Yet this account of the state has not been without its critics, and it is clear that even if only for analytical reasons this account of the state is simply too broad, and acts as a barrier to the analysis of the complex interplay of elements that make up the state. Moreover, on such a reading of the state it is clear that there is no requirement to deal with and differentiate between individuals and/or groups within the state. Few would argue that this is a realistic account of the state, and this account is normally supplemented by some additional caveats.

In particular, it is commonplace among positivists, or methodological individualists, to treat the state as a synonym for the government, or the group of individuals that control the state. David Easton takes this view. Insofar as we can refer to the state it is either the officials that comprise it, or it is little other than a metaphor, or, as he calls it, a 'ghost in the machine' (Easton, 1981: 316).

From a totally differing theoretical perspective, Erik Ringmar suggests that although the state 'may consist of all kinds of bureaucratic structures, institutional mechanisms and other body-like organs', these need not concern us (Ringmar, 1996: 452). For the only reality of the state we can have contact with is a succession of metaphors that are then constructed into a 'narrative concept of the state' (Ringmar, 1996: 441). As Ringmar puts it:, 'we as subjects are nothing more and nothing less than the stories we tell and that are told about us' (Ringmar, 1996: 452). Thus the state, for Ringmar, appears to be nothing other than a story which we tell ourselves and through which we live our lives. Cynthia Weber takes a similar view, arguing, in a phrase reminiscent of Easton's, that '[t]he state is a sign without a referent' (Weber, 1995: 123).

Contra this, however, the scientific realist ontology that I adopt allows us to escape the empirical, linguistic and conceptual ontology to which Weber, Ringmar and Easton are wedded and incorporate non-observable entities into our theories. In fact, while we can only know of the state by its effects and through the observation and interpretation of the concrete practices and organizations of government and the process that constitute what Easton calls the political system, the theoretical concept of the state is necessary in order to *explain* these phenomena. The concept of the state thus refers to an underlying social structure that is real but not empirical, nor merely linguistic, or conceptual. We cannot observe it, though we can experience its power through the activities of its officials.

As an underlying social structure, however, it is important to differentiate the state from other elements in the social field, but also to consider its component parts. In particular, the state is not the same as the government. The government is that aspect of the state that governs the state. However, governments can and do change while the state remains essentially the same. Hence, in democracies electorates can vote in a new government, but we would not consider this to be a new state. In addition, governments are essentially composed of groups of people, whereas people, resources, ideas, and various functional organizations and institutions constitute a state. The state is also not the same as the territory it administers, or the people that are said to be part of the state. The state is best considered to be a complex ensemble of institutions that provides a range of goods, resources and services within a well-defined territory for a well-defined group of people.

Recent attempts to rethink the state within IR theory have been a direct consequence of the intrusion by sociologists into the sovereign territory of IR (Evans, Rueschemeyer and Skocpol, 1985; Giddens, 1985; Halliday, 1987). Although this burgeoning literature is important, it ultimately fails to address the ontological status of the state, and more specifically, whether or not the state can be considered an agent. This issue is important since it relates to the definition of terrorism I will defend in Chapter 4. In short, I intend to argue that the state is a structure that displays agential properties, but that these properties can only be mobilized by human agents empowered by state structures to act in certain ways. Thus a given state, due to its structuring in a certain way, would, on this reading, constitute a structure with a certain set of powers derived from its constituent elements and organization. A state, then, can be considered a structure constituted out of many structured organizational entities and institutions, which are themselves structured in certain ways. That is to say, that the organizations and institutions which (in part) constitute the state stand in complex relations, hence are structured into a certain form. The entities that stand in these relations are ontologically varied and encompass both material and social aspects of existence. And, of course, given the sheer complexity of the modern state it would be very difficult, if not impossible, to say that all aspects of the state operated in the service of a particular class interests. However, because any particular state is itself located in a wider structure composed largely of capitalist economic relations, then ultimately at least we can see how, whether intentionally or not, the state does serve some interest over others.

Within a given state one could identify economic organizations and institutions; political organizations and institutions; ideological organizations and institutions; cultural organizations and institutions, and so on. And whilst not all of these could be said to be explicitly organized towards the maintenance of particular class interests, the very history of the state and its embeddedness in a capitalist economic order ensure that state interests are always the interests of some or other party. In part, these organizations and institutions, as well as the social groups and individuals that inhabit them, will have different components, but in large measure the same components related differently. And it is the totality of this structured ensemble that is the state. Moreover, when protest against the state emerges it is these specific institutions and the individuals that occupy places and roles within them that should be the proper focus of dissent, and perhaps violence. These state agents, then, are legitimate targets for insurgent groups, but once these groups begin to attack non-state actors they have moved into the terrain of terrorism.

Even accepting this, however, there are still many outstanding questions relating to the state. Is the state a political subject, an organism, or a machine? Is it a social relation that reflects divisions within society, or a forum for the negation of political conflict? Should we define the state in terms of its legal form, that is, as a 'legal person'? Does the state have moral responsibilities? What are the most important aspects of the state, its coercive capacities, its institutional and/or organizational composition and boundaries, or its place within the international system, or society of states? How are we to understand the relationships between the state and law, the state and politics, the state and civil society? Can the state be studied on its own, in isolation from both the domestic and international conditions of its possibility? To what extent is state power autonomous from the flows of power within the wider social field? What are the sources and limits of state power? Clearly, answers to these questions are important, although equally clearly, they are beyond the scope of this book. But there are some things we can say of the state.

The state is a 'structured organizational and institutional ensemble'; it does not and cannot exercise power. It is not a unified subject that possesses the power to exercise power. Rather than talk of the power of the state we should refer to the various state capacities inscribed in it as an institutional and organizational ensemble (Jessop, 1990). How far and in what way such powers are actualized will depend upon the action, reaction and interaction of specific agents. In short, the state does not exercise power, but facilitates the exercise of power by agents. The powers of the state are only ever activated through the agency of structurally located political actors located in specific structural conjunctures. It is only these agents who bring into play specific powers and state capacities that are inscribed in particular state institutions that act.

Marx argues that the state is a 'real-concrete' object, formed through 'the concrete synthesis of multiple determinations' (Marx and Engels, 1967: 100). However, insofar as these complex multiple determinations will necessarily consist of organizations and institutions they will also be dependent upon the practices and discourses of those agents whose practices constitute those same organizations and institutions through which the state is constituted as a 'concrete object'. This is the 'duality of practice'. It means that the state is also, to some extent, constituted as a changing discursive object of discourse and is best considered, not only as a 'real-concrete' object, but also as a 'product-in-process'. Hence, in common with most social objects, the state has a dual existence; it has both its concrete form and its discursive form. Therefore there will never be a moment when we achieve a full account of the identity of the state.

The sheer complexity of the state is derived, in part, from its placement and function in society. That is, the state is only one of many institutional orders in any given social field. But modern states also play a major role in the legitimacy and maintenance of social order, which provides the structural framework in which non-state institutional orders function. Hence, the state guarantees the legitimacy of the institutional order, which, in turn, guarantees the legitimacy of the state. Thus, although the state plays a unique role in a given society, it is not simply one institutional order among others. The state is the pre-eminent institutional order. But there are significant areas of overlap between state activities and other institutional orders. Equally, differing institutional orders have differing structures, and they each have their own mechanisms and organizations through which they maintain their own institutional order and influence other institutional orders. Thus, although playing a role in all of these institutional orders, the state may not enjoy direct and unmediated access to them. However, where elite membership of the various institutional orders overlaps to a significant extent, then state officials may be able to play a direct role in non-state institutional orders, and managers of non-state institutional orders may be able to exert a greater influence on state projects.

The fact that the state is a 'complex institutional and organizational ensemble', constituted in and through material resources, state practices and discourses and differing structural configurations, and is endowed with political responsibility and recognized as a juridical subject, does not entail that it is a moral or psychological subject capable of independent action. It may be possible to argue that the 'reason of state' becomes so deeply internalized by state officials that they orientate their actions totally in accord with this 'reason of state', such that it forms an essential part of their identity. In such circumstances, one might begin to talk of the state as a collective subject, or individual. I would reject this, not only in virtue of the sheer complexity of the state as a complex institutional and organizational ensemble, and thus to talk of this collective subject is really only a reference to part of it (the state officials), but also because this portrays state officials as mere throughputs; machines, that is, whose actions are totally determined by this 'reason of state'.

Thus, and to reiterate, the state, as a complex institutional and organizational ensemble, can only exercise power insofar as its structural imperatives are realized in the practices and modes of thought of state officials. The state cannot exercise power independent of those agents that act on its behalf. How far and in what way such powers are realized will depend upon the action, reaction and interaction of specific social forces located within and beyond the complex ensemble. In short, the state does not exercise power, but constrains and/or enables embodied agents to act. It is these agents who activate the specific powers and capacities of the state inscribed in particular institutions and organizations.

Because of this, it follows that these structural powers and capacities and the manifold ways in which they are activated cannot be understood by focusing solely on the state. Thus the state appears as a complex ensemble of competing forces that offer unequal chances to groups within and outside the state to act for differing political purposes. Bob Jessop is correct to highlight the manner in which the state displays an element of 'strategic selectivity', wherein some groups benefit from the particular form of a given state to the detriment of other groups. In this sense the state is 'strategically selective' (Jessop, 1990: 367). Equally, although the state does have its own distinctive resources and powers, and although these are never activated in the absence of agency, it also has distinctive liabilities that emerge due to its need for resources that are produced elsewhere in the social field.

Thus the state cannot be examined in isolation from the domestic and international system, or society, in which it is constituted. The state must be related not only to the broader political system but also to its wider social and cultural environment. This should not be taken to imply that the state has no distinctive properties and can therefore be derived from, or reduced to, and explained independent of, other factors and forces in the social field. For as an emergent entity and structure the state is still characterized by its distinctive structural make-up that endows it with a unique set of powers, properties and liabilities. In this very limited sense it may be possible to talk of state rationale, or 'reason of state'. However, this 'reason of state' should not blind us to the fact that the state remains only one part of a complex social field and therefore must be related to this wider social locale. The state can only be understood by examining the emergence of individual initiatives to develop and/or safeguard collective projects. Agents, after all, are agents of something. This also means that the attempt to explain international phenomena in terms of isolated levels of analysis is flawed. The international emerges out of the social, not the domestic; hence the analytical dividing lines drawn around the state provide an illusory picture of simplicity in a complex world.

Late modern societies, in particular, are incredibly complex and differentiated such that no element or structural principle could be said to be 'determinate in the last instance'. Nor could any one structure form the apex of a singular hierarchy of command whose rule extends everywhere. If there is a global political system its logical form would be heterarchical, even if this was not the actual form in which it manifested itself (Donnelly, 2009: 64–6).

Finally, it is clear that the state functions can only be fulfilled insofar as embodied agents feel predisposed to carry out those functions. Equally, the state is also a site of political practices that seek to deploy its various institutions, organizations and capacities for specific purposes, and this invokes human agency; although, of course, that agency is itself dependent upon the structural resources and context within which it is embedded. Rather than attempt to define the core of the state in *a priori* terms we need to explore how its boundaries are established through specific practices within and beyond the state. As such, the state is not a unified, unitary, coherent ensemble or agent, but an ensemble of institutions that, taken together, collectively constitute the state.

What the above discussion implies is that states are emergent structural phenomena that are themselves subject to various and conflicting structural principles. This suggests that the contingent structure of the state cannot, *pace* state-centred approaches, be defined independently of the state projects, if any, which happen to be particularly hegemonic or dominant at any given moment. There is never a point when the state is finally built within a given territory and thereafter operates according to its own fixed and inevitable logic. Nor is there ever a moment when a single state project, even war, becomes so hegemonic that all state officials will simply follow universal rules that define their duties and interests as members of a distinct governing class. For no matter how often constitutions and international law declare and attest to the unity and sovereignty of the state as a juridical subject, there are always conflicting patterns of relationships within states, and hence the ever-present possibility that protest against the state might emerge.

In terms of a consideration of terrorism, two things follow from this approach to the state. First, whilst never a unitary actor, and accepting the fragmented nature of state agency, it is clear that all the institutions and structures of the state are complicit, to varying degrees, in facilitating state projects. Moreover, and depending on the particular structural configurations that make up individual states, it is clear that the complicity of each state institution (executive, judiciary, military, social welfare, etc.) will also vary. This issue will have a bearing on how legitimate we consider attacks on certain state institutions to be. In a highly fragmented state structure it may well be the case that certain state institutions are in opposition to state projects not supporting them. Nonetheless, even if this is the case, it can only be decided on a case-by-case basis and the theoretical possibility of attacks specifically targeted against state institutions and agents is an act of war, not terrorism.

Second, although state projects are dependent upon, and only possible in, particular structural and institutional frameworks, those institutions are embodied through the practices of human agents. Moreover, state agents within state institutions are differentially located, particularly in terms of their power to shape both the projects of the specific institution, and the contribution of that institution to shape the larger state project it is a part of. Thus just as states are fragmented to varying degrees, then so are state institutions. This means that the responsibility of all of those state agents pursuing state projects is not equally spread. Nonetheless, since those agents are agents of that state institution, and insofar as that institution is contributing to a state project that some might object to, then if those objecting to that project determine that violence is the only option, state agents all the way down may be considered legitimate targets. This does not mean that they 'are' legitimate targets. But it does mean that the test of their status needs to be determined. However that is decided, on the account I will develop in the following chapters it would not be terrorism. Collateral damage, perhaps, maybe even justified casualties of a conflict. But given the place of violence in constituting and maintaining the state, the state agents involved in the maintenance of the state might well be legitimate targets of action against the state, even if that action is violent.

Conclusion

The modern state, then, is a complex ensemble of institutions that are designed to fill the functions of that state. The state is not the government, it is not the nation and it is not synonymous with a given territory. States occupy and control a given territorial domain and the population resident in that territory, but states are not the same as the people. Nor are states the same as the government. The government, or regime, can be considered as a control centre for the state. But the state is the complex of institutions and organizations that governments control on behalf of the people. Although the particular configuration of individual states varies, all states use violence as a last resort in order to control their territory and populations. Even if this violence is not actualized at any given moment, the possibility of its deployment acts as an effective form of deterrence and control.

How one views the legitimacy of this recourse to violence on behalf of the state affects one's judgement of differing types of protest against the state. In an authoritarian state that rules through the use of brutal repression, it seems natural to support those that protest against their subjugation. Yet whatever the attractions of representative democracy, it remains a blunt tool for dealing with differences in society. Our attitude to protest against the state is dependent upon our views of that state, and its policies and its historical constitution. Nothing demonstrates this better than reaction to the state of Israel, which for many people is a state that promotes its democratic credentials at the same time as it brutally suppresses the Palestinian people. Israel, of course, would claim that its treatment of the Palestinians is necessary to ensure its security. We do not have to settle this dispute here, or even come to a position on it. What matters is only that this example startlingly illuminates how any moral judgement of protest against the state can only be made through an analysis of that state, its history, constitution and practices. What is surprising is why the terrorism industry has so far failed to grasp this mutually constitutive relationship of the relationship between violence, terrorism and the state.

3
Political Dissent

In this chapter, I address the issue of both violent and non-violent protest against the state, concentrating on 'civil disobedience', but situating this in the context of 'legal protest' and more radical and violent forms of political action. However, by violent forms of political action I do not yet mean 'terrorism'. Not all forms of violent political protest are 'terrorism', and it is important to differentiate between different kinds and modes of violence. This is particularly necessary in the post-9/11 world, where the term terrorism is deployed in a wholly inappropriate manner by states, the media, publics and academics. In Chapter 1, the state was seen, inter alia, to be a site of institutionalized and legitimized violence. It is also, of course, at least when viewed historically, a mechanism for the appropriation of resources, populations and territory. Thus, this expansionary state project had clear winners and losers; even if in the modern liberal-democratic state it is not always clear that this has been the case. Given this, the question becomes; when is it appropriate for those who feel they have suffered at the hands of the state, or perhaps feel no loyalty towards it, to protest against the state, and by what means?

Terrorism is only one possible response. But the use of such political violence is almost universally abhorred, and there are very few overt defences of the deployment of terrorism as a legitimate, and morally acceptable, means of redressing political grievances. No one wants to own the label (terrorism); yet everyone seems to want to deploy it. If we consider terrorism to be a form of political protest, and we consider political protest in terms of a continuum, then we may ask the question as to whether there are other forms of protest that might legitimately be deployed against the state. For it is clear, given the close relationship between the state and violence, that it is not violence itself (pacifists excluded) that we find wholly objectionable. As we have seen, violence is embedded within the state, and even though in most modern states consent is the primary mode of social control, violence is still the ultimate, and last, resort of the state when challenges to its pre-eminent social position emerge. We react negatively to violence even as we accept the necessity of it in certain circumstances.

Yet is violence is the most appropriate form of protest, or even the most effective? Before we consider the form and scale of violent protest against the state, we should consider if there are alternative forms of protest that might be more legitimate, morally more acceptable, and perhaps even more effective (Chenoweth and Stephan, 2011). There are various ways in which non-violent protest against the state can be registered, and many of these come under the term civil disobedience.

However, there is considerable disagreement on what civil disobedience is and on how it might be justified (Herngren, 1993). Must, for example, civil disobedience be non-violent, or can it ever take a violent form? Must those engaging in civil disobedience remain committed to the general framework of existing political and legal systems, even though they may be objecting to specific aspects (laws, rules, norms) of that framework? Or to put it another way, can civil disobedience be revolutionary in intent?

Civil disobedience can be contrasted with two other forms of political protest. An extreme form is revolution, which, in a political context, typically involves an attempt to overturn the institutions of the state as a whole, the aim being the replacing of existing structures of authority with an alternative set of institutions, often organized according to an alternative set of political ideals. Revolution usually, although not always, involves political violence – violent acts committed with a specifically political aim. Moreover, revolution can also involve acts of terrorism. Hence in this respect revolution constitutes the wider context within which civil disobedience, lawful protest and terrorism may reside. As such, revolution can be seen as both the process through which political change is achieved, and the end point towards which political protest and action aspire. Of course, revolution is not always the desired end of all forms of political protest, and in some instances the aim of the protesters is simply an alteration in one specific part of the political system; a change in law or policy, perhaps. However, at other times wholesale political change is the desired end and in those instances we refer to it as a revolution (Foran, 1997, 2003, 2005; Goldstone, 1992; Proudhon, 1989).

A less radical form of political action than that of revolution is lawful political protest, which usually involves opposition to a specific law or policy, but which does not involve the breaking of any laws to represent disagreement with the policy. Legal, political protest takes place within the law and is often organized with the full knowledge and cooperation of the state. Civil disobedience lies between these two forms of action in the sense that it is generally more limited in its aims and methods than revolution, but it contrasts with lawful protest on the grounds that it falls outside the law, and indeed, often involves unlawful activity. In practice, the boundaries between these differing forms of political action are often blurred, which is why a consideration of the justification underpinning any political action is necessary. Equally, the validity of any form of protest against the state requires a judgement of the action itself and the political context in which the action takes place. Hence, John Rawls (1971), for example, argues that it is not difficult to justify civil disobedience in an 'unjust regime', but that the situation is more difficult in a 'nearly just regime'. According to Rawls, civil disobedience constitutes a method through which a minority of dissenters can force a majority to reflect upon whether the validity of acts of civil disobedience are in accordance with its sense of justice or not (Rawls, 1971: 333–91).

For now, I will define civil disobedience as those politically orientated acts that are illegal, committed openly and conscientiously within the framework of the rule of law, and with the intention of frustrating or protesting some law, policy or decision of the government. I have deliberately left the issue of violence out of this definition, although inevitably this is an issue to which I must return.

Situating Contemporary Protest

In 2011 *Time* magazine named the 'protester' as the person of the year (*Time*, 2011). Political protest has a long and venerable history, yet the dynamics of protest have changed dramatically with the advent of the internet and as the landscape of global politics has become transformed. The decision to name an unidentified protester as person of the year, and to place an image on the front cover of the December 2011 edition, reflects the momentous influence and scope of protest throughout that year. Indeed, Alain Badiou (2012) has referred to 2011 as the 'rebirth of history'; an explicit reference to Francis Fukuyama's claim that history had ended after the end of the Cold War (Fukuyama, 1992). However, it would be an error to think that the nature of protest had completely changed since the advent of the internet. What has changed is the ability to mobilize and communicate among protest groups, as well as the capability to publicize both the cause underlying the protest and state responses to it. The internet, through message boards, blogs, wikis and social media – such as Twitter and Facebook – has enabled disaffected groups and individuals to enlist support and mobilize protest at a speed and scale unthought of before its advent (Gerbaudo, 2012: 5, 9–13).

The organization of contemporary forms of protest typically emerges in cyberspace and quickly, almost instantaneously, spreads through the process known as 'going viral'. According to Niklas Luhmann, modern protest movements act as if they must defend society against its own political system (Luhmann, 1993: 126–8). As such, appeals from incumbent politicians to 'observe the law', or to adhere to constitutional principles, are often beside the point and often generate more, not less, protest. In many respects, modern protest movements are articulating a different attitude towards the political process, and in some instances their objectives are not embedded within traditional left vs. right forms of politics. Such groups aim to influence the direction of a society, but they are not themselves involved in the pursuit of political power. Of course, in some instances, such as the Arab Spring, control of political power is precisely the issue, but even then many of the protesters are expressing dissatisfaction with the prevailing order through an 'open-ended revolutionary dynamic' that requires a new political vocabulary, rather than engaging in limited attempts to gain control of that power for themselves (Dabashi, 2012: 2, 97; Howard and Hussain, 2013: 103–26). This lack of a desire for political power and control should not, however, be understood as implying any sense of satisfaction with the prevailing political order; if anything, quite the reverse is true. In fact, many modern protesters, and protest movements, express a quasi-anarchist version of politics, believing, as they do, that the current political system is beyond reform (Aragorn, 2012; van Gelder, 2011: 1–12, 51–68).

Political protest shares with terrorism a desire to communicate as much as exercise control; hence the natural allies of contemporary protest movements are often the mass media. Traditional media provide both a conduit for the transmission of the message, but also add their own unique spin onto events, often highlighting, creating and distorting elements of scandal, alarm and urgency, as they seek to maintain or increase their audience share. More importantly, however, new forms of social media allow almost instantaneous dissemination of both the message and coordination of acts of protest. The new social media played such an influential role in protests in Turkey in 2013 that Prime Minister Recep Tayyip Erdoğan declared: 'There is now a menace which is called Twitter. The best examples of lies can be found there. To me, social media is the worst menace to society' (Costanze, 2013). Philippine President Joseph Estrada likewise blamed the 'text messaging generation' for his downfall in 2001 (Shirky, 2010). This seems to suggest, at least in the minds of some political leaders, that the new social media have emerged as a potent political force. As Andrew Sullivan has put it:

You cannot stop people any longer. You cannot control them any longer. They can bypass your established media; they can broadcast to one another; they can organize as never before. It's increasingly clear that Ahmadinejad and the old guard mullahs were caught off-guard by this technology and how it helped galvanize the opposition movement in the last few weeks. (Sullivan, 2009)

What make the new social media particularly effective in this regard are two things. First, they facilitate the rapid and effective formation of groups (Tormey, 2015). Second, they allow the recipients of the message the ability to reply, reformulate and disseminate communications themselves; in effect, even a sympathetic causal observer can become part of the complex communications loop, and in important ways contribute to and change the content of the message. Moreover, the individuals who tap into this system can 'edit' any of the scripts they receive and, in the process, redraft them and resend them as they choose. Thus, involvement at a distance becomes a legitimate part of the protest movement and the dissemination of the message. Contrast this to the tendency of more traditional social movements, who largely attempted to control the process of dissemination and insisted on a uniform account of events and a narrative that was consistent with the underlying ideology of the party or movement, in order to justify a unified line of struggle. Often these more traditional movements are notoriously intolerant of any communication from members that does not conform to the party line.

In some respects, this lack of conformity in terms of message and acceptance of leadership is what differentiates new forms of protest from more traditional ones. The new forms of protest tend to be extremely large in scale precisely because they draw participants who come from various affiliations and who are not expected to conform to any party line on all issues; what unites them is their common commitment to 'this' cause, and this cause alone. As such, modern protesters are difficult to transform into long-term political formations and projects such as parties. Their openness to new supporters of the issue makes membership in the movement precarious and unstable. But this is not to claim that they are incapable of carrying out successful protest, or lack the ability to bring about political change. The mistake of most governments has been to underestimate the seriousness of their demands because of their polycentric character and apparent lack of a unified command to sustain action. All this makes us think of modern protests as a system that is distinct from political movements. They create not so much new political formations as a protest environment that is open to a diverse array of issues. Moreover, the issues are not rooted in any single worldview or ideology, and what seems to unite them is no more than a general disaffection with the existing order.

This raises an obvious question for government around the world: How does the ubiquity of social media and new forms of protest affect state interests, and how should policy makers respond to it? As new forms of technology emerge and the communications landscape gets denser, more complex and more participatory, the networked population is gaining greater access to information, more opportunities to engage in public speech, an enhanced ability to undertake collective action and increased opportunities for the monitoring of state activity (Shirky, 2008). In the political arena, these increased freedoms can help loosely coordinated publics demand change. In some cases, the protests ultimately succeed, as in Spain in 2004, when demonstrations organized by text messaging led to the quick removal of

Spanish Prime Minister José María Aznar, who had inaccurately blamed the Madrid transit bombings on Basque separatists. In Moldova the Communist Party lost power in 2009 when massive protests coordinated in part by text message, Facebook and Twitter broke out after an obviously fraudulent election. There are, however, many examples of activists failing, as in Belarus in March 2006, when street protests (arranged in part by email) against President Aleksandr Lukashenko's alleged vote rigging swelled, then faltered, leaving Lukashenko more determined than ever to control social media. During the June 2009 uprising of the Green Movement in Iran, activists used every possible technological coordinating tool to protest but were ultimately defeated by a violent crackdown (Dabashi, 2011; Nabavi, 2012).

Despite this mixed record in terms of success, social media have become coordinating tools for nearly all of the world's political protest movements (Castells, 2012), just as most of the world's governments are either trying to limit access to them, or use such media as forms of social and political control (Morozov, 2011). Yet, as with most new forms of technology, the implications of the new social media are not clear. There are two ways of looking at it. First, the optimists, such as Clay Shirky (2010) and Paul Mason (2012), view it in positive terms and argue that the political use of 'social media' has the potential to enhance freedom:

> Social tools create what economists would call a positive supply-side shock to the amount of freedom in the world. ... To speak online is to publish, and to publish online is to connect with others. With the arrival of globally accessible publishing, freedom of speech is now freedom of the press, and freedom of the press is freedom of assembly. (Shirky, 2008: 172)

This assumes that new media have predominantly positive effects and have the potential to bring about radical change; 'social tools are dramatically improving our ability to share, cooperate, and act together. As everyone from working biologists to angry air passengers adopts those tools, it is leading to an epochal change' (Shirky, 2008: 304). One the other hand, pessimists, such as Malcolm Gladwell (2010), argue that activists in revolutions and rebellions inevitably risk their lives and risk becoming victims of state violence as a result of their participation in protest. The courage required to face these dangers needs strong social ties and relationships with others in the movement. Political activism involves high risks. 'The kind of activism associated with social media isn't like this at all. The platforms of social media are built around weak ties' (Gladwell, 2010: 45). As such, Facebook and Twitter activism would only succeed in situations that do not require protesters to make real sacrifices. Indeed, according to Gladwell, social media would 'make it easier for activists to express themselves, and harder for that expression to have any impact' (Gladwell, 2010: 49). Social media 'are not a natural enemy of the status quo' and 'are well suited to making the existing social order more efficient (Gladwell, 2010: 49).

Others are even more scathing about the potential for social media to bring about political change. Evgeny Morozov uses the term 'slacktivism' to refer to

> feel-good online activism that has zero political or social impact. It gives those who participate in 'slacktivist' campaigns an illusion of having a meaningful impact on the world without demanding anything more than joining a Facebook group ... Slacktivism is the ideal type of activism for a lazy generation: why bother with sit-ins and the risk of arrest, police brutality, or torture if one can be as loud campaigning in the virtual space? (Morozov, 2009)

For Morozov the notion of 'Twitter revolution' is based on a belief in cyber-utopianism – 'a naive belief in the emancipatory nature of online communication that rests on a stubborn refusal to acknowledge its downside' (Morozov, 2011: xiii) that, combined with internet-centrism, forms a techno-deterministic ideology. Likewise, Jodi Dean claims that slacktivism engenders a form of post-politics:

> Busy people can think they are active – the technology will act for them, alleviating their guilt while assuring them that nothing will change too much. ... By sending an e-mail, signing a petition, responding to an article on a blog, people can feel political. And that feeling feeds communicative capitalism insofar as it leaves behind the time-consuming, incremental and risky efforts of politics. ... It is a refusal to take a stand, to venture into the dangerous terrain of politicization. (Dean, 2005: 70)

There is research that suggests that the impact of social media in major protests is overstated (Fuchs, 2012). However, there are also plenty of examples and anecdotes of its effectiveness. Clearly, more research is needed before we know the full impact of new forms of technology and its relationship to political activism. What is clear, however, is the paradoxical nature of these technological developments. On the one hand, they seem to afford those keen to monitor, expose or criticize state authorities new opportunities. Wikileaks (Beckett and Ball, 2012; Leigh and Harding, 2011; Sifry, 2011) and the NSA revelations from Edward Snowden (*Guardian*, 2013) are powerful examples of the potential of technology to expose state practices that political elites would prefer remained hidden. On the other hand, these examples also demonstrate the immense possibilities such technologies afford state authorities to monitor and control individual behaviour (Morozov, 2011). Irrespective of how we understand these developments, protest itself has a longer history.

A Brief History of Civil Disobedience

Debates surrounding political disobedience have a long history. In a celebrated early example, Crito argued that Socrates should flee prison in order to escape an undeserved, although legitimately arrived-at, death penalty. Jews and Christians persistently disobeyed the demands of Roman law and rejected its claims to supreme authority. Indeed, religious doctrines of various forms have traditionally advanced the idea of passive obedience when confronted with what are perceived to be inappropriate secular demands. Given this, it is perhaps surprising that academic theories of civil disobedience are relatively latecomers to the scene. Until John Rawls explicitly addressed the issue, theories of civil disobedience developed largely out of political practice; key figures in this development are Henry David Thoreau, Mahatma Gandhi and Martin Luther King. It is John Rawls, however, who formalizes these practices into a distinct academic theory of civil disobedience (Rawls, 1971: 361–90).

To my knowledge the phrase 'civil disobedience' was first used by Henry David Thoreau (Thoreau, 1993), who in the 1840s, refused to pay his poll tax. Thoreau intended his withholding of taxes to be a principled symbolic objection to the Federal government's aggressive war against Mexico, its support for slavery in the southern states and what he perceived to be the continued violation of the rights of the native Indian population. Although Thoreau's actions had no immediate impact on these perceived injustices, his ideas were nonetheless a good example of how actual practice can yield theoretical reflection.

The concept of civil disobedience only emerged as a term of academic engagement, and a subject of public debate, in the early 1950s. The Montgomery Bus Boycott of 1955 in the United States represented the beginning of a long struggle by black Americans for equality under the law. Although academic theory has been slow to follow political practice in this regard, there have been some major interventions in terms of our understanding of civil disobedience. The use of non-violence as a deliberate political tactic has been a regular occurrence throughout history. There are many examples of groups using non-violent forms of political protest to challenge perceived injustices (Sharp, 1968, 2012). However, the combination of organized mass protest and non-violence is a relatively new phenomenon.

It originated with Gandhi in 1906 with the emergence of a campaign in South Africa for Indian rights. Gandhi's notion of *satyagraha* – or resistance to tyranny through mass civil disobedience – was first developed and put into practice in South Africa. However, as Gene Sharp notes, Gandhi and his associates were aware of, and influenced by, other non-violent struggles before they adopted such methods themselves (Sharp, 1979: 26). In India, and again, largely under Gandhi's influence, the struggle for independence from British control included a number of successful non-violent campaigns. Perhaps the most notable of these was the Salt campaign during the 1930s, in which 100,000 Indians were jailed for intentionally violating the Salt Laws (Gandhi, 1996: 72).

In Britain the militant campaign for women's suffrage deployed a mixture of non-violent tactics such as boycotts, non-cooperation, property destruction, marches and demonstrations (Pankhurst, 1911). Non-violent civil disobedience was also an important reason in women gaining the right to vote in the United States (Perry, 2013: 126–56) and the use of mass non-violent action in the 1960s civil rights movements changed the face of the American politics forever (Perry, 2013). During a period (1955–68) of sustained protest, acts of non-violent civil

disobedience required a fundamental rethinking of race relations in the US (Perry, 2013: 59–93, 212–46). Some of the most
famous, and successful, forms of protest were the Montgomery
Bus Boycott (1955–56) in Alabama, the 'sit-ins' at Greensboro in
North Carolina (1960) and the Selma to Montgomery marches
(1965) (Perry, 2013). The success of these protests can be measured in terms of the changes in legislation that followed them.
Notable among these are the Voting Rights Act of 1965, that
restored and safeguarded voting rights; the Civil Rights Act of
1964 that declared all US-born people to be citizens and crimi-
nalized discrimination in employment practices based on 'race,
color, religion, or national origin'; the Fair Housing Act, also in
1968, which banned discrimination in the provision of public and
private housing, and which ensured that all US citizens could buy
and rent property (Luders, 2010).

Opponents of the Vietnam War (Hagopian, 2009) also used
civil disobedience in an efficient manner, through the burning of
draft cards and mass demonstrations, such as the 500,000 who
took to the streets in Washington, DC, in 1969. In addition,
sit-ins, the blocking of recruitment centres, tax resistance and the
May Day march of 1971, which led to the arrest of 13,000 people, were also effective forms of communicating dissent (Gottlieb,
1991; Hagopian, 2009: 27).

Formed in Britain in 1957, the Campaign for Nuclear
Disarmament (CND) had initially argued against civil disobedience
or any kind of unlawful action. This position led one of the leaders
of the movement, Bertrand Russell, to resign from the Campaign.
Russell argued that direct action was needed because the danger of
nuclear war, or nuclear accidents, was so high; hence it was essential to keep the issue in the public domain through increased media
attention. Russell also believed direct action was necessary to disrupt government preparations for nuclear war (Russell, 1961). In
the 1980s, and under the influence of the women's anti-nuclear
protest at Greenham Common, CND reversed its opposition to
civil disobedience, and it became part and parcel of organized
nuclear protest within the movement (Minnion, 1983).

Inspired by the success of direct action in the civil rights
campaign in the United States during the 1960s, the anti-
apartheid movement of the 1980s also found the tactic to be
a strategically effective way of promoting peaceful change
(Skinner, 2010: 101–17, 200). Civil disobedience was also a key

tactic deployed by those protesting against US interference in Central America. In addition, non-violent direct action has also been an integral part of activism in the lesbian and gay community, the animal rights movement, and in the promotion of green politics. More recently, mass civil disobedience has played a fundamental role in protests against globalization. Perhaps the most famous of these was the 'battle for Seattle' in 1999, when over 40,000 people took to the streets in Washington to protest against world leaders gathering to attend the World Trade Organization ministerial conference (Hillyard and Edmonds, 1999; Thomas, 2000).

Finally, there was the striking use of non-violent civil disobedience during the Velvet Revolution, which eventually led to the fall of the Soviet empire (Wheaton and Kavan, 1992). Equally, non-violent civil disobedience has been an integral part of the Arab spring (2010–11, and Egypt in 2013) (Dabashi, 2012), the 'green revolution' (2009–10) in Iran (Dabashi, 2011; Nabavi, 2012) and protests in Turkey in 2013, to name but a few. The outcome of these protests is not always easy to predict, and it remains to be seen how effective and long-lasting democratic reform might be in the Middle East. What is undeniable is that protest against the state can generate successful political change. However, whilst we have, thus far, been content to outline protest in a very generic way, in societies where protests are permitted, it is questionable if all forms of political protest constitute civil disobedience. Not all acts that take place in a particular protest might be civil disobedience, and the lines between it, and more violent forms of political protest, are often blurred. Hence, within a lawful protest march, for example, there may well be individual and collective acts that might well be considered to be civil disobedience, and some that are deemed to be violent direct action. Thus, we need to differentiate politically motivated actions, such as demonstrations against corrupt and tyrannical regimes, from the kind of activity that characterized the London riots of July 2011 (Reicher and Stott, 2011). Thus, we need to examine the concept of civil disobedience in more detail.

A Theory of Civil Disobedience

Perhaps one of the first recorded attempts to grapple with the concept of civil disobedience is that of Étienne de La Boétie, a

French judge and diplomat, who wrote an essay entitled *Discourse of Voluntary Servitude* (*Discours de la Servitude Volontaire*) in 1552 (La Boétie and Kurz, 1975). Although only published after his death in 1576, the essay circulated in pamphlet form prior to its publication. La Boétie deals with the relationship between the individual and state power, and in particular, the question of why individuals consent to their subjugation. Or, to put it another way, why do most people obey the commands of the government? La Boétie considers the widespread and general consent to despotism to be puzzling. When he drafted the pamphlet despotism was the dominant form through which political order was maintained, and it is indeed puzzling how individual leaders were able to exercise such firm control over their subjects, particularly given that they were in the minority. It is clear that many of the conditions that puzzled La Boétie about an individual's acquiescence to state power are not relevant in the context of the modern state. What was puzzling for him was how the few could control the many.

In the modern state, with a vast security and surveillance apparatus, the explanation of how the few control the many can be located in the structural apparatus of state control and a high degree of consensus that a democratic state is legitimate. Hence, one might wonder whether it is anachronistic to look at his theory in relation to contemporary democratic states. Nonetheless, La Boétie's treatment of these issues goes to the heart of the relationship between the individual and political power, and in particular, as to how consent in political systems is manufactured.

According to La Boétie, the submission of the many primarily arises out of consent, not fear. It is not cowardice that prevents the people from rising up against political authorities, but indifference. La Boétie bitterly opposed tyranny, but he finds the public's consent to its subjection equally troubling. His opposition to this subjection rests on a theory of natural law and a natural right to liberty. As he puts it: 'If we led our lives according to the ways intended by nature and the lessons taught by her, we should be intuitively obedient to our parents; later we should adopt reason as our guide and become slaves to nobody' (La Boétie and Kurz, 1975: 55). Obedience to our parents, then, is a necessary part of the natural life cycle, but once we reach maturity we should be slaves to no one; we should use our own reason, a reason which resides in us and is a natural aspect of our being. La Boétie's work can be considered an early articulation of a theory of civil disobedience; mass non-violent resistance as a method for the overthrow of tyranny. Indeed, La Boétie concludes that there is no need to use violence to overcome any tyrant, because he can be defeated if the population refuses to consent to its enslavement. If tyranny rests on mass consent, then the means for its overthrow is mass withdrawal of that consent. 'I do not ask that you place hands upon the tyrant to topple him over, but simply that you support him no longer; then you will behold him, like a great Colossus whose pedestal has been pulled away, fall of his own weight and break in pieces' (La Boétie and Kurz, 1975: 53).

The removal of tyranny, then, will not require force or the shedding of blood, but only the removal of funds, resources, and importantly, consent. If tyrants are disobeyed they become powerless. La Boétie claims that the oppressed can free themselves by refusing to supply the tyrant with the instruments of their oppression. Put this way, it is almost as if we conspire to oppress ourselves. Freedom lies in our ability to recognize this and remove our consent. La Boétie's theory of non-violent political transformation is radical in terms of its outcomes. For the violent overthrow, or even death, of a ruling tyrant is nothing more than an isolated individual act within an existing political system. Thus, political assassinations rarely lead to the complete overthrow of a political regime since they often lead to the mere replacement of one leader with another. Mass withdrawal of consent, on the other hand, is a direct, non-violent, act by the mass of the people, and it is genuinely revolutionary insofar as it can transform the system itself.

There is, however, a potential naiveté to La Boétie's position. For he has no theory, or account, of how the individual withdrawal of consent can be turned into mass withdrawal. In short, he has no account of mass mobilization. Without this, those in power can easily pick off individuals who withdraw consent. History is replete with examples of when leaders have done exactly this. Marx, on the other hand, saw only too clearly that mass mobilization and the possible use of force was the only way to overturn oppressive regimes. The potential naiveté of La Boétie's position is demonstrated in Roland Bleiker's (2000) excellent *Popular Dissent, Human Agency, and Global Politics*, which draws heavily on La Boétie in an attempt to articulate a new form of resistance in the contemporary world. Bleiker argues that social change is best brought about through a transformation of values, and adaptations in language and discourse (Bleiker, 2000: 273–82). According to Bleiker, cultural forms such as poetry, for example, are efficient means of effecting this transformation (Bleiker, 2000: 244–72). Privileging micro-resistance at the level of the individual behaviour over more organized forms of resistance, Bleiker's position seems politically naïve, given the vast institutional and normative power the state can draw upon. Individuals may feel they are engaging in resistance, but when faced with the vast institutional power of the modern state and the contemporary global political order, small changes in individual behaviour are unlikely to have much effect long-term political effect.

This is not to deny their place in political protest, but merely to indicate the necessity of political action that goes beyond the individual, and that needs to be organized. However, despite its inherent weaknesses, La Boétie's account of the relationship between people and state power provides an underlying rationale for the deployment of civil disobedience as a technique orientated towards effecting change in political outcomes. Most theories of civil disobedience that follow La Boétie are far less radical and are orientated towards political change around particular causes rather than the wholesale transformation of the political system. But what, then, is civil disobedience?

First, civil disobedience generally involves the breaking of some or other law. Consider, for example, any law to which an individual is subject and supposed to obey. If they are uninterested in this law, or approve of it, then they will probably comply. However, what if they do not agree with the law? Then they must decide what to do, and can choose among several possibilities. First, is to comply yet keep the disapproval quiet; perhaps out of fear of punishment if they do not comply with the law, or out of a concern with public attention and criticism. Second is to comply, but only after voicing disapproval; I, that is, the voicing of disapproval is itself allowed. Where such open dissent is permitted, compliance, even if done under public protest, and perhaps after efforts to nullify the law, is not civil disobedience, for nothing illegal has occurred, and no law has been disobeyed. Much the same can be said of all forms of lawful protest such as strikes, boycotts and marches. Where these acts are methods of lawful protest they do not count as civil disobedience as that term has commonly come to be used.

Third, when confronted with a law that one disagrees with, one possibility is to refuse to comply yet keep that non-compliance hidden in order to avoid the unpleasant consequences that typically follow when unlawful conduct is openly committed. Does this count as civil disobedience? It certainly counts as disobedience, but is it civil? Neither Martin Luther King nor John Rawls thought so, and their view is the dominant one. In the case of Socrates and Thoreau the position is less clear-cut. For Socrates, the issue was whether he should bribe his jailer to escape the death sentence. Such a course of action would not have been in open defiance of the law, but a fraudulent evasion of it involving lying and corruption of public servants. As for Thoreau, for several years he made no effort to make his non-compliance with the poll tax public, and since what he later wrote on the subject of civil disobedience was formed by his own conduct and experiences, it is unlikely that he meant to exclude his own illegal conduct (silent evasion of taxes) from the reach of his argument (Richardson, 1986).

Crucial to the question under consideration is what one believes to be the point, or purpose, of breaking the law. What is it that turns some, but not all, disobedience into civil disobedience? If the rationale for one's disobedience were nothing more than an attempt to avoid having to comply with a given law, then non-public disobedience at the individual level would suffice. But in the conduct of Gandhi, as well as that of Martin Luther King, and in the theory of John Rawls, indeed in virtually all modern discussions on the subject, there is a distinctive public purpose to civil disobedience; to frustrate and then change the law, by making an appeal to the conscience of the authorities and the conscience of the majority of the public. Civil disobedience, then, can be understood as an exercise in public and moral education, as a tactic to achieve law/policy reform. Such disobedience is properly called civil because it is part of the civic life of the society.

However, no appeal to the public conscience can be made unless the illegal conduct is done openly, in the public domain, as a political act. Another problem with the concept of civil disobedience is the normative power that comes from aligning oneself with it. Thus, some protesters who break the law may attempt to secure public approval by describing their conduct, whether correctly or not, as civil disobedience. Hence, for example, it is possible to conceive of someone breaking a law and then retrospectively claiming that it was an example of civil disobedience only after his or her lawbreaking activity has been uncovered. For these reasons, then, it is unlikely that illegal conduct covertly undertaken can be regarded as civil disobedience. For, insofar as one accepts the proposition that the purpose of civil disobedience is, in part, the moral education of society, then it is impossible to achieve that aim without making public the fact that one has broken the law in the service of such moral education (Bedau, 1991: 7, 55; 1969).

Thus, much like terrorism, civil disobedience is concerned centrally with communication. It is a form of political communication. The public and communicative aspects of civil disobedience can also be highlighted if we contrast civil disobedience with conscientious objection. The primary purpose of a conscientious objector is not typically to educate the public but rather a matter of private exemption; not political change but a personal rejection of violence. When the conscientious objector violates the law, he or she primarily does so in order to avoid conduct that runs counter to personal conscience, even though that same conduct might be required by public law. Setting an example for others, or forcing society to re-evaluate its support for the law, is a secondary consideration, but such a personal rejection of violence could conceivably become civil disobedience if the objector uses his or her actions primarily to change the public's perception of such violence.

A second problem is the relationship of non-violence to civil disobedience. Pacifists such as Gandhi and King reject, on principled grounds, the use of violence to resist even unjust laws. But for others, the decision to act violently emerges as a tactical, not a principled matter. Ideally, political discourse is, or should be, non-violent, and insofar as advocates of civil disobedience remain committed to the 'rule of law', then any acts of violence shift attention away from the core demands on to the violent means of attempting to achieve them. Those in power who support the legal status quo often show no hesitation in putting down non-violent illegal protests with violent counter-measures, but should those engaged in civil disobedience also move to violence in response? The difficulty is that the protesters are claiming the moral high ground, and accepting the consequences of their actions in order to highlight some perceived injustice and perhaps bring about political and or social change; any resort to violence may negate the claim to occupy this moral high ground.

Likewise, critics of civil disobedience also often object that it is self-serving of protesters to present their illegal conduct in the language of civility, when their behaviour is little different from that of ordinary criminals. There is clearly a significant difference between crime and civil disobedience. Criminal activity is usually motivated by the possibility of personal gain, whereas civil disobedience is motivated by respect for some moral principle which, in the judgement of the protesters, has been violated by an unjust law. In this sense, civil disobedience is not an outright rejection of the law itself. But rather, it is a rejection of a particular law, or set of laws, which in the viewpoint of the protesters, is unjust. Undoubtedly, Thoreau, Gandhi and King based the legitimacy of their approach to civil disobedience on an appeal to higher moral principles. Hence, any assessment of the justification of civil disobedience requires a consideration of the nature of the moral principles upon which the protest is based. Evidently, not just any moral principle will serve to justify illegal conduct. For surely, some acts of civil disobedience are unjustified no matter how committed the protester might be to the cause.

For Socrates, justifiable illegal conduct is virtually impossible to contemplate, and no matter how unjust the outcome may be, the law must be obeyed, even to the point of personal sacrifice. In Thoreau's case, on the other hand, what justifies his refusal to pay the poll tax is that he refuses to become complicit in the injustices done to others. For Thoreau, payment of his taxes would contribute to the injustices he wishes to stop. In King's case, several principles are mentioned, all of which attempt to establish the injustice of legally enforced racial segregation (King, 1968). However, a theoretically sophisticated approach to the justification of civil disobedience cannot be found in the work of Socrates, Thoreau and King. For this we have to turn to the work of John Rawls (1971: 293–335).

For Rawls, the fundamental question was whether civil disobedience was ever justifiable in a constitutional democracy. His answer sets the bar high, and he suggests that even in a nearly just society, a person can be assumed to have the right to engage in civil disobedience only when three conditions are met. First, that it is initiated in response to an instance of substantial and manifest injustice. Second, that it is unmistakably undertaken as a last resort. Third, that efforts to coordinate activity with other minority groups are taken into consideration. Effectively, this is the same as asking whether breaking the law can ever be consistent with respect for majority rule in a political system that protects minority rights. Rawls argues that it can, but only under very particular circumstances and conditions. In short, for him, principled lawbreaking is justified only if the lawbreaker willingly accepts his or her punishment. Rawls believes civil disobedience to be non-coercive because it is non-violent. Essentially, it is a form of public argument. He also suggests that the justification for civil disobedience requires that the moral position underpinning the protest be consistent with the moral, or constitutional, principles shared by the general public. For Rawls, the line between non-violent and violent disobedience can clearly be drawn, and he claims that, in a constitutional democracy, only non-violent disobedience is justifiable (Rawls, 1971: 326–31).

The idea that civil disobedience must be a public demonstration of non-compliance with the law can also be found in the work of Martin Luther King. King's more famous statement of civil disobedience can be found in his letter from Birmingham city jail written in 1963 (King, 1968). In this letter, King formulates a reply to those who ask how African Americans can urge others to obey the 1954 school desegregation decision while themselves breaking laws. For King, the answer lies in the fact that there are two types of laws; those that are just and those that are unjust. King attempts to provide some rules of thumb that distinguish just from unjust laws, whilst insisting that respect for the law itself is a position that is compatible with the breaking of an unjust law. Thus, a person who violates an unjust law must do so 'openly, lovingly, and with a willingness to accept the penalty' (King, 1968: 3). According to King, 'an individual who breaks a law that conscience tells him is unjust, and who willingly accepts the penalty of imprisonment in order to arouse the conscience of the community over its injustice, is in reality expressing the highest respect for the law' (King, 1968: 3). Indeed, such behaviour is not only permitted but demanded: 'we must learn that passively to accept an unjust system is to cooperate with that system, and thereby to become a participant in its evil' and 'to cooperate passively with an unjust system makes the oppressed as evil as the oppressor' (quoted in Bedau, 1991: 92).

At the heart of civil disobedience is a moral claim. This is often said to be embedded within a commitment to conscientiousness. However, as we have already seen, we need to distinguish conscientious objection from civil disobedience. Certainly it may be that moral convictions underpin both; the conscientious objector may object to going into conflict, for example, because they believe it immoral to take another's life under any circumstances. However, in general, a conscientious objector is generally opting out from some or other activity on personal moral grounds. For the political activist engaged in civil disobedience, on the other hand, the moral ground for their actions goes well beyond that of personal beliefs. And thus, for those engaged in acts of civil disobedience the breach of law is necessary, not only in terms of personal self-respect and moral consistency, but also to serve the interests of the greater social whole. Thus, acts of civil disobedience aim to highlight the unjust nature of laws or policies that require change. In short, civil disobedience is required under certain circumstances in order to preserve the very character of the society itself. It may be that conscientious objection and civil disobedience can be related to one and the same act. Thus, for example, draft dodgers during the Vietnam War who publicly discussed their reasons can be considered to be both engaged in conscientious objection on personal grounds and also civil disobedience insofar as they make their position subject to public validation and critique.

The public aspect of civil disobedience highlights the fact that, just like terrorism, it is a form of political communication. The communicative aspect of civil disobedience is an essential part of it, since in publicly disobeying a law the political actor seeks not only to convey his or her rejection and condemnation of that law, but also to draw public attention to the issue in the hope of instigating change. According to Rawls, covert or secret acts are not civil disobedience; civil disobedience is a public expression of protest at some law or policy. Indeed, Rawls adds a further stipulation, arguing that properly conceived acts of civil disobedience would require not only the public claiming of responsibility for the actions, but also giving the legal authorities prior notice that such acts of disobedience were going to take place (Rawls, 1971: 366).

However, the stipulation of prior knowledge to the authorities is problematic, and if followed through in all cases would probably ensure that civil disobedience is an ineffective tactic to employ. If a person publicizes their intention to breach the law, then they provide political opponents and legal authorities with the opportunity to abort their efforts to communicate. So, for example, animal rights groups would have little to gain, and everything to lose, by giving fair warning to the authorities that they intended to break into a particular laboratory and release the animals. For this reason, covert disobedience is often preferable to actions undertaken with fair warning, and all that is required is that the dissident political actor publicly accepts responsibility for the acts after they have taken place.

Another problematic issue is the question of whether civil disobedience must necessarily always be non-violent. According to Rawls, violent acts, particularly those likely to injure others, are incompatible with civil disobedience. Thus, for him, any form of violent action would not be civil disobedience. 'Indeed,' argues Rawls, 'any interference with the civil liberties of others tends to obscure the civilly disobedient quality of one's act' (Rawls, 1971: 366). This non-violent approach to the concept of civil disobedience is certainly embedded within the practices of Gandhi and Martin Luther King, yet it is not universally accepted, and there are clearly problems in terms of how to specify an appropriate notion of violence.

For example, what would be a suitable scope of acts that were disallowed under the principle of non-violence? What about damage to property or injuries suffered by police or other actors in the course of attempting to deal with civil disobedience; would these count as violence (Morreall, 1991: 130–43)? Moreover, non-violent acts of civil disobedience could, potentially at least, cause more harm than individual acts of violence. Acts of civil disobedience, for example, that disrupted power supplies could have far-reaching consequences. According to Rawls and Peter Singer, the use of violence in acts of civil disobedience lessens the communicative aspect of the act (Singer, 1973: 86); presumably because attention is focused on the violence and not the principled reasons for the committing of the act. There is no doubt that the increased communicative potential of an act of limited violence could, potentially, raise public awareness of the cause. Nonetheless, most advocates of civil disobedience argue that non-violent protest is preferable to violent forms. A commitment to non-violent civil disobedience avoids increasing the total amount of violence in the system, and there is always the danger that violent forms of civil disobedience could lead to increasingly reactionary, and potentially violent, reactions to the civil disobedience. Moreover, violent civil disobedience could, potentially at least, risk an adverse public reaction to the violence and antagonize other groups of protesters that might be future allies (Raz, 1979: 267).

We have already seen how the public aspect of civil disobedience differentiates it from common crimes. Criminals rarely, if ever, willingly admit to their crimes or publicly announce them in advance. Another significant difference between civil disobedience and common crimes, however, is the willingness of the political actor engaged in acts of protest to accept the legal consequences and the punishments that may follow acts of civil disobedience. Indeed, the willingness to accept punishment functions as an indication of the commitment to the rule of law. In addition, as Martin Luther King argues, the acceptance of punishment can serve to increase the moral justice of the cause (King, 1968). Moreover, a willingness to accept the legal consequences may help the silent majority to realize that there is an issue of great significance at stake; an issue that, up until the acts of civil disobedience brought them to the public's attention, they were mostly indifferent to (Singer, 1973: 84). Yet again, however, and depending upon how harsh the punishment is, it may be that the overall effectiveness of a sustained campaign of protest suffers if too many political actors prepared to engage in disobedience find themselves incarcerated in state prisons. The numbers willing to participate in civil disobedience might be small if prison is one of the possible outcomes.

One major problem for all forms of political protest, apart from legal protest, is whether such action is ever justifiable. The issue here is whether people should ever disobey the law in societies that are democratic and reasonably just. In such societies, there is an assumption that there is an obligation to follow the law. In general, two arguments are often advanced in defence of this obligation. First, if it is wrong to do harm to others then one does not a have a right to harm the state, which consists of the generalized other of society. Here any harm enacted on the state will necessarily harm other individuals in the state. Second, citizens of a given state enjoy the protections, rights and benefits provided by that state and hence they have tacitly agreed to follow the laws of that state. But, of course, citizens born into a society have not necessarily agreed that all the laws of that society are just, so how can they be expected to obey every law, particularly if they have a moral disagreement with some of them? Once again, in complex modern societies it is impossible to apply this rule, since there are far too many laws that were enacted in periods that existed prior to when individuals might have been born. However, citizens do, generally, enjoy certain benefits as members of a particular state and as such the assumption should be that the law should be followed. However, given the history of state development, this assumption should allow space for principled dissent against particular laws or even widespread political action orientated against an unjust regime.

Assuming that we accept the general principle that citizens should normally follow the law, then it also follows that they have an obligation to use proper legal channels and legal protests to redress any grievances. Non-legal political protest, then, in whatever form, can only be employed as a last resort. But how would we know when we had reached the last resort? Moreover, given the structures of power in modern states it may well be that the legal system provides support for those in power. It would be naïve, given that the legal system is part of the state, to assume that it benefits all sectors of society equally. The legal system, like any other aspect of the state, is a function of the history of that state. Thus, legal channels of protest may well prove to be ineffective. Rawls suggests that if protesters are engaged in legal forms of protest, the outcome of which has not led to change, then it may well be that further legal protest might be considered impractical; hence, civil disobedience might now be regarded as a last resort. In short, for Rawls all that is required is a demonstration that legal channels have been the first resort (Rawls, 1971: 369–74).

Legal Protest

The key difference between legal protest and civil disobedience is that a legal protest remains within the limits of the law. Protest marches, sit-ins, refusing to vote (unless voting is compulsory), writing letters and hunger strikes are all forms of legal protest. Many of the features of civil disobedience are found in legal protest, which is essentially a communicative demonstration against some law or perceived injustice. Moreover, there is also a moral dimension to legal protest insofar as it justifies political action in terms of changing some law or policy; hence legal protest also embodies an attempt at public moral education. It might be argued that the unlawful nature of civil disobedience requires a stronger moral argument than that needed by legal protest. However, as David Lyons (1998: 36) argues, the status of the moral argument concerning protest changes depending on the nature of the political regime in which obedience is demanded. Thus, for example, there can be no moral presumption concerning obedience to the law in regimes that are themselves not moral. Hence, in immoral regimes there is no requirement for an additional moral justification for acts of civil disobedience. The unjust nature of the regime covers both legal protest and civil disobedience.

An additional reason for favouring civil disobedience over legal protest is that it is often difficult to get one's case across when the controllers of mainstream media tend to give proponents of dissenting views limited space to make their case. The sensational aspects of illegal methods, such as engaging in civil disobedience, can lead to the wider dissemination of a position. These points, however, have not been lost on terrorists and the question remains as to what limits are permissible to publicize one's cause, no matter how strongly one feels the moral case is.

Revolutionary Protest

The revolutionary protester uses forms of communication that are unlikely to persuade others of the merits of his or her position. Since the aims of the revolutionary are far more extensive than that of legal protest or those engaged in civil disobedience, then the tactics employed will likewise be more extreme. Here we have a difficult problem. We have seen that for many writers civil disobedience must always be non-violent. This means that a sharp dividing line is suggested between political protest that is non-violent and political protest that is violent. Civil disobedience sits on the non-violent side of this line; anything that involves violence, it is argued, cannot be considered to be civil disobedience. Unfortunately, social practice takes no heed of the attempts of academics to draw such lines.

We have now moved onto the terrain of radical revolutionary political protest that goes beyond civil disobedience. In general, revolution and other forms of radical protest do not aim to persuade governments to change established policies.

However, revolutionary action may seek to persuade a society that a change in government or regime is required. Yet revolutions can take place peacefully. In India, for example, Gandhi had some success with non-violent revolutionary action, as did the Velvet revolutionaries who contributed to the end of the Cold War. But peaceful revolutions are not the norm, and very few revolutions take place in the absence of some violence. Large-scale protest and resistance that deploy terror are different activities from the non-violent resistance that distinguished, for example, Gandhi's protest in India. Moreover, because people can engage in protest for numerous reasons, acts of civil disobedience guided by conscientious commitments can also emerge from revolutionary aims; hence the dividing lines are difficult to draw.

Differing forms of protest are only differing tactics employed by various parties engaged in protest against some perceived injustice. As such, the differentiations made between various forms of protest above do not always reflect the messy patterns that emerge when protest unfolds. What we have is not a one-dimensional continuum from weak to strong forms of dissent, but a multi-dimensional continuum of protest, full of complexities, paradoxes and fluid points of contrast that blur the lines between legality, violence, harm, communication, motivation and persuasiveness. As protest on the ground unfolds, the idealizations of the theorist meet the messy reality of the protester, who may begin with the best of intentions, but who can find themselves wrapped up in situations that break free of idealized theoretical boundaries.

Conclusion

Some theorists have argued that civil disobedience is an outdated view of political protest that fails to reflect current forms of political activism. Empirically this may well seem to be the case, with more and more extreme modes of political protest at the forefront of political engagement. Herbert Storing has suggested that 'The most striking characteristic of civil disobedience is its irrelevance to the problems of today' (Storing, 1991: 85). Certainly, there have been shifts in the form civil disobedience has taken in recent years; yet these shifts have still occurred mainly within the framework of conscientious communication. The historical examples and beliefs of Gandhi, Martin Luther King, the Suffragettes and

Nelson Mandela are as relevant today as they were when these examples of civil protest engaged in it. Such idealized disobedience contrasts with much contemporary civil disobedience, which in many respects has tended to take a more direct, and often violent form.

Civil disobedience and other forms of protest may be seen, in part, as responses to a breakdown in the mechanisms available for citizens to engage in the decision-making process. One way to think about this lack of mechanisms is that of a democratic deficit (Markovits, 2005). Such deficits may be an inevitable part of contemporary democracies. As such, disobedience undertaken to correct this deficit can be interpreted as attempts to protect and revalorize the democratic ideal. Thus, civil disobedience remains today very much a vibrant part of political life, and it is of particular importance, both theoretically and practically, to maintain the distinction between it and more radical forms of protest. It should be clear, however, that the appropriateness of civil disobedience depends on the context, and in particular the nature of the state in which such protest is considered. If a state is particularly brutal and oppressive, then perhaps civil disobedience may not be appropriate in terms of bringing about radical change. This again only serves to highlight the fact that any consideration of the appropriateness, or justice, of any form of political protest can only be made within the context of a consideration of the nature and history of a particular state (or political system) under which the protest occurs.

4

Political Violence: Situating Terrorism

Writing in 1988, Alex P. Schmid and Albert Jongman suggested that there are at least 109 definitions of terrorism (Schmid and Jongman, 2005: 5–6). In 1999 Walter Laqueur could only detect 100 (Laqueur, 1999: 6). Perhaps Laqueur's figure represents some form of progress, yet post-9/11, we can presume the figure is on the rise again. Indeed, by 2001 Jeffrey Simon identifies 212 definitions (Simon, 2001: 29). Despite the claim by some scholars (Laqueur, 1977: 4) that the definitional problem surrounding terrorism does not need solving, the need for a definition is pressing. As Kofi Annan, former secretary-general of the United Nations (UN), has put it, 'the moral authority of the United Nations and its strength in condemning terrorism have been hampered by the inability of Member States to agree on a comprehensive convention that includes a definition' (Annan, 2005: 26). To most people the idea that terrorism is hard to define must seem absurd. Surely, events such as 9/11 and the London 7/7 bombings present us with graphic displays of what terrorism is. Indeed, why do we need a definition of terrorism at all? Is not it the case that we all know it when we see it? It is perhaps the assumption of being able to identify terrorism when we see it that is, in part, responsible for the confusion surrounding the label. Moreover, any scholarly enquiry into terrorism cannot rely on the 'know it when I see it' response, particularly if the aim of such an enquiry is to demonstrate that the obviousness of seeing is more problematic than it seems. Here is the nub of the problem; terrorism is an emotional and politically charged subject that suffers conceptual stretching by the media, governments, state officials and members of the public.

Academic discussion of terrorism is no less confused. Few would disagree that terrorism involves indiscriminate attacks on people and property, that the intention is to spread fear and terror, and that it is politically motivated. Beyond this broad agreement, however, there is little consensus. Moreover, which acts meet the criteria are the subject of heated debate. Failure to reach agreement on the definition of terrorism is not a new phenomenon. Despite the presentism that infuses most contemporary discussions of terrorism post-9/11, the definitional problem has always constituted a serious barrier to any coherent academic and theoretical discussion of the issue.

Some authors take an alternative view. Thomas Mockaitis, for example, argues that we need a functional, rather than a theoretical definition of the problem (Mockaitis, 2008: 2–3). In the attempt to develop a functional definition, Mockaitis draws the analogy between a hunter, who when pursuing a dangerous animal, 'does not need to know its genus, species, and phylum, but he/she must be able to recognize clearly the beast and be intimately acquainted with its behaviours and vulnerabilities' (Mockaitis, 2008: 3). This is question begging and assumes that there is agreement on which dangerous animal is the subject of the hunt. However, it is precisely this that is missing when attempting to deal with terrorism. For it is clear from the heated political debate that surrounds the issue that we do not all know it when we see it. For some people, tigers are dangerous wild animals; for others they are an endangered species.

Others (Avard, 2010) attempt to avoid the definitional problem altogether through a complete avoidance of the term. This is no more successful than the approach of Mockaitis. Essentially, this constitutes a form of 'ostrich enquiry'; as if putting our heads in the sand will make the problem go away. It will not, and most academics who take this approach invariably end up using the term, but refuse to tell us what they mean by it. The assumption being, once again, that we all know it when we see it and that we all agree with the implicit and hidden definition of the academic who seemingly has no use for the term. In effect, a Humpty Dumpty approach to the term is employed: 'hence when I use the term it means exactly what I wanted to mean, no more and no less'. Whatever the problems with the academic and political use of the term, this cannot be an acceptable solution. Indeed, one major problem that emerges when we adopt the 'we know it when we see it' approach is that it leaves open the possibility of state practices orientated towards the eradication of terrorism to be introduced, despite the fact there is no definition of terrorism. Thus, for example, almost all states provide criminal codes, repressive measures, punishments and penalties for terrorist crimes, in the absence of a clear definition of terrorism. This, of course, allows them to declare as terrorist almost any activity they find reprehensible, and once behaviour is named as terrorist it becomes subject to some of the most draconian laws and procedures a society can construct. As, Ben Golder and George Williams put it, the 'danger is that if terrorism is not so defined, the powers of the State may extend very far indeed' (Golder and Williams, 2004: 272).

Walter Laqueur, a well-known and well-respected expert on terrorism, argues that 'no definition of terrorism can possibly cover all the varieties of terrorism that have appeared throughout history' (Laqueur, 1977: 7). The irony here is that in the absence of a definition of terrorism, Laqueur cannot possibly identify 'all the varieties of terrorism that have appeared throughout history'. This is a classic example of having a hidden definition of terrorism, whilst at the same time denying that such a definition is needed. Moreover, Laqueur also argues that to say that 'terrorism cannot be studied until such definition exists is manifestly absurd' (Laqueur, 2001: 5). Yet to carry on in the absence of such a definition ensures only that one's own account of terrorism will be replete with confusions about which acts of political violence amount to terrorism and which do not. Such an approach may also lead to the flattening out of the differences between varied and different acts of political violence, and an arbitrary categorization of certain acts under the terrorism label, whilst others will be arbitrarily classified under other labels. As Jack Gibbs has put it, '[l]eaving the definition implicit is the road to obscurantism' (Gibbs, 1989: 329).

If academics have failed to solve the definitional problem, practitioners, government agencies and international organizations have fared little better. Most states adopt definitions so broad as to be all-inclusive and meaningless. For example, the US military currently defines terrorism as

> The calculated use of unlawful violence or the threat of unlawful violence to inculcate fear; intended to coerce or to intimidate governments or societies in the pursuit of goals that are generally political, religious, or ideological. (US Department of Defense, 2001)

Whilst this definition does seem to cover most instances of what might be considered terrorism, it lacks the fine details and nuances that would allow us to distinguish terrorism from other forms of political violence. Indeed, this definition is so flexible it can be applied to almost all forms of unlawful political violence. Crucially, of course, this definition gives us no critical purchase on how to distinguish between differing types of political violence. Equally, and to compound matters further, nine departments of the US government have come up with nine different definitions of the term.

The UN has also struggled to agree on a common definition of terrorism, preferring instead to take a pragmatic approach and simply list those acts deemed to be terrorist. Of course, given the political structure of the UN it may be unsurprising that it has been unable to reach a coherent definition of terrorism, but it is no less lamentable. However, the UN does recognize that the lack of a coherent definition is a problem for the international community:

> The question of a definition of terrorism has haunted the debate among states for decades ... The UN Member States still have no agreed-upon definition. Terminology consensus would, however, be necessary for a single comprehensive convention on terrorism, which some countries favour in place of the present 12 piecemeal conventions and protocols. The lack of agreement on a definition of terrorism has been a major obstacle to meaningful international countermeasures. (UN, 2007)

The importance of such a consensus on the definition of terrorism came to the fore after the 9/11 attacks.

UN Security Council Resolution 1373 was unanimously passed on 28 September 2001, and because it was adopted under Chapter VII of the UN Charter, it is binding on all UN member states (UN Security Council, 2001). Resolution 1373 called on all states to 'ensure that terrorist acts are established as serious criminal offences in domestic laws and regulations and that the seriousness of such acts is duly reflected in sentences served' (UN Security Council, 2001). The resolution, however, includes no definition of terrorism, and the UN attempted to address this problem in resolution 1566, which was passed in 2004 (UN Security Council, 2004). Resolution 1566 condemns terrorism as one of the most serious threats to peace and security, and calls on all countries to prosecute or extradite anyone supporting terrorist acts or participating in the planning of terrorist operations. The resolution also includes what might be considered an attempt to define terrorism:

> criminal acts, including against civilians, committed with the intent to cause death or serious bodily injury, or taking of hostages, with the purpose to provoke a state of terror in the general public or in a group of persons or particular persons, intimidate a population or compel a government or an international organization to do or to abstain from doing any act, which constitute offences within the scope of and as defined in the international conventions and protocols relating to terrorism. (UN Security Council, 2004)

However, by referring these 'criminal acts' back to previous international conventions and protocols relating to terrorism, 1566 takes the issue no further forward, since these conventions and protocols themselves fail to reach an agreed definition of terrorism. It had been thought that the UN had resolved the definitional issue in 2005 when the then secretary-general Kofi Annan declared: 'In addition to actions already proscribed by existing conventions, any action constitutes terrorism if it is intended to cause death or serious bodily harm to civilians or non-combatants with the purpose of intimidating a population or compelling a government or an international organisation to do or abstain from doing any act' (Annan, 2005: Ch. 3, para. 91). Mr Annan also called on world leaders to 'unite behind it and to conclude a comprehensive convention on terrorism before the end of the sixtieth session of the General Assembly' (Annan, 2005: Ch. 3, para. 91). Unfortunately, there has been little or no progress in this area.

The definitional confusion surrounding the issue of terrorism means that it is almost impossible to answer pressing political questions concerning the phenomenon, and hence the term becomes a political football kicked around and deployed by a varied array of actors keen to legitimize their own view of the world and delegitimize those of others. Consider, for example, the words of Osama bin Laden:

> what happened in September 11 [in New York and Washington] and March 11 [in Madrid] are your goods returned to you ... Since we have reacted in kind, your description of us as

terrorists and of our actions as terrorism necessarily means that your actions must be defined likewise ... Our actions are but a reaction to yours, your destruction and murder of our people, whether happening in Afghanistan, Iraq, and Palestine. (bin Laden, 2005: 234)

Here is a clear example of how the confusion surrounding the term allows its deployment in the service of extremist causes. Many academics, keen to demonstrate the hypocrisy at the heart of state practice, provide an easy legitimation of such views through an ever wider-ranging critique of state practices labelled as terrorist. Little wonder, then, that bin Laden and other extremists have found intellectual support for the moral and political legitimacy of their actions. Such a political impasse, itself based on a conceptual and definitional impasse, can only increase the amount of violence in the world, and provides us with no conceptual tools with which to further the cause of peace and resolve genuine injustices. Yet how are we to deal with this problem? Is it really the case that 'one man's [*sic*] freedom fighter is another man's [*sic*] terrorist'? Most of the problems associated with this position arise from our inability to reach agreement on key terms that are already politically charged. Thus, for example, we might say freedom fighters never attack innocents, or non-combatants. Yet the terms innocents and non-combatants are also politically charged and the subject of heated debate. To most Palestinians, for example, no Israeli citizen can be innocent, and doubtless the Israelis feel the same about Palestinians.

Indeed, bin Laden has explicitly denied the possibility of any innocents in Western democracies that vote for and support their governments (bin Laden, 2005: 70, 119). Linking terrorism to the issue of the state, however, does, I suggest, provide us with a way forward through the concept of non-state actors. The argument here is deceptively simple. Insofar as the state is founded on violence, and given that the state project has had winners and losers, political space must be enabled for forms of protest against the state. Of course, protest against the state does not always have to be violent, as we have seen in Chapter 3. Non-violent forms of political protest have been shown to be highly effective in achieving political outcomes (Chenoweth and Stephan, 2011), and there is evidence that terrorism does not work (Abrahms, 2006). However, given that there is always the possibility of groups that may feel they have no alternative other than violence, then we need a means to distinguish between those that may have a valid case for the use of violence and those that do not. I examine the moral case for terrorism in Chapter 5 and conclude that once a definition of terrorism embedded within the concept of non-state actors is accepted then there are no legitimate grounds on which it can be justified. However, insofar as actors and groups orientate their activities, whether violent or not, against state actors and officials, then given the history of state development, we can consider these to be freedom fighters. We may not agree with the cause, we may not agree with their tactics, but unless we are ourselves intimately either for these groups or against them, then we have no moral or political right to deny them effective protest and tar them with the terrorism label. In accepting this position, we are, of course, rejecting the Kantian standpoint that no disobedience to the law is justified (Kant, 1966: 86).

An issue that has rarely, if ever, been discussed in relation to the definitional problem are the criteria on which we might judge the definition to be adequate. Here we must turn to the philosophy of social science to help, for the definition of social objects cannot follow the same procedure as that employed in the natural sciences. As a social construct, and one deeply embedded within political worldviews, terrorism is not just 'out there' such that we could point to it and say, 'look, our definition is correct'. This does not mean that there is no such thing as terrorism, and terrorism is undoubtedly, and unfortunately, all too real. However, the fact that there is so much disagreement on what the term means is hardly surprising, given that the actors engaged in the practice of perpetuating terrorism and those intent on eradicating it themselves disagree about how the term should be understood and used. So the academic confusion surrounding the term terrorism is, in part, an accurate reflection of how the term is deployed in social practice. Being aware of this, however, is part and parcel of how we deal with conflicts and lessen the impact of political violence throughout the world.

In short, we face a set of political and moral choices about whether we want to lessen the confusion surrounding the term. Certainly the UN, and the international community, recognize the need to reach a definition of the term. Likewise academics, despite some like Laqueur, generally bemoan the lack of a clear definition. Given this, what criteria might we use to enable us to assess the validity of the definition of terrorism?

When thinking about terrorism we need to be careful to avoid falling into the trap of assuming that to terrorize is the same thing as terrorism. To terrorize simply means to instil terror in other individuals or groups. Many groups and individuals terrorize others; criminals, for example. But it would be a mistake to confuse this with terrorism. Thomas Schelling, for instance, argues that '[m]y dictionary defines terrorism as "the use of terror, violence, and intimidation to achieve an end" … to coerce by intimidation or fear"' (Schelling, 1982: 66). If we accept Schelling's account, how does terrorism differ from violent criminal activity? Criminals routinely use terror as a deliberate tactic to achieve their ends. Indeed the protection rackets that were widespread among mafia organizations would seem to be a paradigmatic example of 'coercing by imitation or fear'. Equally, a husband can terrorize his wife, a father his children, or the director of a horror movie can attempt to terrorize his audience. Indeed, if we accept Schelling's definition, almost any legal system would constitute a form of terrorism, since legal systems ultimately depend on the use of coercion against potential and actual lawbreakers. None of these examples are what we normally mean when we use the term terrorism. Terrorism generally denotes a particular form of political communication that is often violent. The conflation of the deployment of terror with the concept of terrorism is most apparent in discussions concerning state terrorism.

Annamarie Oliverio, for example, argues that 'Terrorist activity occurs daily, at different levels of analysis, especially within technologically advanced societies and societies whose structures, institutions, and organisations privilege hierarchy and domination' (Oliverio, 1998: 27). Thus, for Oliverio, terrorism can be examined 'as a form of social control, fundamental control and … [the] … apparatuses of the state may be viewed as terroristic' (Oliverio, 1998: 27). Oliverio goes even beyond this, suggesting that 'rape, spousal or child abuse, racism, gang violence, environmental destruction, poverty, or even gross medical malpractice' should be recognized as terrorism (Oliverio, 1998: 140). This is close to arguing that any and every form of social control is terrorism, and once we get to the point where 'gross medical malpractice' is deemed to be terrorism we seem to have lost all critical purchase on the issue.

Ironically, Oliverio's position on terrorism runs counter to one of her stated aims. According to her, most people 'perceive terrorism as more threatening to life, peace, and security than handgun ownership or highway travel. Yet the death rates as a result of terrorism, versus handgun and/or highway deaths, suggest just the opposite' (Oliverio, 1998: 3). In this context, Oliverio is surely correct to argue that 'incongruities in the actual and perceived social harm of terrorism ... should lead us to examine and understand the nature of the construct of terrorism' (Oliverio, 1998: 4). Given her inflated definition of terrorism, why are handgun attacks and highway deaths not also terrorism? But if handgun attacks and highway deaths are terrorism we will have flattened out all differences between different forms of violence, and this is a serious barrier to analytical rigour. We will also, of course, have multiplied the amount of terrorism in the world exponentially, and given the ability of the state to use the fear of terrorism as a driving force for enhanced social and legal control, a broad definition of terrorism would be counter-productive to any approach that attempts to show that terrorism is not, and should not, be viewed as a major security threat to either individuals or the stability of the international global order.

Since terror is an integral aspect of all violence and can be used by a variety of different actors – states, insurgent movements, criminal organizations – any definition of it that we employ has to be able to differentiate between these groups of actors and between the differing forms of political violence. In short, since all forms of violence instil terror in victims, we need to distinguish between 'to terrorize' and terrorism. We may not be able to reach a completely watertight definition of terrorism, and there will always be fuzzy cases that provide challenges, but we need to politically and morally differentiate between forms of political violence.

Clearly, states have employed violence repeatedly throughout the centuries, and I have tried to bring this violent aspect of state development to the fore in Chapter 1. Equally, they have often used violence as an explicit form of communication. The Romans, for example, crucified thousands of prisoners following slave rebellions as a warning to anyone else considering rebellion. Likewise, it would be possible to argue that the bombing of Dresden by the British Royal Air Force served no other strategic purpose than to communicate to the Nazi regime and the German people the probable costs of continuing the war (Addison and Crang, 2006; Heribert, 2011). The bombings of Hiroshima and Nagasaki also represent clear instances of states using massive violence to communicate a clear message to another state. Indeed the term terrorism was first coined in the French Revolution, when the revolutionary forces unleashed a 'reign of terror' aimed at all enemies of the regime.

Dictators in the twentieth century became experts in the use of state terror and aimed to engender an environment of fear so all-encompassing as to intimidate their populations and ensure that they would not even think about mounting opposition to the regime. Even contemporary democracies are well-versed in the use of state terror, despite their professed liberal principles. Indeed, left liberal critics of the war on terror have almost begun to equate the war on terror itself as an act of terrorism (Jackson, 2005; Jackson, Murphy and Poynting, 2010), with extraordinary rendition, human rights abuses in military prisons and the use of torture all deemed to be terrorism. It would appear that terrorism is everywhere and that there is a great deal of it. We seem to have moved from a position where terrorism denotes a very particular form of political violence to one where any act that instils terror becomes terrorism. Yet, however reprehensible terror perpetrated by states is, do we gain anything by using the term state terrorism for these acts?

We need to pursue an approach to the issue of political violence, and threats of violence, that can deal with differences between forms of violence. For apart from those pathological individuals who seem to possess no fear, an act of violence always induces terror in those confronted by it. In which case, perhaps we should just label every act of violence as an act of terrorism. This is clearly not what governments, policy makers, politicians and members of the general public understand by terrorism. Moreover, to label every act of violence or threat of violence as terrorism inflates the amount of terrorism in the world. This has the effect of legitimating more and more state responses to it. Since 9/11, international terrorism has come to be seen as one of the major threats to the stability of the international political system. Yet horrific as international terrorism is, instances of it cause relatively few deaths in the international political system in comparative terms. Compare, for example, figures for international terrorism with those of the deaths of infants who failed to reach the age of 5 (UN Statistics, 2006). Alternatively, consider the number of global deaths from road accidents in comparison to deaths from international terrorism (Wilson and Thomson, 2005). Inducing fear in global populations is one of the aims of terrorism, and states might also support an inflationary approach to terrorist threats insofar as it allows them more freedom to act unencumbered in security arenas.

In many respects, since terrorism is not simply out there await-ing a description and definition, we could move to a situation where we agree to use a coherent definition. However, if this is the case then it is probably also the fact that many actors, and possibly academics, simply do not want to arrive at a definition of terrorism. For those prepared to engage in political violence, the confusion surrounding terrorism provides a welcome bulwark, allowing them to label violence used against them as terrorism and violence used by them as legitimate. Given this, the question is how to move the debate forward. I suggest that any definition of terrorism has to be sufficiently narrow such that the number of acts that fall under the definition is limited. Any definition of ter-rorism has to take into account how the term is commonly used in public debate, and in particular, how it differs from alternative forms of violence used by states and against them.

If the definition of terrorism is so broad as to include nuclear war, conventional war, guerrilla war and insurgency, the term loses any useful analytical meaning. If both a suicide attack on a government building by a small insurgent group and the strategic bombing of an enemy population by a superpower in a war are 'terrorism', then social scientists, policy makers and legislators can have little use for the term apart from its deploy-ment as a term of political abuse. If the concept of 'terrorism' is to have any utility in political analysis, it ought to be limited to identify a very specific type of phenomenon, clearly differen-tiated from other forms of political violence. As Ariel Merari puts it:

> [d]espite the ambiguities and disagreements ... the concept of terrorism in modern usage is most commonly associated with a certain kind of violent actions carried out by individuals and groups rather than by states, and with events which take place in peacetime rather than as part of a conventional war. (Merari, 1993: 216–17)

Forms of Political Violence

At the most basic level, political violence is the use of physical force to achieve political ends. Violence here is used in the common-sense meaning of the term; behaviour involving physical force intended to hurt, damage or kill someone or damage something. In concentrating on this form of violence, I do not mean to lessen, ignore or deny the importance of structural violence (Galtung, 1969). Structural violence is clearly prevalent and causes many deaths. However, the focus of the book is on the relationship between forms of protest against the state, and not the production of violent (harmful) outcomes due to structural power, inaction or neglect. Political violence takes many forms. In a perceptive examination of the issue, Walter Benjamin distinguishes between violence as the means by which law is instituted and preserved and violence as the source of law: 'Lawmaking is powermaking, assumption of power, and to that extent an immediate manifestation of violence' (Benjamin, 1996: 248). Thus, laws within the state rest ultimately on violence, not only for their preservation, but also for the moment of their production. Violence is the condition of possibility for law, and law serves to protect the place of violence in a society and the state's ownership of it.

Viewed from the historical perspective of state development, this is unsurprising. States make laws, but the right, and power, to make law was derived through the deployment of political violence. Once the state had used violence to gain lawmaking power it then used the law to claim ownership of violence for itself and delegitimize all other forms of violence. This claim regarding the legitimate ownership of violence has largely been accepted with the global spread of the modern state. This means, however, that state violence and violence conducted by non-state actors require different forms of justification. The use of violence by non-state actors always begins with the assumption that it is illegitimate. Even in instances where violence is deployed in response to existential threats to one's survival, the burden of proof rests on the individuals' ability to prove the violence was purely for purposes of self-defence.

Likewise, violence conducted in the pursuit of personal or collective gain is always a crime (against the law) if it emanates from non-state actors. State-sanctioned violence, on the other hand, begins with the assumption that such violence may be warranted precisely because it is the only legitimate form of political violence recognized. This is not, of course, to say that state violence is always warranted or justified. More often than not state violence far exceeds what is warranted or justified. But in such instances states always begin with the assumption that such violence was warranted. Non-state actor violence always begins with the opposite assumption. This places a higher burden of proof on non-state actor violence. It also means that a political cause can have widespread public support, but the use of violence in support of that cause is universally criticized. Of course, state violence can also be criticized, but states can always, and do, point to the fact that it is their legal duty to uphold the law through the use of violence if necessary.

The distinction between the use of state violence versus the use of violence by non-state individuals and/or groups is one useful way to distinguish between differing forms of political violence. Effectively it is a means of identifying who deploys the violence. Another, important aspect, however, is the target of the violence. States, for example, can use violence against other states or their own citizens, and groups within the state can use violence against the state or other groups within the state. This allows us to begin to differentiate between different forms of political violence.

State political violence deployed against other states is typically described as war; understood here as simply large-scale military conflict conducted by armies. But clearly, states have also used violence against other states in ways that would not be considered to be war. In fact, overt declarations of war are becoming less common. Targeted drone attacks are one example, but limited air-force strikes, commando raids and political assassinations are other ways in which states can deploy violence against competitor states. In all instances, however, if the acts are planned, coordinated and resourced through the state apparatus we can call them acts of state violence. Moreover, since the state and politics are inseparable then they are political violence. In some instances, however, the role of the state is not always so clear. Plausible deniability is a concept political leaders often use to insulate themselves from critique if covert state operations that use violence go wrong. However, insofar as these acts can be traced back to functional institutions within the state, the Central Intelligence Agency (CIA), for example, then the fact a political leader denies them does not negate the fact these are still acts of state violence.

The use of violence by states against their citizens comes in many forms. One is the obvious deployment of violence as a part of the legal system through which state law is enforced (Sarat, 2002). This can range from the simple act of depriving citizens of their freedom to the use of violence to control riots, break strikes and apprehend criminals. Often, however, states will use clandestine, often illegal forms of violence designed to intimidate and terrorize their citizens with the intention of preventing them from opposing the regime.

Common crime is typically the kind of violence we think of when considering citizen-against-citizen violence, but since it is not, mostly, politically motivated it would not count as political violence. The boundaries become blurred, in instances such as when drug cartels or large-scale criminal organizations use violence against political elites and institutions to exercise control over their chosen domain (drugs, gambling, prostitution). Even in these examples, however, the primary aim of attacking political targets is to safeguard the criminal activity and not to affect the political environment per se. Citizen-against-citizen violence can also emerge as a result of racial, ethnic or ideological conflict. Groups within a state can attempt to exercise violence against other groups as a way of exercising political control over them, or perhaps even banishing them from the region through ethnic cleansing (Naimark, 2001). In addition, citizens or groups inside the state can use violence to attempt to influence political outcomes in relation to issues such as abortion, the environment or animal rights.

The use of violence by citizens against the state comes in many forms. Often, in riots or demonstrations, for example, it is not planned but spontaneous. The fact that it is unplanned or uncoordinated does not negate its political character, and political dissent expressed through violence, however spontaneous, is still political violence. Sometimes it is used to overturn a government, and sometimes just to bring about change in a policy area.

In terms of protest against the state, revolution is the most generic concept, insofar as most forms of political violence can be encompassed within it. However, not all of the other forms of violence deployed against that state are necessarily attempting to bring about revolution. A revolution usually refers to radical social, political or economic change. However, it can be applied to such things as technology, or military affairs. As such, revolution typically refers to an outcome; the overturning of some order or other (Foran, 1997, 2003; Skocpol, 1979, 1994). But the concept of revolution is ambiguous, since it can also be used to refer to a process rather than an outcome. Citizens can revolt, and when they take to the streets we talk of a revolutionary process the outcome of which is yet to be determined. The French Revolution of 1789, for example, can refer to the momentous changes that took place at that time, or to the process and events that brought about the change. Revolutions do not always involve violence. In some cases, revolutionary change of the system can be achieved with little or no violence (e.g. the so-called Velvet Revolution in Czechoslovakia that played a role in ending the Cold War (Wheaton and Kavan, 1992)). Often, however, revolutions involve enormous suffering and bloodshed, as in the Russian Revolution, the French Revolution or Chinese Communist Revolution (Skocpol, 1979). When thinking of revolution as a process we can see that some revolutionary changes take place over protracted periods and others are relatively quick.

When political and social revolutions are under way the actors promoting the revolution may use various tactics; some violent, some not. A typical example of this is a coup d'état, which can be described as the forcible overthrow of a government. Often a coup d'état takes place over a relatively short period and involves the seizure of power by individuals or groups. In many instances, it is carried out by persons who already control important positions in the state's machinery, and who wrest power from the government (Luttwak, 1979), for example when elements of the military decide to remove the government to preserve order or to take control for other parts of society. A coup that emerges from outside the ranks of the army will inevitably need the cooperation of the army after the coup, or at least a well-armed body of supporters able and prepared to defend it. The success of a coup often depends upon surprise, in order to catch the government off guard. When compared to other types of insurgency, a coup often involves little or no violence and bloodshed. Not all coups can be described as a revolution. A coup d'état can be an attempt to gain control of the political apparatus of the state to stop revolutionary forces.

Riots are another form of political action that can occur in revolutions, and they are essentially a form of mob violence. They are usually unorganized, in that a leader does not normally control the rioters. Nor are they typically structured in units or other hierarchies. However, in some instances dissenting political groups can use riots as a particular strategy to destabilize a regime. As such, riots can be seen to be part of an insurgent strategy, although once unleashed they are often difficult to control. Riots, however, are not always political. Moreover, even when riots are politically motivated they are not always attempts to bring about revolutionary political change. Indeed, many riots are simply the spontaneous expression of some deep dissatisfaction.

Many revolutions also involve guerrilla warfare; a type of war typically fought in relatively small formations, against a stronger enemy. It is not always a form of revolutionary war, nor is it restricted to non-military forces. Guerrilla warfare can serve as an auxiliary tactic engaged in by military or non-military personnel, often operating behind enemy lines. In many insurrections against state power, however, guerrilla warfare was, at least for a while, the dominant form of struggle.

The *Oxford English Dictionary* defines an insurgency as 'an insurrection against an existing government, by a group, lacking the official status of a belligerent' (*Oxford English Dictionary*, 1989). This is confusing, since a belligerent is normally defined as someone, or something, engaging in war, or warlike activity. As such, any definition of an insurgent not having the status of a belligerent seems to rely on a very limited, and restrictive, definition of war. Those involved in the insurgencies in Iran and Afghanistan, for example, would clearly consider themselves to be at war with the US forces and the governments they support. An insurgency occurs when groups within a state decide to take violent action against the state, often in the form of attacks on state officials and property. The aim of the insurgency can be to take control of the state, or sometimes to secede from the state in order to form the group's own political community. Insurgency is a direct and overt challenge to the authority of the state, and it is not surprising that most states will refer to insurgent groups as terrorists, whilst reserving the term freedom fighters for insurgent groups it deems to be fighting against oppression.

However, the distinction between freedom fighters and terrorists does not stand up to scrutiny. Terrorism is violence in pursuance of some political goal. But that goal could still be freedom, and terrorism is the chosen means to achieve that goal. In effect, terrorism is one strategy among many that groups fighting for freedom can use. We might, and often do, conclude that groups that use terrorism as a strategy are not worthy of our support, but that is a comment on the particular means, not the validity of the cause. In fact, there may be, and often have been, very good reasons why groups within states feel they have no alternative but to resort to force. In this respect, we need to separate the cause of terrorism from the means of achieving it. We need to differentiate terrorism from other forms of violence that insurgent groups deploy.

I treat insurgency as a form of political protest. All insurgents attempt to mobilize support for their cause amongst the wider population. They dispense information through various means, often pointing out the shortcomings of existing authority structures and explaining how things will become better once the insurgents gain power, or how they are able to gain significant concessions. As such, insurgent groups use forms of communication as well as force, or they can use force as a form of communication. In this respect, insurgency is a form of communication and terrorism might be one of the chosen methods through which it achieves its aims. When insurgents do this, however, the aim is not to terrorize the general population so much as terrorize the political elite. Insurgents need large-scale support and the acceptance of the general population; hence they will often seek to avoid actions that alienate large sections of the community.

Insurgents generally target government facilities, assassinate or kidnap politicians and officials, and sometimes murder specifically targeted people who aid the authorities; but in general, they avoid inflicting indiscriminate mass casualties. Often the form of terror they employ is not wholly indiscriminate because they have no desire to alienate the population upon whose support they depend. This does not mean that insurgent attacks are random, even if they are terrorist in form; far from it, the attacks are often well-planned, and the targets carefully chosen. However, terrorist violence used by insurgent groups is indiscriminate insofar as it does not matter who the specific people are that are targeted. Insurgent attacks that are not terrorism, however, will typically select targets on the basis of their relationship to the state. Of course, in insurgent attacks, as with standard military actions, it may well be the case that non-state actors also become victims. When state-sanctioned violence produces such casualties they are often referred to as 'collateral damage' (Crawford, 2013). There seems no reason why this notion should not also apply to insurgent groups that did not deliberately target those non-state actors. Acts of terrorism, on the other hand, do explicitly target non-state actors. When an insurgency against an oppressive regime moves from guerrilla war to terrorism, we can still support the aims of the insurgents without supporting the means.

Often a key aim of insurgents is to provoke a violent reaction from the state such that the state uses disproportionate force and alienates disaffected people, potentially driving them into the arms of the insurgents. Provoking a heavy-handed state response is also often employed as a deliberate tactic to gain international support and recognition, and possibly even intervention on their behalf. Insurgency generally involves irregular forces operating out of uniform and often in loose formations. Historically, such groups have attacked small regular military units, isolated outposts, police, and government paramilitary forces. In general, insurgents do not carry out indiscriminate attacks on the general population. Indeed, an insurgent group that moves beyond attacks on state actors, officials and property and explicitly targets non-state actors has, I would argue, entered the terrain of terrorism. This is not surprising. Conflict, even an insurgent one, can involve a wide range of tactics. Terrorism might be just one of them.

In order to maintain analytical coherence, we need to differentiate between those forms of violent protest directed against the state and those that randomly target on non-state actors. Once insurgent groups move into the terrain of targeting non-state actors they have moved into the domain of terrorism, since, as I will argue, it is only the distinction between non-state and state actors which allows us to distinguish between violence that may have a moral justification and that which does not. In addition, it is worth restating that violence used to generate terror is not necessarily terrorism.

Criminal organizations and gangs also make use of terror to maintain their control and achieve their objectives. However, as long as their use of terror is confined to the occasional murder of rival members or perhaps traitors within their own organization, then such violence will not normally produce a strong public reaction, and such violence would certainly not be subject to laws relating to terrorism. Equally, the aim of criminal activity is generally to make money, not advance specific political ends, so criminals have a vested interest in ensuring that publics do not become so concerned with their activity that they put pressure on governments to intervene. When the criminal use of terror does generate widespread public concern, a government crackdown on the criminal activity through the organizations of state is often bad for business. Indeed, criminals will generally keep their use of terror at relatively low levels to avoid unwanted public attention.

The boundaries between criminal activity and politics can become blurred. For example, drug cartels in parts of Latin America have become powerful enough to represent a direct challenge to state security institutions, and, even if only temporarily, have managed to control entire provinces. In some respects, this moves their activity from the criminal arena to the political, and they have not hesitated to murder judges and other government officials and at times to engage military forces. However, this kind of activity is orientated at gaining political control only to ensure that profit levels are maintained and that government interference in their business is minimized. None of this negates the general point that criminal groups do not routinely engage in indiscriminate acts of terror against the general population. Indeed, criminal use of terror largely relies on the fact that people must know what actions will make them a target of such terror. For criminals, profits are the primary motive, and anyone who interferes in the profit-making potential of a criminal organization risks serious harm. At times this can include state actors, but the aim here is to attempt to stop these state actors from interfering with the criminal activity and not necessarily to bring about political change. No matter how irrational we might find terrorist behaviour, like most forms of political violence, it normally has a political rationale, not one orientated around profits.

Post-9/11 it has been become commonplace to refer to something called the new terrorism (Laqueur, 1999). Often referred to as religious or apocalyptic terrorism, these new forms are often claimed to be irrational, hence outside the realm of politics (Ignatieff, 2001). New terrorism, it is argued, pursues broad ideological/religious goals so utopian as to be unattainable in the real world. Contemporary Islamic terrorism only appears to be religious from a secular perspective. I deal with this issue in more depth in Chapter 6, so it will suffice for now to indicate that contemporary Islamic terrorism is political through and through and, indeed, rests on a fundamentally different conception of sovereignty (Ahmad, 1958).

We are now in a position to proceed to define terrorism in a consistent manner that will allow us to make sense of the analysis and the rest of the book. Terrorism is a tactic used in pursuit of political aims. This does not mean that all acts of violence in pursuance of political ends are terrorism. Attacks on political leaders, for example, are not terrorism, for political leaders are a paradigmatic example of a state actor. State security services, for example the police, the military, and those branches of the secret services, are likewise state actors. Judges and Crown prosecutors are also state actors, whereas defence lawyers are not. There are some problematic aspects to this approach. University educators, and some workers in the welfare and health systems, are paid employees of the state in many countries. Are these workers not also state actors?

Much depends upon the definition of the state that one adopts. Under a Gramscian account of the 'expanded state', for example, educators and intellectuals are clearly state actors (Buci-Glucksmann, 1980: 48). Gramsci (1971: 350) regarded every hegemonic relationship as an 'educational' one. That is, hegemony entails the education of individuals and groups in order to secure consent to the dominant group's agenda. This is taking things too far. We need to distinguish between those individuals and organizations that are an integral aspect of the state, from those individuals and organizations that play a role for the state, and indeed may be funded by the state, but which are not an essential element of it. Hence, it is conceivable, for example, that an education system might be wholly privatized, but a state without a security apparatus could not function as a state.

In many respects, my line of thinking here follows that of Michael Walzer (Walzer, 1978: Ch. 12). For Walzer, terrorism is a totalitarian form of war and politics that shatters the war convention and prevailing political and moral codes. As such, it violates moral limits by failing to make moral distinctions between the targets of terrorism. Terrorism is totalitarian war because the differences between citizens in the state are flattened out. For terrorists all the citizens in a state who lend even tacit support to a regime are legitimate targets; they kill anybody in order to promote their cause, sometimes even killing people who have no relationship at all to the target audience (Walzer, 1978: 197–206). Indeed, estimates suggest that over fifty of the victims of the 9/11 attacks were Muslims.

Rather than the distinction between state and non-state actors, however, Walzer's analysis is based on those who might be deemed to be working in the service of the state and hence subject to assassination. Walzer essentially sees three categories. First, government officials who are part of the presumed oppressive apparatus are potential targets. Second, other persons in government service, who are not related to the oppressive aspects of the regime (e.g. teachers, medical service personnel, etc.), make a questionable category. As he puts it: 'the variety of activities sponsored and paid for by the modern state is extraordinary ... it seems intemperate and extravagant to make all such activities into occasions for assassination' (Walzer, 1978: 202). Third are private persons, who according to Walzer are not morally acceptable targets for assassination.

The danger of taking the definition of terrorism too far is clear in Carl Wellman's treatment of the issue. In his article 'On Terrorism Itself', Wellman argues that although violence often enters the picture, as it is one of the most effective ways of causing terror, it is not central to terrorism and, in fact, most acts of terrorism are nonviolent (Wellman, 1979: 251). But it seems to make little sense to talk of nonviolent terrorism, particularly if we include threats of violence in our definition. This problem arises because of Wellman's very broad definition of terrorism, which, he suggests, is simply the 'use or attempted use of terror as a means of coercion' (Wellman, 1979: 250). As we have already seen, terrorism is not reducible to 'to terrorize', unless, that is, we are prepared to admit that all sorts of human activity constitute terrorism. If we accept this definition, there is much more terrorism than we had previously thought. Indeed the absurdity of Wellman's position becomes clear when he admits to terrorizing his own students:

> I must confess I often engage in non-violent terrorism myself, for I often threaten to flunk any student who hands in his paper after the due date. Anyone who doubts that my acts are genuine instances of terrorism is invited to observe the unwillingness of my students to hand in assigned papers on time in the absence of any such threat and the panic in my classroom when I issue my ultimatum. (Wellman, 1979: 252)

Another important aspect of any account of terrorism is the random or indiscriminate nature in which the use of violence is deployed. We need to be careful here, and it is not correct that terrorists strike blindly and pointlessly; on the contrary they plan their actions carefully, thinking through the options and aiming for a course of action that will best promote their objectives. What is meant by the indiscriminate nature of terrorism is the manner in which the violence, or threat of violence, fails to discriminate between the guilty and the innocent.

Terrorism generally has two targets. First is the immediate target of the act; that is, the immediate subject of the violence. The immediate subject of the violence, however, is often only a means, not an end. The target of the attack is simply a cipher and has to suffer the violence so that the message can be transmitted to the secondary and most important audience. Hence, terrorism also involves the attempt by someone to force another person or group to do something they would otherwise not do. When this is achieved by intimidation, and when this intimidation is brought about by the use of violence against innocent people (for now defined as people whose behaviour is not subject to the desire of modification), or by the threat of violence, then the strategy is that of terrorism. This is an important aspect of terrorism. It is fundamentally a form of political communication. Thus, terrorists may attack a group of civilians with the aim of intimidating the civilian population at large and getting it to change its behaviour, or they may attack it with the purpose of altering the behaviour of the government such that it accepts their demands.

The problematic terms here are civilians and innocents. Many writers have attempted to draw clear distinctions between morally acceptable targets and morally unacceptable targets. For example, Igor Primoratz argues that what constitutes the innocent in this respect is that they are not attacking the terrorist directly; hence his/her actions cannot be justified as self-defence. Innocents are not responsible, in any plausible sense of the word, for the 'perceived injustice, suffering, deprivation, which is inflicted on [the terrorist] or on any of those whose cause he has embraced' (Primoratz, 2004: 17–18). The problem is that there are many terrorists who hold to an extremely broad notion of collective responsibility and argue that the mere membership of an ethnic or religious group, or perhaps citizenship of a state, entail at least a minimum level of responsibility. Moreover, in democracies, of course, there is something to this argument, given that the right to vote can be understood as partaking in the selection of a government in some way. To hold publics wholly responsible for the activities of their governments is stretching the notion of responsibility too far. For even in democracies there are always large sections of the population that did not vote for the government. Moreover, even those citizens that perhaps did vote for the government may not be in favour of the policy that is implemented and objected to by the terrorists.

However, given the history of the development of the state, we do have to accept the possibility that some may want to take issue with certain state practices, and thus the state agents who explicitly work for the state become potential targets. This does not imply that as soon as opponents of a certain regime are satisfied that the regime is unjust that they have a moral licence to kill and maim its officials, but it does suggest that if they do so, their actions will not be terrorism but political assassination. Also, this does not mean that we have no means of condemning their practice. To claim that an action is not terrorism but political assassination is not to justify it, or excuse it. So to reiterate, groups that explicitly target only state actors should not be labelled terrorists. Hence by indiscriminate or random, we simply mean that terrorism does not discriminate between the guilty and the innocent.

This position is diametrically opposed to that of Laqueur, who argues that many terrorist attacks are not indiscriminate. Laqueur can only make this argument because he confuses political assassination with terrorism. As he puts it: 'terrorist operations have been quite selective. It can hardly be argued that President Sadat, the Pope, Aldo Moro or Indira Gandhi were arbitrary targets' (Laqueur, 1987: 143–4). But if the targeting of non-state actors is an essential aspect of terrorism, then none of the examples Laqueur provides can rightly be considered terrorism. In general, people are not born into positions of political authority or influence; hence one becomes a state actor by joining the army or the security services, or by holding office in a regime that is organized around the political institution of the state. However, anyone who has not and does not play such a role should not be the subject of violent attack by non-state actors, and when they are this is one element of terrorism.

Terrorism is too politically and morally loaded a term to use loosely. States seeking sympathy for their own causes all too often use it irresponsibly as a public relations move. The best way to ensure that 'terrorism' has a practical and enforceable meaning, that it facilitates rigorous analysis, and is useful in public discourse, is to use it in very specific, and narrow, ways. Thus, we should restrict the use of the term terrorism to the violent activities of non-state actors in the pursuance of political aims. Of course, states can and do use their power unlawfully, and when necessary they should demonstrate their legitimacy by abiding by well-established international law. They should also be prepared to defend their use of violence in international organizations able to prosecute illegitimate state violence, such as the UN and the International Court of Justice (ICC). Although far from perfect, these bodies can take action against individuals and state agents accused of war crimes and acts of violence that terrorize non-state actors (civilians). Moreover, where these organizations fail to bring cases the appropriate response is to strengthen them, not retreat to treating political violence as being all of a kind. People rightly concerned about state abuses of human rights and state aggression should direct their attention towards ensuring that these institutions become more effective rather than engaging in a futile attempt to get states to accept the label of state terrorism.

I want to conclude this chapter by pulling the discussion together and setting out the core elements of my account of terrorism. Rather than attempting a pithy definition I deal with some of the elements I deem to be essential to any coherent account of terrorism.

Terrorism Involves the Deliberate Targeting of Non-state Actors and Institutions by Non-state Actors

This is a key aspect of my approach and rests on the symbiotic nature of the relationship between the state, violence and protest. In using the designation non-state actors, as opposed to innocents or non-combatants, I recognize the central role of the state in the political organization of society and the constitutive role of violence within that process. For insofar as state actors play a role in the maintenance of state projects, and if those projects have groups and individuals that object to them, then the means to react to the state must be accepted. Thus, politicians, the police, military and security services, civil servants, diplomats, members of the judiciary and public prosecutors – indeed, any actor that can be said to be engaged in the direct maintenance of the state – can be considered a legitimate target of groups that object to that state. This does not mean that the morality of violent acts against the state and its institutions is not subject to question. Nor does it imply that that such attacks are something I support. Such attacks are neither good nor bad in and of themselves independent of context, and the determination of support can only be made on a case-by-case basis. But ultimately, groups that confine their violent, or nonviolent, expressions of political discontent to state actors and state institutions should not be labelled terrorists.

Of course, there is still a problem of those fuzzy areas concerning actors that may be said to be agents of the state but who are not actually working for the maintenance and functioning of the state apparatus; examples here might be university educators, nurses, or local authority employees. Answers to this question will depend upon the definition of the state that is adopted and the specific structural form of the state in question. There is no doubt that views will differ on this issue. In fact, in totalitarian states, this might be a valid argument if the tentacles of the state reach into all aspects of society. However, even in totalitarian states, it is the state that intrudes into civil society and not civil society that has chosen to play a major role in the maintenance of the state. In theory, however, it is possible that if the population is almost wholly supportive of the state, and works towards its explicit maintenance, then the category of non-state actors is massively reduced. This is only a theoretical possibility, and in most states the identification of non-state actors is relatively unproblematic.

I am aware that by insisting that terrorism is always carried out by non-state actors against non-state actors I am, by definition, ruling out the possibility of state terrorism. This is not an oversight; it is a deliberate strategy to limit the scope of the range of acts that might come under the label. We need a robust deflationary account of terrorism so that we might grasp its role, function and place in the contemporary world and begin to assess just how much of a problem it represents. Only then are we able to assess government claims that our freedoms should be limited in order to fight terrorism.

Terrorism is a Form of Violent (or Threatened) Political Communication

Political communication that is non-violent, or does not involve threats to violence, is not terrorism. Groups within societies always, potentially at least, have disagreements. In general these disagreements will revolve around competing visions of how the world is, how it came to be, and what it might become. This is why I believe that ontology lies at the heart of politics. If there were no basic ontological differences about how we conceive the world then there would be no politics (Wight, 2006). Accepting this, however, should not lead us to accept that the only way to settle these differences is through the use of violence. A terrorist act is primarily a means of publicly demonstrating these ontological differences, through the use of violence or the threat of violence. Those who adopt terrorism as a specific form of political violence generally do not expect that the use of such violence will lead directly to state action aimed at addressing the terrorist cause.

The aim of the terrorist is to publicize the cause; spread fear, in the hope of getting publics to pressure governments to act to acquiesce to the terrorist demands; or engender a violent counter-response from the state that generates sympathy and support from the cause. Terrorist acts rarely lead to successful outcomes; terrorism, at least at one level, does not work (Abrahms, 2006). However, whilst individual acts of terrorism aimed at specific outcomes, the releasing of prisoners, for example, may not work, as a long-term strategy aimed at extracting concessions of a political nature there can be little doubt in its effectiveness for some actors. Where it has achieved this, however, it is largely as a result of its communicative aspect, not any strategic value associated with individual terrorist acts.

The Victims Are Not the Intended Recipients of the Political Message

The victims of terrorist acts are not the intended recipients of the message. Indeed, terrorists use the victims in an instrumental way as a means of communicating. The victims are not targeted in any precise manner, but rather, any victim will do. The message is important and the victim is simply the conduit for the message.

This does not mean that terrorists do not choose their targets in a well-formulated way. They do. But the choice of target is not based on the actual individuals killed or injured, but rather the symbolic value of the overall attack. Hence the 9/11 attacks on the Twin Towers, for example, were targeted on the centres of economic power and not the individuals working in them. For the terrorists it did not matter who was in the buildings at the time. What mattered was that the symbols of the supposed US Empire and financial system were attacked. Equally, when considered in light of the other dimensions of my account of terrorism, it should be clear that while the attacks on the Twin Towers can be considered to be terrorism, the attack on the Pentagon was not. This is so because there is a legitimate case that can be made that the Pentagon was a legitimate military target, whilst the Twin Towers were not. Certainly, whilst non-state actors were killed in the attack on the Pentagon, if the attack was primarily aimed at the military heart of the United States, then those non-state actors who died as a result of the attack can be considered collateral damage; in the same way we consider innocent victims of drone attacks to be innocent but unavoidable casualties of war.

Terrorism Is Always Illegitimate Violence

In the contemporary world, only the state has a legitimate right to exercise violence. This means that any violence carried out by non-state actors is illegitimate. This does not mean that such violence lacks a justification or that violent protest is denied. The onus, however, is on non-state actors to justify their use of violence. Given the violent history of state development it is always possible that groups and individuals have grievances against the state. When such violence is directed against state actors, it remains illegitimate, but it might be justified. Violence conducted for a political cause that targets non-state actors is neither legitimate nor justified.

Conclusion

Terrorism is a very specific form of political violence. Not all political violence is the same, and the dynamics, modes of operations, functions and outcomes of differing forms of political violence need to be acknowledged. Max Abrahms has grouped terrorist scholars into two groups, 'lumpers and splitters' (Abrahms, 2010). The 'lumpers' tend to treat differing forms of political violence all of a kind, whereas the 'splitters' insist on recognizing the differences between various forms of political violence. I agree wholeheartedly with Abrahms that '[c]onflating conceptually unlike units may occasionally have normative appeal, but risks yielding ambiguous, misleading results that obscure rather than inform counterterrorism strategy. For this reason, splitting – not lumping – is the future of terrorism studies' (Abrahms, 2010). However, I prefer the distinction between an 'inflationary' account of terrorism and a 'deflationary' one because it highlights the political nature of the definitional problem. Inflationary accounts inflate the potential threat that terrorism poses to individuals, societies, states, or the security of the international system. Deflationary accounts place terrorism in context and allow the nuances of that context to form the basis of analysis.

Context always matters, and violence always has a context and the state is always part of the context of any terrorist act. Violence, when considered theoretically, is a structure. It is a fundamental force and has played a major role in the development of the political realm. Indeed, it continues to play a major role in that realm. There is no general theory of political violence, and hence it must be examined through its specific forms and manifestations. Thus, theories of violence must be as varied as the practices and contexts within which it emerges. To flatten out these differences and attempt to deal with differing modes of violence under the one descriptive term is a serious error. It is an error that is compounded when there is little, or no, consensus on that term. In order to make sense of the context of terrorism, we need a clear sense of what it is, and what it is not. As such, the definitional problem will not go away.

5
State Terrorism

This chapter tackles the issue of state terrorism. State terrorism is an important issue because although the emergence of 'critical terrorism studies' (Jackson, Smyth and Gunning, 2009) should have been a welcome development, much of the work emanating from that approach has become bogged down in a critique of state terrorism (Jackson, Murphy and Poynting, 2010). By focusing on state violence and deeming it to be terrorism, they have failed to provide a critical account of terrorism itself. As such, critical terrorism studies have not provided the promised critical perspective on terrorism. There is certainly a need to move the state to the centre of analysis of terrorism, but not in terms of state terrorism. The state is a condition of possibility for terrorism, not a perpetrator of it. On the other hand, the majority of mainstream approaches to terrorism lack a theoretical and philosophical grounding of the concept in terms of its structural relationship to the state. Clearly the definitional problem has been a major barrier to this. The most important moment for any field of study is to define the parameters of its object domain. In the absence of even a minimal consensus on the definition of terrorism, there is no consensus on what should be the object of analysis (Richards, 2013). Hence, whilst I fully support the move to link terrorism to the state, I argue that this is not in relation to state terrorism, but the state considered as a condition of possibility for terrorism. In short, terrorism, in the form we find it today, can only be analysed as a particular form of political violence and understood in terms of its structural relationship to the modern state under conditions of globalization.

State terrorism is one of the most contentious areas of research into terrorism and no doubt my position is going to be the subject of much disagreement from those scholars keen to present their work as critical (Blakeley, 2009; Gareau, 2004; Goodin, 2006; Jackson et al., 2010; Stohl and Lopez, 1988). Yet, the determination of what is, and what is not critical, cannot be made purely on some claim to the label. If critical, in the political sense, is to mean anything, then the outcomes related to the deployment of critical concepts, such as state -terrorism, have to be shown to be advancing the stated political aims of the critical theorist; in this case a critical stance on state practices and through this, the potential alteration of those practices; or emancipation. If, on the other hand, the academic validation of concepts, such as state terrorism, leads to political ends that run counter to the aims of the critical theorist, then that theorist has an obligation to rethink their conceptual framework. I argue that the academic validation of the concept of state terrorism provides no additional critique of state practices beyond that which we already possess. But, in addition, it allows state managers the ability to label enemy states as terrorists (a practice that is almost universal), introduces confusion into debate surrounding differing forms of political violence, and lends support to state practices aimed at controlling populations on the basis of the threat from terrorism. These cannot be the aims of any critical theory worthy of the name.

Put simply, we should dispense altogether with the notion of state terrorism. Let me be clear lest my position is misunderstood. What the analysis of the state contained in Chapter 1 demonstrates is that violence and terror are constitutive of the state. Granted, state control in the contemporary world is largely exercised through consent, yet this is consent guaranteed by an ever-present threat of violence if protest against the state goes beyond certain socially acceptable, and legitimate, forms; 'acceptable' and 'legitimate', that is, according to definitions and boundaries set by states. That states use violence against their citizens and citizens of other states is beyond doubt. That states kill more people, often their own citizens, than terrorism, is clear. That states deliberately set out to terrorize groups of people for political ends is also not in question. Yet terrorism, if it is to have any analytical purchase, cannot be equated with simply the production of terror. All kinds of individuals, groups and complex institutional forms use terror in society, but we would not wish to call all forms of 'terror production' terrorism. The conflation of terror with terrorism occurs in all attempts to construct arguments concerning state terrorism.

The idea of state terrorism is not new. Noam Chomsky is perhaps the most vocal, and well-known proponent of this view (Chomsky, 2001), and he clearly equates terror with terrorism, arguing that the United States is the 'world champion in generating terror' (Chomsky, 2014). Edward Herman makes the reduction of terrorism and terror explicit, arguing that '"Terror", according to the dictionary definition, "is a mode of governing, or of opposing government, by intimidation"' (Herman, 1982: 21). Likewise, Michael Stohl and George Lopez explicitly embrace the idea that coercive dimensions of state foreign policy are equivalent to state terrorism (Stohl and Lopez, 1988: 1–12). Other examples of state terrorism can be found in Alexander George (1991) and Jonathan Friedman (2006: xxx). In all of these examples, it is the assumed conflation of terror with terrorism that does the work. The problems with this are clear when Herman's dictionary definition is placed within the context of the state as detailed in Chapters 1 and 2. If the mere production of terror equates to terrorism then just about everything the state does would fall under this label; states are the ground of the political, and they ultimately enforce their will through the production of terror. Hence, in order to situate terrorism as a specific kind of political practice, we need to dispense with the confused notion of state terrorism.

Equally, my deflationary account of terrorism provides no support for more traditional studies of terrorism that have also generally been happy to dispense with the concept of state terrorism (Laqueur, 2003: 237). For on my account, many of the events, activities and phenomena typically considered to be terrorism are not. Thus, for example, political assassinations, bomb attacks – such as those conducted on the Conservative government of Margaret Thatcher in Brighton in 1984 – and attacks on military targets, state officials and security forces would not constitute terrorism and should not be considered as such. Recall that terrorism, as I define it, is a form of violent political practice deliberately targeted at non-state actors with the aim of communicating political grievances in the hope of forcing state managers to enact political change.

My argument in relation to state terrorism has three aspects. First, is a conceptual one; the state and terrorism are two concepts which, when properly considered, form a complex conceptual matrix. Moreover, both the state and terrorism are highly contested concepts, and it is difficult to reach consensus on just one of them, let alone attempt to arrive at a composite conceptual term. Putting the two together forms a 'conjunctural concept' that makes agreement on what it means impossible to reach. Equally, those keen to talk in terms of state terrorism will need to come up with a definition of terrorism able to generate at least some form of consensus; and as we have seen thus far they have failed. Moreover, they will also need to come up with a definition of the state. None of the authors keen to defend the notion of state terrorism present a clear account of what they mean by the state; it is assumed rather than elaborated.

Robert E. Goodin (2006), for example, arguably one of the most sophisticated advocates of state terrorism, treats the state as a given, unproblematic term. He fails to unpack its form, its relationship to violence or its place in the wider social field. The state, for Goodin, simply is, and it requires no specification. Likewise, Ruth Blakeley, who effectively extends the definition of terrorism to encompass all state activity, provides a lengthy defence of her definition of terrorism, and state terrorism, yet never specifies an account of the state. Blakeley provides a discussion of state agents but not an account of the state (Blakeley, 2009: 36–42). This is a serious theoretical problem that the advocates of state terrorism have neglected to address. Definitions of the state are as varied and contentious as that of terrorism, and a coherent account of state terrorism is impossible when one side of the conceptual couple remains implicit rather than explicit. When both are implicit, the problem is magnified.

Second, and again drawing on the philosophy of social science, is the fact that our definition of terrorism must have some resonance with how political actors and publics understand and use the term. In the social sciences, the practices of the actors we study are embedded within self-understandings that draw on concepts that the social sciences are trying to explain. Hence, the social scientists' accounts of the phenomena under study have, in some ways, to map onto the understandings of the actors involved in the study. Or, as Conor Gearty has put it, the meaning of terrorism

> is moulded by government, the media and in popular usage, not by academic departments ... The manipulators of language are no respecters of academic integrity, and, simply to keep up, political scientists who believe a definition is possible have had to broaden their attempts so extensively that the exercise becomes rather pointless. (Gearty, 1991: 6)

Bringing state violence under the umbrella of terrorism is one such broadening that has led to this unfortunate trend. Moreover, if academics begin to use terms in ways that do not resonate with those agents engaged in the practice under consideration, then due attention has not been paid to how social objects are constituted. All social objects are concept- and activity-dependent, and academics cannot construct theoretical accounts of particular fields of social activity that do not take into account the concepts held by actors engaged in the activity. How those actors define their practices is part of the ontology of what the practices are.

Thus, when analysing terrorism, for example, part of the specification of that object must be the beliefs and concepts of the actors involved in the practice (broadly conceived). By this, I do not just mean the concepts and beliefs of the terrorists themselves (setting aside for a moment the definitional problems with the term). Rather, since terrorism is a public political practice we have to include in our accounts what lay actors and publics think terrorism is. We do not have to give these lay accounts precedence, and it may well be that social scientific explanations correct the lay accounts of terrorism in fundamental ways. After all, we have no reason to assume that the actors involved in a given practice will always understand the totality of that practice, and politicians and the media cannot be given sole authority to use a term in any way they desire.

However, even when a correction of a given actors' set of beliefs around some phenomenon is demanded, it can only take place through an engagement with those concepts. In terms of terrorism, the consensus of public discourse treats the issue as related primarily to non-state actors. Assuming for a moment that these public understandings of terrorism are flawed, then any academic account that attempts to correct them has to be able to demonstrate why these accounts are so prevalent, as well as explaining how more expansive views are an improvement on them. In short, the social scientist has to demonstrate why the lay actors' accounts are wrong and why the academic account is better. Social scientists simply cannot say that these actors have it wrong and begin using terms commonly used in public discourse in a fundamentally different way from how they are used by the actors. In the context of state terrorism, this can only be achieved through sustained engagement with the problematic concepts of the state and terrorism. Thus far, terrorism studies have not satisfactorily resolved the definitional issue of terrorism, let alone the issue of state terrorism.

Hence, just as I argued that the concepts employed by agents involved must be taken into account when defining terrorism, then the same is true of state terrorism. Although most individuals would consider state violence to be abhorrent, they would not consider it to be terrorism. In this regard, Sir Jeremy Greenstock, the Chairman of the UN Counter-Terrorism Committee, argued in a 2002 meeting that the 'twelve previous international conventions on terrorism had never referred to state terrorism, which was not an international legal concept, and that when states abuse their powers they should be judged against international conventions dealing with war crimes, international human rights and international humanitarian law, rather than against international anti-terrorism statutes' (UN, 2002).

Third is a pragmatic political consideration. One argument of this book is that we need a deflationary approach to terrorism. Terrorism, as I define it, is simply not a major cause of deaths in the international system, nor is it a threat to international security and stability. Indeed, it is rarely even a serious threat to the security of individual states, let alone the international system. It is, in fact, a very marginal form of political violence, engaged in by very few, and directly affecting a few.

However, if our measures include all those activities that might reasonably fall under the definition of state terrorism, then there is certainly much more terrorism in the international political system than we previously thought. If this is the case, then citizens would be well advised to be concerned about levels of terrorism and governments would be equally well advised to follow policies and procedures aimed at controlling it. The more terrorism there is, the more political control we seem to accept to deal with it. One does not have to be a conspiracy theorist to see how states might use rising figures relating to terrorism to implement ever more coercive and restrictive laws. Interestingly, Goodin (2006: 3), despite claiming to develop a deflationary account of terrorism, argues that states participate directly in terrorism by amplifying the fear of terrorism, even as they try to exclude themselves from the category. If amplifying the fear of terrorism is itself terrorism, then how is this deflationary? How does the incorporation of many instances of state violence in our definition of terrorism produce a deflationary account? It doesn't – it inflates it.

Of course, since Goodin (2006: 2) claims that terrorism is fundamentally nothing other than 'frightening people for political advantage', then it is not surprising that he would consider 'amplifying the fear of terror' to be a form of terrorism. This is an extremely broad definition of terrorism and one that is too all-encompassing to be of analytical value. It also fails the test of conceptual coherence with the accounts of terrorism that circulate in public debate. Moreover, although Goodin accepts that there are political tactics that involve frightening people for political advantage that do not constitute terrorism, he provides no guidance on how we might differentiate these from that class of acts that do constitute terrorism. There is no doubting that Goodin's argument has been influential. Ken Booth and Tim Dunne (2012: 39) provide what looks to be a compelling argument against my position through their acceptance of Goodin's account.

'In logic,' argue Booth and Dunne, 'one must ask why to terrorise is not to engage in terrorism if the act of terror has a political end, the target is the public, and the aim is to communicate a brutal message' (Booth and Dunne, 2012: 39). At first sight, there would seem some similarities between their position and my deflationary account. Terrorism, according to Booth and Dunne, is a political act, it is communicative, and the acts are committed against the public (my non-state actors). However, there are some subtle differences between our respective accounts that have serious implications for how we understand terrorism. First, is it not clear, if by insisting that the target is the public, that Booth and Dunne would accept my view that attacks on state agents are not terrorism? Let us assume for the moment it does; for Booth and Dunne, terrorism always involves acts against the public. Second, although the immediate targets of terrorist acts are the public, the communicative target is not. Terrorists commit violent acts against non-state actors (Booth and Dunne's public) to communicate a political message to state managers. Yes, the fear that emerges out of a terrorist act might spread through the public, but the aim of the terrorist is for that fear to put pressure on state managers to change some or other political practice. A classic example of this was the decision of Spanish Prime Minister, José Luis Rodríguez Zapatero, to pull Spanish troops out of Iraq after the 2004 Madrid bombings (Baird, 2012). Third, there can be no assumption that the aim is to 'communicate a brutal message'. The act that transmits the message might be brutal, but the message itself might be morally and politically valid; as in, 'stop oppressing our people'. The fact that the transmission mechanism for this message is brutal can have no bearing on the validity of the message. Of course, this does not make the act morally justifiable, and I would argue that on my deflationary account of terrorism, nothing could ever justify the resort to terrorism.

Fourth, the use of 'acts' (and Booth and Dunne do not specify that these acts need to be violent) to instil terror in publics to communicate a political message essentially suggests that all state activity is terrorism. After all, the very existence of a prison system linked to a judicial system and framed on laws made by the state can be considered to be a state mechanism to instil in publics a fear of committing crime; thus ensuring state control of that public. At the margins, one might say that this is criminal not political activity, yet anything that involves the state is by its very nature political. Prisons, courts and the legal system are all aspects of the state aimed at controlling populations; what could be more political? In addition, of course, many acts of war would come under their definition. In the final analysis, I would simply turn the question around and ask Booth and Dunne what we gain by labelling as terrorism 'state activity that aims to spread terror with a political end, where the target is the public, and the aim is to communicate a message'.

Ultimately, what drives Booth and Dunne's argument is the fear that not to label state violence as terrorism somehow lessens our moral critique of that violence. As they put it, to suggest that states cannot be terrorists 'lets them off the hook'; moreover, '[s]tate authorities often exceed what is morally and legally acceptable in terms of using violence' (Booth and Dunne, 2012: 41). Indeed they do, yet such activity can be called state oppression, or state violence, and still be subject to robust moral critique, without introducing the analytical confusion that follows from the deployment of the term state terrorism. Indeed, as Goodin himself puts it, 'If that wrong is not technically termed "terrorism" ... that fact is of no moral consequence' (Goodin, 2006: 55–6). Exactly: we do not need to label state wrongs as terrorism in order to subject them to moral critique.

Equally, once we accept the notion of state terrorism we fall rapidly into a relativist morass where each state can claim that the activities of other states are terrorism. Faced with this, the political analyst advocating the concept of state terrorism has no theoretical devices left to assess, or critique, such claims. States, since they are embedded within a logic that has violence and the production of terror at its core, simply are terrorists. This is deeply problematic and means that academic accounts of terrorism become politicized and are unable to bring analytical clarity to such debates. I suspect that there is a hidden agenda behind many claims concerning state terrorism. It is an attempt to introduce into the study of terrorism a supposed moral equivalence between violent acts committed by non-state actors against publics, and violent acts committed by state actors against publics. There is no moral equivalence. State violence against publics is much more prevalent, much more damaging, and causes innumerably more deaths than violent activity committed by non-state actors against publics. What we need to do is challenge the idea that terrorism is the most heinous form of political violence, not expand the use of the term to the point that it ceases to have meaning.

Hence, I would dispense altogether with the notion of state terrorism and the equally problematic and overused term terrorist state (Chomsky, 2001). Goodin claims that any definition that includes a reference to non-state actors as the perpetrators of terrorist acts constitutes a 'definitional ploy' precluding the 'possibility of "state terrorism" purely by definition' (Goodin, 2006: 55–6). I agree that including a reference to non-state actors in any definition precludes the possibility of state terrorism, but it is not a ploy, it is an explicit attempt to claim that state violence is not terrorism. Equally, that argument works both ways, and a definition of terrorism that simply means the frightening of people for political purposes is designed to ensure the inclusion of state activity under the label of terrorism. Through this, advocates of state terrorism arrive at a definition of terrorism broad enough to encompass those activities conducted by states that they consider to be state terrorism. It is easy enough to see the problem here. Both Richard Jackson and Ruth Blakeley, for example, begin with a set of state practices they find problematic, and then adjust the definition of terrorism in such a way that those state practices can fall under the new definition of terrorism; in effect, they begin from the assumption that there is such a thing as state terrorism and adjust the definition of terrorism to accommodate it (Blakeley, 2009; Jackson et al., 2010). Now, all of the state practices that Jackson and Blakeley want to bring under the label of state terrorism are dealt with comprehensively in the internationasl relations literature, and they are simply not referred to as forms of terrorism. Given the problems surrounding the definition of terrorism, this is not without good reason. Work on repression, ethnic cleansing, genocide and authoritarianism is prevalent in the discipline and cognate areas. Moreover, the concept of state terrorism has also been much debated (Gareau, 2004; Marchak and Marchak, 1999; Oliverio, 1998; Stohl and Lopez, 1988). Despite the existence of this and other literatures dealing with state violence, Jackson still asks why state violence is not studied as state terrorism (Jackson et al., 2010: 2). Of course, one could reverse this and ask just what we gain by dealing with such violence as state terrorism. Indeed, if such literature is widely available, what do we gain by encompassing it under the confused rubric of terrorism? Yet following Goodin (2006), Jackson, Blakeley, Booth and Dunne and Goodin are effectively asking: why is it that similar acts of violence (such as a bomb on a plane) are treated as terrorism when planted by non-state agents, but as something else when planted by state agents?

Now this implies that the act itself is the sole determinant of how it should be understood. This is a very behaviourist account of social action, and it also highlights the important point of taking serious ontological issues derived from the philosophy of social science. Consider the following example. Imagine two human subjects who die after being administered lethal injections. The act in both instances remains the same. Have both subjects been murdered? How could we tell? Both acts are identical, but we simply lack sufficient information about both cases to make a judgement. One of the subjects, for example, could have been inadvertently administered an incorrect drug. One could have been a prisoner subject to a lethal injection. In both cases, and devoid of further knowledge, to treat them as murder is, potentially at least, to misdescribe them. Likewise, consider two humans undergoing procedures to remove a limb. Are both being tortured, or is one being tortured and the other subject to life-saving amputation? The act (the removal of a limb) is the same, but does the same description fit both acts? The same can be said about the bomb example; it only makes sense to compare the two acts as one and the same if we already assume some important details are the same in both instances; details we do not actually have. So were the state agents acting with, or without, the authority of the state? Were the people on the plane civilians, military personnel, or fanatics of some kind or other intent on flying the plane into a shopping centre or some other public space? Surely, if it was the latter and state agents had exploded a bomb on the plane to protect national security, and prevent a great number of deaths on the ground, then would this not be considered terrorism? Context matters in any assessment of political violence, and part of the context is some account of the intentions of the actors. Typically, scholars of a positivist persuasion have shied away from intentions and motives because of the methodological and epistemological difficulties of coming to know them. Motives, beliefs and intentions, on the other hand, are intrinsic to any non-positivist account.

To say that there is a similarity between two acts is not the same as saying they are identical. In this respect, the 'ism' matters, and not all social practices that involve terror are terrorism. The ethical and political motives of Jackson, Goodin, Booth and Dunne and Blakeley are admirable; it is the tactic that is confused. All are concerned to demonstrate how the violence perpetrated by states is worse than that perpetrated by non-state actors. I agree, but argue that nothing is gained, apart from analytical confusion, through discussing such violence as terrorism. In effect, all advocates of state terrorism essentially accept the problematic argument that terrorism is the worst form of violence we encounter and want to increase the field of actions covered by this definition to include state violence. We should certainly highlight the fact that state violence is an horrific form of violence, but we do not need to confuse it with terrorism in order to make this claim.

But social concepts cannot be assessed in this way. Booth and Dunne, Jackson, Blakeley and Goodin all seem to assume that there is something we call terrorism 'out there' in the world, and that all we need to do is refine our concepts and bring them into line with that thing. Critical social analysis cannot proceed in this way. We cannot simply deal with the validity of our concepts through an examination of how well they fit with our chosen objects. For the critical theorist, other factors have to be taken into account when determining conceptual validity, and one of these has to be the consequences of adopting some definitions and not others. As such, analytical confusion and unwanted political outcomes seem to be to be good reasons to reject the notion of state terrorism. Of course, as a critical realist, I am not saying that the relationship between our theoretical concepts and the objects we study is of no consequence. Terrorism certainly exists, and we should attempt to do all we can to ensure our theoretical accounts capture that object in all its complexity and as accurately as possible. But as already indicated, the object is not just the specific act, but the concepts and beliefs held by publics trying to grapple with the meaning of such acts as well as the context within which the act takes place.

Blakeley addresses this issue in some depth, but her account is confused. First, she rejects Laqueur's argument that 'there are basic differences in motives, function and effect between oppression by the state (or society or religion) and political terrorism. To equate them, to obliterate them is to spread confusion' (Laqueur, 1986: 89). This, Blakeley argues, proves that Laqueur's analysis of terrorism is 'actor based, rather than action based. Even if the motives, functions and effects of terrorism by states and non-state actors are different, the act of terrorism itself is not' (Blakeley, 2009: 26–7). But this makes little sense; the act itself, as argued above, is given meaning by the context in which it is placed, and part of that context is the intentions and motives of those involved. In fact, Blakeley is unable to maintain this strict act-based, or behaviouralist account, and later argues that state terrorism involves 'the deliberate targeting of individuals' (Blakeley, 2009: 31), that 'what differentiates state terrorism from other forms of repression is the intent of the actor to create extreme fear' (Blakeley, 2009: 33), and that a 'further indication of intention concerns the reasonably anticipated likely consequence of an act' (Blakeley, 2009: 41). Hence, whilst she rejects Laqueur's attempt to argue that motives and intentions are important when trying to differentiate between differing forms of political violence and insists that 'acts' are all that matter, she then reintroduces intentions as a central category to form her own differentiation between state repression and state terrorism. However, if we can differentiate state repression from state terrorism on the basis of intent, why is Laqueur wrong to do so when differentiating between differing forms of violence? Short answer; he is not.

Indeed, most people, even those I am arguing against here, have an implicit account of terrorism that naturally leads to the assumption that these are acts committed by non-state actors. In fact, Jackson often removes state terrorism from his account on many instances and assumes a definition of terrorism predicated on non-state actors. After all, if Jackson wants to claim, as do I, that terrorism is not as prevalent or as big a danger as states would like us to believe, then he cannot be including state terrorism in his definition. As such, the distinction between terrorism and state violence underpins much of Jackson's work. In particular, his blog entry of 25 May 2011 explicitly excludes figures relating to state terrorism in order to demonstrate how the threat of terrorism is small when considered in relation to other causes of death, such as smoking and car crashes (Jackson, 2011). If state terrorism were included in these figures, then, the argument would not hold up to scrutiny. Jackson appears to move from one definition to another depending on the purposes of his argument. This might be a reasonable political strategy, and politicians employ it all the time, but it is not one that any coherent science can adopt. Imagine if the meaning of a 'gene' were to change according to the political point a biologist wanted to make. Or if the meaning of 'mass' were to change depending on how the physicist wanted to deploy it.

If the relationship between our theoretical constructs and the objects we study was the only available measure to assess the validity of our theoretical concepts, we would all be positivists. Critical theory, on the other hand, demands that we place our concepts in a wider context, taking into account the consequences of adopting one concept rather than another. This is one important aspect of reflexivity (Bourdieu, 2004). Positivism has the easier path; critical theory is harder, but intellectually and politically more honest.

Perhaps the main problem with the conflation of terror and terrorism is that almost every aspect of state practice could be considered an act of terrorism on this account. Indeed, this is how Jackson and Blakeley seem to treat it. Thus, if we define terrorism, as Jackson does, as 'the threat or use of violence against one group of people in order to terrify or intimidate another group of people as a means of preventing or changing their political practice', then all sorts of state practices come under the rubric of terrorism (Jackson, 2008: 385). This definition is simply too broad to be analytically useful.

To his credit, Jackson is quite explicit about this, arguing that '"state doctrines and practices of nuclear deterrence", "coercive diplomacy", "constructive engagement", "sanctions" and "certain peace settlements involving making pacts with groups who have engaged in widespread use of terror" can also constitute state terrorism' (Jackson, 2008: 387). I fail to see what we gain here. If all of these state practices are terrorism, then it is difficult to see what state practice cannot come under this definition. Do we really want to view 'peace settlements', however unjust they may be, as forms of terrorism?

Blakeley's analysis has a similar problem. According to Blakeley, state terrorism involves the following four key elements:

1. A deliberate act of violence against individuals that the state has a duty to protect, or a threat of such an act if a climate of fear has already been established through preceding acts of state violence;
2. The act must be perpetrated by actors on behalf of, or in conjunction with, the state, including paramilitaries and private security agents;
3. The act or threat of violence is intended to induce extreme fear in some target observers who identify with that victim; and
4. The target audience is forced to consider changing their behaviour in some way. (Blakeley, 2009: 30)

There are various problems with this definition. First, it seems strange that Blakeley would claim that state terrorism always involves violence against individuals that the state has a duty to protect. Many of the examples of state violence that are normally addressed in the literature on state terrorism are based on violence against the citizens of other states; the bombing of Dresden, for example. Many of the examples of state terrorism that Blakeley provides are acts perpetrated by states against individuals who are not citizens of the state committing the act; US torture of non-US citizens suspected of terrorism, for example, or extraordinary rendition, again of non-US citizens; in which case, the state concerned has no duty to protect them. After all, states are typically only considered to have a duty to protect their citizens and not the citizens of other states. Blakeley attempts to pre-empt this criticism by arguing that if a state has prisoners of war it has an obligation to protect them; but even this qualification does not help in terms of extraordinary rendition, where it is doubtful that those being held are 'prisoners of war'. But equally, extraordinary rendition and the treatment of those held in Guantánamo Bay are forms of state practice shrouded in secrecy, so they seem to fall foul of the communicative aspect of terrorism embedded in her points 3 and 4.

What is particularly puzzling about Blakeley's discussion is that she accepts that it is counter-productive to define state terrorism in relation to domestic law, since when states violate such laws they normally justify themselves in terms of some emergency powers (Blakeley, 2009). She attempts to deal with this issue by arguing that state terrorism can be examined in relation to international norms and laws, specifically those concerned with human rights (Blakeley, 2009: 31). This seems correct, but it is not clear why a violation of human rights or international norms needs to be described as state terrorism, particularly since state terrorism has not been codified in international law, whereas the violation of human rights has. Indeed, adding the label state terrorism to these issues is likely to make the cases harder to prosecute, as states will obviously react strongly to any attempt to label their actions as terrorism. Moreover, Blakeley argues that 'it is deemed illegal and inhuman when non-state actors commit those acts [acts Blakeley considers to be terrorism] and it is no more humane if the perpetrator is a state' (Blakeley, 2009: 33). Clearly, it is no more humane to say that the state has committed the act, but it adds nothing to the moral judgement of such acts to call them terrorism. It is puzzling that Blakeley accepts that there are already international laws in place to deal with these state practices, but still wants to apply the label of state terrorism to them. To repeat, nothing is added by doing so apart from analytical confusion and possibly a less successful outcome in terms of the prosecution of states who commit such acts.

A related problem with Blakeley's discussion of state terrorism concerns the level of secrecy that states may exhibit in relation to their activities. Terrorism is normally considered to be a public demonstration of violence, or the threat of it, that symbolically spreads fear around a larger population for political ends. Blakeley argues that secrecy is not such a problem in relation to state terrorism, because even in those incidents when states 'do all they can to avoid their actions being exposed, they are nevertheless seeking publicity among a particular, albeit small, audience' (Blakeley, 2009: 33). It is difficult to see how Blakeley can substantiate this claim. If states deny outright that they had been involved in a particular act, how can Blakeley, or anyone, even those in the supposed target audience, know that the state is intentionally attempting to spread fear? Moreover, in cases such as extraordinary rendition, those involved are not normally innocents in any meaningful sense, or at least, the state does not think they are innocent. These people are specifically targeted because of their presumed direct involvement in the conflict, and if the state intends to send a message, it is to others similarly engaged in acts against the state. But how can that message be spread if the state keeps these acts secret? On the other hand, if extraordinary rendition were not kept secret, it could be viewed as a form of social control aimed at changing the behaviour of both those subject to the rendition, and others in the target group who might fear they would suffer the same fate. In this respect, it is no different to the kind of message the states routinely send to criminals via the legal and penal system. This is not to say that we should always believe everything that the state officials say or do, even their denials. But it does mean that determining this cannot rest on the claims of a few that may see the exercise of state power and conspiracy everywhere.

In fact, when Blakeley discusses specific examples of state terrorism it is difficult to see what activity would not come under this definition. To name but a few: disappearances, illegal detention, torture, assassinations, intelligence gathering, kidnap, interrogation, torture, bombing campaigns, the killing of enemy combatants that had been disarmed, the legal targeting of civilians, other humiliating and degrading treatment, extraordinary rendition, and so on (Blakeley, 2009: 35–51). Blakeley goes further, arguing that even if the intention was not the explicit intimidation of a target audience beyond the victim, states can still be accused of state terrorism if fear emerges in some audiences (although not a target audience, for a target implies intention); terrorism by accident, presumably (Blakeley, 2009: 42–4). As she puts it, even 'when terror is not the primary intention, but a secondary effect of some other act, it still constitutes state terrorism' (Blakeley, 2009: 43). Admittedly, she adds a caveat here arguing that such state -terrorism is not the 'unintended secondary effect of some good or indifferent act. It is a consequence of a policy which is itself illegitimate, repressive and ... evil' (Blakeley, 2009: 43). So, for example, if a state is attacking a military base and some audience observes the testing and decides that aliens are about to invade, and that audience spreads fear among the general population, then the state (and presumably the audience who wrongly transmitted the message?), having spread fear, however inadvertently, are, for Blakeley, guilty of state terrorism.

The problems with this should again be clear. Blakeley extends the definition of terrorism to all forms of political activity, even those that do not involve intentional violence, or the intention to produce terror or fear. This is the main problem with the use of the term state terrorism; it begins to look like every state activity is, or potentially can be, a form of state terrorism. As already indicated, I do not deny that states engage in activities intended to spread fear and terror among populations. Often the target audience of such state activity will be the citizens of state themselves, and sometimes they are citizens of another state. Such state actions are morally reprehensible and should be challenged and rejected whenever possible. What I do not accept is that we need to call this terrorism, and nor do I understand what we gain in doing so.

All the activities discussed by Blakeley in her account of state terrorism could be, and have been, covered through notions of state violence and suppression. To label these activities as state terrorism simply because of some superficial similarities surrounding the production of terror adds nothing to the debate. Moreover, there are already procedures for prosecuting state action deemed to be illegitimate or outside international norms. These can involve prosecution for war crimes or for the 'unlawful use of force' as defined in the UN Charter and by the UN Security Council. If states have abused their power, and there is no doubt that they do so regularly, then they should be judged against international conventions dealing with war crimes, international human rights conventions and international humanitarian law. Thus, if it is believed that a state has exceeded its legitimate authority, there are already mechanisms for dealing with it in the international system. Moreover, these existing provisions will be more effective if applied without resorting to the use of the term terrorism. In addition, we already have international laws, conventions and rules and a consensus around when they apply. In terms of terrorism, no such consensus exists, hence taking these practices outside an already accepted consensus and placing them into a discourse where no such consensus exists is not likely to lead to a greater moral critique of them, or legal prosecutions of them.

However, three potentially problematic cases require consideration. The first concerns state violence aimed at modifying the behaviour of a population beyond those who are the immediate victims of an attack. Thus, if a state randomly selects certain members of a community, perhaps one in ten, and executes them with the aim of sending a clear political message to the rest of the population, might this be considered a form of terrorism? Horrific as this practice is, it should be dealt with under procedures relating to human rights abuses or war crimes. The problem here is one of legality. Terrorist acts are always criminal acts, and can the act of the state ever be considered criminal, given that it is the state that determines what is and what is not a crime? This is exactly what Carl Schmitt meant when he claimed that 'sovereign is he who decides on the exception' (Schmitt, 1985: 5). Certainly, these offences can be dealt with under international law, and procedures to do so already exist. But there are no such procedures to deal with these issues as instances of state terrorism. It is simply not a category that is accepted in international law.

For Schmitt, every government capable of decisive action must include within its constitution the possibility of a dictatorial moment, or process, which frees the executive from any legal restraints to its power that would normally apply. Of course, individual state agents can commit crimes, but can the state itself ever be deemed to have done so in its own jurisdiction? It may be possible to argue the case, but I am unaware of any successful examples. Even in those instances when the state might be deemed to have violated its own laws, such as the National Security Agency (NSA) revelations of 2013, it simply changes the law, or ignores the judgement. Hence in this instance, if this activity is within the laws of the state then it cannot logically be considered an act of terrorism. This does not mean that we think this action is morally appropriate and, in fact, a deeper critique emerges not only of this particular act, but the laws of a state in which such an act could occur. Likewise, an example such as this would be considered as a war crime under international law, and adding the concept of state terrorism to this charge would only confuse the issue given the lack of agreement at the international level on the concept of terrorism.

The second example is that of 'death squads', such as those used in Nazi Germany and in Argentina and Guatemala (Campbell and Brenner, 2000; Jonas, 1991; Langerbein, 2004; Mazzei, 2009). Here I think we need a much more disaggregated notion of the state (Wight, 2004, 2006). States are not the unitary actor presented in much IR theory and assumed in terrorism research. Often 'death squads' emerge when the security apparatus of the state begins to act alone and without the knowledge or consent of the country's rulers. In these instances, the death squads are non-state actors. That is, if discovered by state leaders we can expect these death squads to be subject to the rule of law. Moreover, states will often go to great lengths to distance themselves from such acts, disclaiming involvement and responsibility (Campbell and Brenner, 2000; Mazzei, 2009). If this is the case, then how is the message being transmitted, and how are the target populations to understand who is issuing the message? In addition, when states have used sections of their security apparatus in a manner consistent with a definition of death squads, the targets of such squads are not randomly chosen, but carefully selected because they are members of the group the state wishes to control. No doubt, these 'death squads' can spread terror among the group and the wider population, but the targets of 'death squads' are normally carefully chosen precisely because they send a message to the target group that anyone else engaging in that activity might well be subject to the actions from the 'death squad'. Hence, death squads are typically very selective about whom they attack.

Third, what about situations when states use their agents to carry out attacks on foreign soil? For example, when states use their personnel to conduct violent operations against actors in other states; might this not be considered terrorism? Again, my answer is no. First, such acts are normally conducted against specific opponents of the state that may have fled to other countries. These could be political dissidents, exiled political leaders, human rights activists and journalists. Thus, for example, the murder of Russian Alexander Valterovich Litvinenko in 2006 would not normally be considered an act of terrorism (Goldfarb and Litvinenko, 2007). Moreover, if a state sends its agents into another state to attack the citizens of that state, this would be normally be considered an act of war, and not terrorism. Some have also argued that US drone attacks should be considered a form of state terrorism (Hagopian, 2014). However, whilst non-state actors clearly suffer in these attacks, the actual targets are the individual terrorists whom the United States considers to be enemy combatants and a threat to the security of the US state. And again, to use the label state terrorism in relation to such acts serves no function other than a form of moral critique, rather than putting in the place the conditions under which such acts might be prosecuted as war crimes.

It is clear that states do use terror as a deliberate tactic. For example, some go well beyond the use of coercion in maintaining state power and institutionalize the use of terror. Often these are totalitarian states; examples might include Nazi Germany, the Soviet Union under Stalin, or Cambodia under the Khmer Rouge (Arendt, 1967; Gleason, 1995). By definition, a totalitarian state tends to dominate all aspects of a society. The means by which this dominance is enforced varies, but a key component is always an ever-present and all-pervasive use of terror, often generated by an omnipresent and omnipotent security apparatus, or secret police. There is no doubt that when such states have employed such techniques the success of them depends to a great extent on the indiscriminate nature of their activities. Thus, one did not have to be a dissident in the Soviet Union to suffer at the hands of the secret police. Moreover, both the Soviet Union and Nazi Germany suppressed opponents and deployed their secret police against potential, and largely unidentified, groups. Paranoia was obviously a key aspect of such regimes. As Karl J. Friedrich and Zbigniew K. Brzezinski so graphically put it, such state terror 'aims to fill everyone with fear and vents in full its passions for unanimity. Terror then embraces the entire society ... Indeed to many it seems as if they are hunted, even though the secret police may not touch them for years, if at all. Total fear reigns' (Friedrich and Brzezinski, 1966: 146). Horrific as such practices are, they do not constitute terrorism, as least as most people would deploy that term. Such practices should be dealt with as human rights violations, as indeed they generally are in the international system (Simpson, 2007).

It is not only totalitarian states, however, that use terror against their own citizens. Dictatorships in South America, for example, have clearly, and often overtly, used their armed forces and security services to terrorize their populations. Terror under these regimes is perhaps less institutionally embedded within the state than under totalitarian regimes, but it is no less horrific. Often these states, aware of the potential problems of international condemnation of their tactics, deploy covert means such as in the death squads of Colombia. Nonetheless, although such activities are clearly an aspect of state control, we do not need to label them terrorism in order to subject them to moral critique.

The literature on state terror also often fails to differentiate between terror deployed by a state against its own citizens from the use of terror abroad; perhaps as a strategic means of conducting foreign policy, waging war or administering an occupation, for example. Now although I reject the idea that the use of terror by a state should be called terrorism, I do want to insist that in almost all instances the deployment of terror as a deliberate tactic by any state, whether domestically or at the international level, is morally worse than terrorism. Here I follow Igor Primoratz (Primoratz, 2004), who claims that the use of terror by states is morally worse than the use of terror by non-state actors for four reasons.

First, is the scale of the issue; the use of violence by states has led to the deaths of substantially more people than that of terrorism. In fact, as we have already seen, violence, and through its deployment, the creation of terror, is embedded within the notion of the state. However, the use of violence by the state is simply that, state violence, and that it produces terror should not lead us to confuse it with terrorism. Despite this, there can be no arguing with the fact that the levels of death and destruction through the use of state violence are far greater than that arising out of terrorism. To give but one example: often claimed to be 'the most devastating terrorist attack in history', the 9/11 attacks are said to be responsible for 2993 deaths. The latest estimate for casualties in the bombing of Dresden during the Second World War is 18,000. Primoratz argues that these figures are hardly surprising, given the vast differentials in terms of resources and power between states and non-state actors (Primoratz, 2004: 118).

Second, is the secrecy, deception and hypocrisy that surround the use of terror by states, which will often go to great lengths to deny involvement in anything that might be construed as the deliberate deployment of terror as a tactic. Often they will hypocritically point how their values rule out such a tactic. Third, is that many of the violent actions carried out by states that involve terror are expressly forbidden under international law. Thus, the deliberate targeting of civilians, for example, is a war crime. Hence, Primoratz argues that as signatories to many of these conventions states have a duty to abide by them; a duty that non-state actors do not have (even if the non-state actors might have a moral duty). However, this makes the point forcefully of why state activity of this kind should be dealt with under human rights regimes or as crimes of war. We gain nothing, apart from confusion, by treating these violations of international law (as does Primoratz) as state terrorism (Primoratz, 2004: 119).

The fourth argument is that non-state terrorism can be justified, or at least its wrongness mitigated, by the fact that there is no alternative. Thus, according to Primoratz, when a people is subjected to a form of rule that includes oppression, humiliation and exploitation, then a liberation movement may legitimately claim that the only effective method of struggle at its disposal is terrorism. Indeed, Primoratz goes as far as to claim that to 'refrain from using terrorism in such circumstances would be tantamount to giving up on the prospect of liberation altogether' (Primoratz, 2004: 119). This is problematic, and whilst my framework allows the possibility of such an oppressed people taking up arms against a state that is oppressing them (attacks targeted on state actors, officials, institutions and property), there can be no moral justification for a resort to attacks on non-state actors (terrorism).

Often the issue of state terrorism is confused with that of state-sponsored terrorism (George, 1991). Moreover, in much of the literature, state-sponsored terrorism is actually referring to state-sponsored insurgency, and it is important to note that under the definition of terrorism advanced in this book, state support for organized insurgent movements that do not intentionally target non-state actors is not state sponsorship of terrorism. Hence, it does not form part of this discussion. State-sponsored terrorism occurs when a government that claims political legitimacy, in a given territorial domain, attempts to achieve some of its goals through the support of groups using terrorist tactics in another territory (Alexander, 1986; Brenchley, 1984; Cline and Alexander, 1986). A state may provide funding, materials, training, intelligence and ideological support to groups using terrorism in the hope of using these groups to achieve their own aims. There is compelling evidence that several states have sponsored many organizations that have deployed terrorist tactics (Byman, 2005).

In many respects, this allows states to engage in war by proxy. Equally, by avoiding committing acts of violence against an enemy state themselves, the risk of direct military confrontation is avoided. Provoking a war against any country, particularly a powerful one, is risky for less powerful states. If there are groups willing to undertake terrorist activities on the sponsor's behalf the risks to the sponsoring state are reduced. The sponsoring state will deny any involvement, yet continue to destabilize another state without incurring danger to itself. This is war by proxy, and in general the state sponsoring the violence does not wish to send a message to the state managers of the target state, but instead wants to destabilize it or cause it to expend resources securing itself again the terrorism (Innes, 2012). If the sponsoring state were attempting to send a message, then it would have to reveal itself as the sponsor, and hence the sender of the message. In general, all states deny sponsoring groups that use terrorism.

State sponsorship of terrorism takes many forms and can include the provision of material and financial support or operational support. Often the sponsoring state provides facilities and training of groups using terrorism, and they can often provide vital intelligence concerning targets. Assistance may also be provided in the form of documents, for example, passports and visas, and sometimes sponsoring states will offer terrorists access to legally protected diplomatic modes of communication, thus offering the terrorist a potential route to smuggle weapons and other resources. Additionally, sponsors can reduce the risk of terrorist operations against themselves by providing sanctuaries for the terrorists. Well-known examples here include 'Carlos the Jackal', who took up residence at a villa in Libya; Abu Nidal, the founder of Fatah, who was based in Baghdad; and Abu Abbas, who found a safe haven in the People's Republic of Yemen.

According to Bruce Hoffman, a pivotal event in the emergence of state-sponsored terrorism was 'the seizure in November 1979 of 52 American hostages at the United States embassy in Tehran by a group of militant Iranian "students"' (Hoffman, 1998: 186). These Iranian students were said to be acting without the authority of the Iranian state, which claimed no responsibility for the taking of the hostages. Hoffman argues that this incident sent a message to other states that acts of violence perpetrated by terrorists secretly working for governments were inexpensive and, if executed properly, were potentially risk-free ways of attacking stronger enemies. Of course, on my account, this example would not constitute an act of terrorism since diplomats are clearly state agents and hence legitimate targets in any war. In fact, evidence suggests that the initial taking of the hostages was not controlled by the Iranian state, and that the reason they did not force the students to release the hostages was that the incident united the Iranian people and provided a focal point for Iranian denunciations of US interference in Iranian affairs (Bowden, 2006; Ebtekar and Reed, 2000).

Given the costs associated with the sponsorship of terrorism, why do states continue to engage in it? One reason is the definitional issue, and they may simply and validly disagree that the groups they support are terrorists. There is no doubt that state sponsorship of terrorism allows the sponsors to pursue specific foreign policy objectives without themselves becoming embroiled in an overt conflict with those states that are subject to their foreign policy initiatives. Despite this, state sponsorship of terrorism is not the same thing as state terrorism.

Since 9/11, the international system has been wracked by a so-called 'war on terror'. In the name of this 'war on terror' major wars have been instigated, nations illegally invaded, and countless humans killed. These include both state actors and non-state actors. Alongside this, civil and human rights have been abused, and wide-ranging legislation introduced at the global and domestic level to control more and more aspects of human behaviour. Those involved in the more radical edge of terrorism studies have decided that the best way to deal with these abuses of state power is to point to some moral equivalence and to claim that this all amounts to state terrorism. The net effect of this, however, is to produce an 'inflationary' account of terrorism. However, there is no moral equivalence, and what states have done and continue to do far exceeds the suffering inflicted by terrorists. In addition, in focusing their attention on state violence they have provided little analysis of what is traditionally thought of as terrorism.

The irony of this is that it seems to suggest that terrorism is more prevalent in the international system than it is. Terrorism, when equated with terror, is everywhere. This simply plays into the hands of states, which can legitimately claim that since terrorism is everywhere, then we need more and more action against it, and thus the spiral continues. Terrorism, whilst terrible in its effects on those individuals who come into contact with it, is not a major security threat to individual states or the international system. On a restrictive (deflationary) definition of terrorism, actual deaths by such acts are few and far between. Certainly they are horrific, but on a relative scale they do not come close to enacting destruction on the scale of poverty, child malnutrition, state neglect or disease, or the unacceptable use of state power, to name but a few. On a 'deflationary' account of terrorism, the resources wasted on a war on terror are both obscene and meaningless. Nothing highlights just how ridiculous the inflated understanding of terrorism has become so much as the recent attempt by members of the US government to label Wikileaks founder Julian Assange a terrorist. Perhaps, in the face of such overuse of the term we should just stop using it altogether. This is not possible.

As previously argued, the concepts and understandings held by actors engaged in the practices we examine are an integral aspect of what any good social science should study. We cannot possibly understand these practices without taking these concepts into account. Of course, we do not have to accept them, but in order to reject them, we would need good, sound, empirical, moral and theoretical reasons to do so. In relation to terrorism, there are no such reasons. What most people mean when they refer to terrorism are forms of non-state violence directed against non-state actors aimed at communicating a political message.

6
Terrorism: Justifications and Explanations

It should now be clear what I mean by terrorism, what is included in that definition, and what is not. Given this, it is now possible to move forward to a consideration of some of the major issues concerning this very particular kind of political violence. In this chapter, I intend to deal with more traditional forms of terrorism, and I will deal with the war on terror, what is sometimes known as Islamic terrorism, and new forms of terrorism in Chapter 7. This should not be taken to imply that there is a fundamental rupture between the terrorism we face post-9/11 and previous forms. Although it makes analytical sense to refer to pre-9/11 terrorism and post-9/11 terrorism, 9/11 here represents simply that moment in time when the possibilities inscribed in the new terrorism became manifest. As a violent reaction against the state that spreads its message by deliberately attacking non-state actors, all forms of terrorism share much in common. However, there is something to the view that the form of terrorism we face today does represent a fundamentally different set of phenomena for states and societies, over and above that presented by more mainstream and traditional forms of terrorism. What these differences are will be dealt with in Chapter 7. However, the definition I have articulated so far allows us to concentrate attention on those acts that fall under the definition. As such, it allows us to see if the phenomenon is radically changing, assess whether it presents a greater or lesser threat than in previous eras, and allows us to think of effective ways we might combat it.

Justifications for Terrorism: Putting the Definition to Work

Political violence, or the threat of violence, against non-state actors can never be justified, unless those actors can be shown to be playing a significant role in the maintenance of the state. This is the case irrespective of whether states or non-state actors commit the violence. In practice, a community, even one with legitimate grievances, always has recourse to alternative strategies to register dissent other than the use of violence against non-state actors; even if the only alternative strategy involves the taking of their own life in such a way that does not involve harming others. Not all political suicides are terrorism (Fierke, 2013). Philosophers will often engage in convoluted arguments, constructing increasingly complex hypothetical situations that they then use as a means of assessing the validity of moral positions that few of us are likely to encounter in practice (Allhoff, 2012: 5.2; Corlett, 2003). Whilst interesting in and of themselves, and providing a moral framework within which to discuss terrorism, these arguments do little to help us deal with the practical cases we confront when violent acts occur. Moreover, despite the complexity of many of these arguments they essentially rest on two prior ethical positions; consequentialist or deontological ethics.

For the consequentialist, the ultimate moral judgement of any act rests on the outcome, or consequences, of the act. Hence, for example, the consequentialist position might be used to defend the torture of a suspected terrorist, if engaging in such practice led to the saving of millions of innocent lives from a nuclear attack (Allhoff, 2012: 87–132; Dershowitz, 2002a; Innes, 1998; Peters, 1996; Rodin, 2007: Chs 8, 9; Stritzke, 2009: 1–62). Here the performance of an immoral act (torture) leads to a better outcome (saving millions of lives). The moral good of the consequences overrides the moral bad of the act. The deontological position, on the other hand, asserts that the torture of humans (perhaps all animals) is wrong and can never be justified. All political violence rests on a consequentialist ethics. The killing of soldiers in war is justified in terms of the greater good of the continued survival of the nation state; violence introduced via the legal system serves the greater good of societal cohesion and order; violent revolution is necessary to remove a repressive regime; terrorism is necessary to redress injustices marginalized groups feel they suffer, and so on.

There are problems with a consequentialist approach to ethics, however. It is almost impossible to know, when faced with a decision in practice, what the consequences will be. This makes the judgement of any initial act in terms of the potential consequences problematic. We could torture a suspected terrorist only to find out there was no such bomb, in which case we would have carried out an immoral act for no good end. Or awareness that a captured terrorist will be subject to torture could force their associates to detonate the bomb through fear that they might be betrayed as a result of it. In which case the knowledge of our preparedness to engage in torture produces the event we hope to stop. Equally, many aspects of the just war tradition hold that actions in war (*jus in bello*) should be proportional to the outcomes (Walzer, 1978). But the fog of war makes such judgements extremely difficult, if not impossible. Of course, this does not mean we should cease attempting to match our moral judgement of actions to potential outcomes. However, if we are to do so we need an a priori set of axioms, which if not strictly deontological, are values we transgress only when our knowledge of potential outcomes is as certain as we can aspire to. Without this requirement, consequentialism legitimates a slippery slope in terms of moral judgement.

The deontological position also has its problems. Taking a firm stance on particular acts seems an attractive and principled moral position, but it is not one most people can adopt in practice. Most people would agree that it is wrong to lie, or to kill, but most people do lie at some point, and most people would kill to defend either their own life, or that of their families. What these two extreme positions illuminate is that moral judgement is a practice, not a philosophical foundation. The world is messy and some situations have no 'right' outcomes. Sometimes, we are simply faced with Sophie's choice. Moral judgement always already begins with some principles we hold dear and that we are prepared to violate only in certain circumstances; sometimes never. Moreover these principles exist on a scale, and the circumstances that would lead us to violate each of them individually are dependent on the commitment we hold to the principles, as well as the context in which the decision becomes imminent. In this way, a consequentialist and relaxed deontological approach to ethics is probably the context within which most people make moral judgements.

Most, if not all, societies place a prohibition on the killing of others at the top of any moral scale. In certain circumstances, we are prepared to suspend this prohibition. But any move to suspend it is generally deemed to be valid only if the argument meets certain conditions. Many of these conditions are subject to dispute. For example, in most Western countries, you can use violence to defend your property, but you should only kill an intruder if your own life is immediately threatened. These positions are always negotiable, and attitudes to them differ across time and place, and change depending on cultural norms and values. What does not change, however, is the fact of justification. All societies expect a justificatory framework for the violation of moral norms. Terrorists push the justificatory framework to ends that are logically untenable. In particular, they extend the concept of political responsibility to breaking point, or they treat their victims as instrumental devices, hence denying their humanity. Whatever problems we face in practice, we should begin from the assumption that deliberately targeted violence against non-state actors is always unjustified. And to repeat, this is the case irrespective of whether such acts are committed by states or non-state actors.

Acts can be considered terrorist when the violence, or threat of violence, is intentionally deployed by non-state actors against non-state actors and used as an instrumental transmission mechanism for the propagation of a political message. The moral critique of such action is heightened when group X has a legitimate grievance against state Y and attacks non-state actors in state Z. For example, imagine a hypothetical disenfranchised community of Russians in the Ukraine. If that group perceives itself to have legitimate grievances against the Ukrainian state, and if that group also decides to employ violent action against Ukrainian state actors, then it would not be terrorism. On the other hand, if that group not only targets state actors within Ukraine, but also targets non-state Ukrainian actors, then those acts can be deemed to be terrorism. Equally, imagine that the same group also targets actors in a European state in an effort to publicize its cause, or to punish the European state for its complicity in the oppression of the group; for the sake of argument, let us use France as an example. Now, if the attacks in France are on non-state actors in France, we can say with certainty that these are terrorist acts. However, what if the attacks are on French arms manufacturers, or French politicians? Here the decisions become difficult, and we need more information. If French arms manufacturers are supplying arms to the Ukrainian state, and if these sales are sanctioned by the French state, then it is clear that their actions might be contributing to the maintenance of the Ukrainian state. As such, certain sectors of the French state and French military complex might indeed be deemed to be legitimate targets for the insurgent group. This makes the judgement more complicated, but in a globalized world this is how the legitimacy of conflict targeting has to be assessed.

The point is that there is no easy way to determine if an act is, or is not, terrorism without closely examining the specifics of each case, and we should be wary of the ease with which governments and the media rush to a judgement when using the term. But this does not mean that we have no way to reach a judgement. What we need are a set of clear guidelines that can be applied objectively and consistently, and which allow us a framework to narrow down the list of acts that might come under discussion. For those acts within the frame of discussion, we can then begin an assessment as to whether the targets can in some way be legitimately argued to be performing some role in terms of the maintenance of the states (or states) involved in the perceived injustice. If the case can be plausibly made that the targeted actors were involved in the maintenance of the state(s) involved in the conflict, then we can determine that these were not acts of terrorism. The aim, in all instances, is to reduce the acts that can be legitimately referred to as terrorism. But can terrorism, as I have defined it here, ever be justified?

The causes that drive individuals and groups towards violence are varied, but the idea that there is no other alternative to the use of violence to address social and political conditions deemed to be unacceptable plays a role in all forms of terrorism. To my knowledge there have been no attempts by groups using terrorism to validate their violence on the basis of a claim that it is simply acceptable to use terrorism without justification. This is an important point; it indicates that terrorists accept the need for moral justification. Most terrorists are not psychopaths, and are aware that their actions have to be located within some moral universe and linked to some political cause.

Virtually all attempts to provide a moral justification for terrorism rely on some version of the 'doctrine of necessity'. However, two supplementary justifications are also worthy of consideration, even if the 'doctrine of necessity' plays some role in them. First is justification via the location of responsibility; non-state actors are legitimate targets because they bear some responsibility for the actions of their state; in effect, there are no non-state actors. Second, is justification in terms of equity of practice; non-state actors are legitimate targets because the state we are in dispute with kills our non-state actors.

Typically, these arguments are couched in terms of innocents, civilians or non-combatants, rather than the concept of the non-state actor. The non-state actor is preferable for three main reasons. First, by using the concept of non-state actor we highlight the fact that terrorism always takes place in a political context within which the state plays a central role. In this way we highlight the structural relationship between terrorism and the state, but also the structural, and historical, relationship between state and violence. Second, the concepts of non-combatants, or civilians, are vague in ways that non-state actor is not. The concept of non-combatants could exclude political leaders, whereas those same political leaders might be the primary causes of the oppression that produces the terrorism. So although not officially combatants, they may be the primary reason (cause) of the oppression. Third, the concept of innocents is simply too value-laden and susceptible to stretching to be of analytical use. For example, Primoratz argues that the concept of innocents is integral to terrorism insofar as 'the terrorist's victim is innocent from the terrorist's own point of view, i.e. innocent even if we grant the terrorist his assessment of the policies he supposes' (Primoratz, 1990: 131–2). This will not work, of course, for as we have seen, many terrorists reject the notion that the concept of 'innocents' has any purchase. There are no innocents as such, and insofar as citizens fail explicitly to reject the policies of their state then they are complicit in the outcomes of those policies.

The concept of the non-state actor obviously has its problems, and there will always be borderline cases. However, in using it we highlight the important issue of political responsibility in terms of political protest, and we acknowledge the central role of the political system and its historical development through the use of violence in the production of terrorism.

H.H.A. Cooper (1977: 18) argues that, in many respects, terrorists are much the same as every other member of society. Terrorists want to belong, and they want to feel accepted and have access to socially generated rewards for their behaviour. In addition to a longing for social acceptance, however, terrorists also feel that there is something wrong with the prevailing social and political order. They often feel that standard channels of protest are no longer valid, or productive, and that violence, or the threat of violence, is the only option; the 'doctrine of necessity'; there is no alternative to violence under particular circumstances (Cooper, 1977: 17).

This does not mean that terrorists are necessarily in favour of violence. According to the 'doctrine of necessity', violence is simply the last option; an option the terrorists consider to be the only choice left. The terrorist believes that the political configuration they inhabit has forced them to embrace violence. Violence is necessary because society or the political order is bad, unjust, or potentially evil. They embrace violence on the basis of a belief that the status quo is worse than the violence caused by acts of terrorism. Violence is necessary because there are no other alternatives available to correct the injustices of their situation. In a world constructed and maintained through state violence these positions seem logical. Hence, the 'doctrine of necessity' may justify political violence, but can it justify terrorism? In fact, only a pacifist could argue that violence is never justified, and however abhorrent we find the effects of violence in societies it remains the underlying basis of social control and order. In fact, the 'doctrine of necessity' also underpins the use of state violence, and articulates a position that certain types of conduct, even if they produce harm, are justified because they avert a greater evil and provide a net social gain or benefit to society. Violence used to control criminals is routinely accepted because it is deemed necessary. Violence is routinely used to provide security for the state because it is deemed necessary. And violence is used for self-defence because it is deemed necessary. Hence, logically, the doctrine of necessity seems sound. But can this argument be extended to violence against non-state actors?

Certainly, there may be times when an oppressed group possesses so little power in relation to their oppressors that it might seem that attacks on non-state actors are the only option, particularly if the aim is to publicize their cause to a wider audience. Many would argue that the Palestinians, for example, are in just such a predicament. I agree that this is indeed the situation the Palestinians find themselves in, but no matter how much I might agree with a particular cause, the justice of that cause can never legitimate the deliberate targeting of Israeli non-state actors, or the targeting of non-state actors from other states. The targeting of state actors, however, who provide the means through which state oppression is maintained, is a different matter. Such targeted violent action, when directed at state agents, is attempting to redress the injustices by engaging with those explicitly engaged in producing or maintaining it.

Deliberate state violence against non-state actors, on the other hand, is never justified and should always be subject to critique, censure and punishment under international law, human rights legislation and the standards of international society administered through international institutions, such as the UN and the ICC. Violence emanating from non-state groups and targeted against non-state actors is unjustified, and, irrespective of how just we think the cause may be, we should never provide support for such action. We may understand the reasons for the political frustration that leads to such violence, but we should never accept it as an appropriate response. Every person who uses, or threatens to use, violence for political ends will have a very clear sense of why they are doing it. Political violence requires justification. Without it, it is difficult to see how we could call the violence political. But that reason for engaging in violent acts cannot legitimate intentional harm inflicted on non-state actors.

Paul Wilkinson links the justification for acts of terrorism to group cohesion (Wilkinson, 1974: 23–5). According to him, members of groups that turn to terrorism enter into a particular ethical universe, shared with other members of the group, which both binds them to that group, and provides a justification for the activities of the group. This is a similar process to that encountered by members of the military in terms of unit cohesion. As William M. Czander puts it:

> Freud maintains that cohesion is found in a group when all members introject the same subject into their ego ideal and then identify with each other ... This phenomenon explains why soldiers willingly give up their thinking capacity and blindly follow orders from their leader ... The soldiers as a group become a cohesive unit because they have all identified with each other. (Czander, 1993: 21)

However, members of the military also enjoy a form of group validation that goes beyond unit cohesion. When a soldier, for example, engages in violent activity on behalf of the state, that activity is generally rewarded, socially acknowledged, and often honoured by the wider society. Thus, the state and society provide social justification for the use of violence by the individuals acting on behalf of the state.

Terrorists, on the other hand, can only receive validation for their actions from the immediate group or the community to which they belong, so unit or group cohesion becomes paramount. This is so, because the terrorist must, in order to function, remain anonymous. Validation from the wider social group is often not forthcoming. This means that the immediate members of the group become tightly bound and, in effect, sacrifice their individuality through the often-unquestioned acceptance of the justification for the violence as articulated by the group. Sociologists refer to this process as 'deindividuation' (Le Bon, 1977; Postmes and Spears, 1998; Stahelski, 2005).

In addition, the sense of secrecy that pervades membership of groups that feel forced to employ terrorist tactics forms a barrier to individuals within the group seeking social acceptance from society at large. This reinforces the separation of members of the group from wider social norms, and it increases the possibility that members of the group will see themselves engaged in something deeply important; something beyond the understanding of the members of the wider community. They come to see themselves as an elite vanguard prepared to sacrifice their lives for the wider cause. This set of dynamics can be applied to any type of group that rejects existing social norms. For example, individuals who join street gangs quickly embrace the mind-set and norms of the gang. Often this is achieved through initiation ceremonies and group rituals that reinforce the bonding. In some instances, the social pressure reinforcing this process is so intense that individual identity becomes subsumed under the group identity and members will sacrifice their own life as a way of affirming their commitment to the group and the cause. The most extreme example of this process is that of the 'suicide bomber'. Robert Pape argues that 'suicide terrorism' can be considered as a form of altruism insofar as individuals are prepared to sacrifice their lives for the larger cause (Pape, 2005: 20–3).

As powerful as these arguments re unit cohesion are, they do not provide a moral justification for terrorism, but an explanation of why some members of groups are prepared to violate moral norms. In effect, they explain some of the processes through which individuals become prepared to violate moral standards, but this does not provide a moral justification for violent acts committed according to this logic.

In many respects, the 'doctrine of necessity' is linked to an understanding of terrorism as arising out of, or caused, by the social conditions in which the groups reside. According to advocates of the root causes of terrorism argument, the resort to violence may not be morally acceptable, but it is understandable when considered in the context of poverty, oppression, and huge disparities in economic distribution (Bjørgo, 2004; Richardson, 2006a). We do not have to agree with the resort to violence by terrorists, but we can understand why they do so. This argument is closely related to another that has emerged post-9/11. This is the idea that terrorists attack us because of our foreign policy and interference in the affairs of their states (Pape, 2005, 2010; Pape and Feldman, 2010). A related argument is that of 'blowback' (Johnson, 2002); the claim that the wars in Iraq and Afghanistan, for example, are said to have increased the membership of terrorist organizations, not decreased them (Bergen and Cruickshank, 2007).

A corollary of this argument concerns the role that religion plays in terrorism. Robert Pape, for example, concludes that religion plays a minor role in the justification of terrorism. According to him, terrorism is primarily a political matter (Pape, 2005: 4). Likewise, Karen Armstrong argues that political, social and economic conditions are the main factors implicated in the production of violence, not religion (Armstrong, 2014a). However, she constructs something of a straw man in relation to the arguments surrounding the role of religion in relation to religious-political violence. According to Armstrong, 'warfare and violence have always been a feature of political life, and yet we [Western secularists] alone drew the conclusion that separating the church from the state was a prerequisite for peace' (Armstrong, 2014b). But the argument has never been that separating the Church from the State was a 'prerequisite for peace'. Who could ever argue this? Two world wars, genocides in Rwanda and Cambodia, the deaths of millions in Stalin's Soviet Union, and Mao's China are just some examples that make clear how secular ideologies can turn to violence. The point is, that in relation to contemporary Islamic terrorism, religion does play a major role. To be clear, it is not the only factor, but in a complex open world of multiple interacting mechanisms, I argue it plays an important part.

There can be no doubt that some terrorists, bin Laden, for example, do justify the resort to violence in terms of a global struggle between good and evil grounded on religious principles, and link these arguments to political interference in Islamic affairs by non-Islamic states (bin Laden, 2005: see index p. 288 for the number of references to the Qur'an). Likewise, it is clear that IS explicitly link religion and politics in the attempt to forge an Islamic state. Only the most arrogant of Western academics and observers can patronisingly tell them that they are confused and that their religion is nothing to do with their lives. In addition, it is of no help to argue that these groups have a distorted reading of Islam; that they are un-Islamic. Debates about the 'true' meaning of Islam, or how to interpret the Qur'an, are beside the point. They cannot be settled. No God is going to come down from above and declare that 'this group' or 'that group' is right. Disagreements about the meaning of religious texts are at the heart of all religions. Indeed, it is precisely because of that fact that secularism was embraced. But the mere fact that one group claims to have the authentic reading, and the other rejects it, displays just how important a role religion plays in these issues. Hence, although it is not always as easy to differentiate one factor from another, as some authors would suggest, there is no doubt that religion plays a major role in contemporary Islamic terrorism. That said, whilst the justification for terrorism can be grounded in religious sentiments, it is not always necessary for religion to play a role.

Terrorists will often concede that the maiming and killing of 'innocent' targets violate basic human rights, but they insist that these actions are justified because they are designed to avert a greater evil: brutal oppression, grave injustices, and the exploitation of their own peoples' lives by the practices of the powers that be. Terrorists believe that there is an 'indispensable necessity' that justifies their resort to violence in order to preserve their way of life, or to free themselves, or their community, from the constraints imposed on them by others.

Some terrorists argue that insofar as the state provides for the continued wellbeing of its population, and insofar as that population benefits from the actions of its state, then all of that population is a legitimate target. Equally, in liberal democracies, publics elect their politicians, hence why should publics not be legitimate targets insofar as they are responsible for the state managers who are enacting the oppressive behaviour? Indeed, bin Laden uses exactly this argument:

> The American people should remember that they pay taxes to their government and that they voted for their president. Their government makes weapons and provides them to Israel, which they use to kill Palestinian Muslims. Given that the American Congress is a committee that represents the people, the fact that it agrees with the actions of the American government proves that America in its entirety is responsible for the atrocities that it is committing against Muslims. (bin Laden, 2005: 140–1)

Obviously this argument does not stand up to scrutiny in authoritarian regimes, when the people have little chance to exercise control over those governing them. Indeed, if this argument were to be applied in such regimes, it would be akin to arguing that an oppressed people could be a legitimate target for terrorist attacks because of their inability to free themselves from oppression. In democratic regimes, on the other hand, bin Laden's argument seems to have more traction. After all, democratic governments are representatives of the people, and come to power through an electoral process. Hence, if the people have elected the government, and it is perceived to be guilty of actions against the community the terrorist purports to represent, then surely, those who elected the government are responsible in some way for the actions of their government.

Whilst prima facie this argument seems plausible, it has two major problems. First, democratic governments come to power through elections in which large sections of the population do not vote for the government that wins. Accepting for a moment that those who do explicitly vote for a government bear some responsibility for the actions of that government, the fact that not all the people voted for the government means that any targeting of non-state actors might not only harm those who explicitly voted for the government, but also some who voted against it. Of course, it might be possible to argue that this situation differs little from state arguments about regrettable 'collateral damage' in military operations. However, the situation is different. When a state attacks a military target and non-state actors are killed or harmed, the argument is still that the intended target was military in nature and hence justified. The 'collateral damage' inflicted on the non-state actors was both non-intended, and regrettable. If there were no military target, this would constitute a war crime. In the case of violent attacks on non-state actors in democratic countries, on the other hand, those responsible for the act cannot know how the targets voted; they cannot know if they are targeting people who voted for the regime, or those that voted against it. Hence, the attacks would be indiscriminate and unjustified.

Second, elections take place in particular moments in time, and in most democracies those elected are representatives of the people. It is conceivable that the people could vote for a government with a large majority and that that government could then engage in action that makes it a target of terrorist attacks. But just because the people voted X government into power at time Y, this does not mean that the people support the action undertaken by the government after the election. 'Not in our name' became a focal point and slogan for protest movements against the invasion of Iraq in 2003 precisely because those protesting did not agree with government actions (Smith, 2010; Stellato, 2012).

The final argument I consider concerns not that of responsibility or that of necessity, but that of justice: that the killing of non-state actors is justified because the state whose citizens are subject to attack has itself killed thousands of non-state actors. Again, bin Laden puts the case forcefully:

> Yes, so we kill their innocents – this is valid both religiously and logically ... Those who kill our women and our innocent, we kill their women and innocent ... The United States and their allies are killing us in Palestine, Chechyna, Kashmir, Palestine [*sic*], and Iraq. That's why Muslims have a right to carry out revenge attacks on the US ... We ourselves are the victims of murder and massacres. We are defending ourselves against the United States. (bin Laden, 2005: 117–19, 140–1)

The logic here is not compelling and, in fact, bin Laden recognizes the weakness of it, suggesting that the perpetrators of 9/11

> did not set out to kill children, but rather attacked the biggest center of military power in the world, the Pentagon ... As for the World Trade Center, the ones who were attacked and who died in it were part of a financial power. It wasn't a children's school! Neither was it a residence. And the general consensus is

that most of the people who were in the towers were men that backed the biggest financial force in the world, which spreads mischief in the world. (bin Laden, 2005: 119)

So bin Laden's argument is no longer 'an eye for an eye', but one that attempts to legitimate the actions in terms of the direct responsibility of those targeted in the production of the oppression and suffering. It is an explicit attempt to argue that those directly involved in the suffering of Muslims bear some responsibility for that suffering, and hence violent action against them is justified. He has a point here, and it is the link to responsibility that is important. For although the outcome was horrific for many, the attacks of 9/11 need to be differentially assessed, with that on the Pentagon not an act of terrorism, whilst that on the World Trade Center was. For, whilst it is clear that the Pentagon plays a major role in terms of the exercise of state power by the United States, the case with the Twin Towers is far more tenuous. And whilst some people in the building may well have been state actors, or closely linked to the state, the vast majority were not.

In the final analysis, bin Laden is either arguing that the attacks were justified because of some assumed link between the US state and those Muslims killed, or advocating revenge. In the former case, the argument has some validity in relation to the Pentagon but not the Twin Towers, and in the latter case retribution rather than revenge would be the morally right course of action. In which case, only those directly responsible could justifiably be subject to attack. Thus, for example, we deem it admissible, and just, to hold criminals to account for their actions, but we do not deem it just to apply the same level of responsibility to their parents, or members of the extended family. Moreover, unlike revenge, retribution is directed only at wrongs, is not personal, should not involve pleasure at the suffering of others, and uses procedural standards (Murphy, 1992).

Bin Laden and other terrorists would likely not accept the moral limitations of the arguments presented here. To a certain extent, they do not occupy the same moral universe, but that is not the point. The issue is not whether the terrorists think their acts are justified; of course they do. The issue is whether we think they are justified, and on what grounds. In the final analysis, there can be no justification for intentional violence on non-state actors in the pursuit of political causes, and in particular, when those non-state actors are treated as instrumental devices through which terror is spread. These arguments apply irrespective of whether it is state agents undertaking the violence or non-state agents. The fact we call one group of acts terrorism, and the other state violence, affects the moral judgement of both not one jot.

Explaining Terrorism

If attempts to explain something are efforts at uncovering causes, then the justifications terrorists provide for their actions will have to provide part of any explanation. All terrorists consider their cause to be just, and they are prepared to sacrifice almost anything for it; their freedom, and, if necessary, their life. This provides a necessary explanation of terrorism, but it is not a sufficient one. In the final analysis, it is probably fair to say that there is no such thing as a typical terrorist, or a single cause of terrorism. Ultimately, what motivates someone to commit acts of terrorism is the unshakeable belief in the cause, combined with a willingness to use violence, and a belief that the prevailing social and political conditions are unjust and require changing. Understanding and explaining terrorism will require a theoretical model able to embrace all aspects. Multiple causes have been suggested. One dominant trend is an examination of terrorist psychology (Bongar, 2007; Horgan, 2005; Reich, 1990). There have also been attempts to examine whether particular kinds of terrorists come from particular social groups (Weinberg and Davis, 1989: 84–96). Other authors have focused on the economic and social circumstances, often referred to as the root causes of terrorism (Bjørgo, 2004; Franks, 2006; Krueger, 2008; Richardson, 2006b).

However, given the variation in the many types of groups that use terrorism and the causes they seek to promote, it is probably impossible to identify simple causal logic. Here, again, attention to issues derived from the philosophy of social science again become pertinent.

Individuals never act in isolation from a social and cultural context (Wight, 2006). Moreover, when individuals act they draw on a range of resources, some material, some social, which enable certain kinds of acts and limit others. This means that the primary drivers of terrorism lie in the political/economic/structural/cultural environment that make it possible, not the psychological makeup of individuals. Certainly this environment will have to convince certain individuals to act in certain ways, but without this environment, the individuals could not act in that way. The actions of individuals cannot be explained without taking the social, political and cultural context into account. Hence, an analysis of terrorism based on individual personality traits, or typologies, attempting to group terrorists into certain kinds of people simply misses the point if we want to understand it as a general phenomenon. Terrorism is primarily a structural practice, and it is at the level of the structure that analysis must begin. In keeping with the critical realist approach, this means that the explanation of why people become terrorists must be embedded in the following dimensions of social existence, with no hierarchy implied among them. These are based on a model developed by Roy Bhaskar, although I have amended them slightly (Bhaskar, 1993: 180). Also, whilst it is possible to differentiate these 'planes', in practice they interact together to form an 'assemblage' in which the various components interact in complex ways (De Landa, 2006; Sassen, 2006):

1. Personal subjectivity.
2. Material relations.
3. Intersubjective relations.
4. Social relations.
5. Social roles.

All social activity involves each dimension. Personal subjectivity should be obvious. We each have a unique way of being in the world based on who we are and our personal biographies. How this subjectivity comes to be is subject to debate. It is possible to argue that individuals are born evil, and that no matter how their life unfolds over time, these innate characteristics will simply manifest themselves at some point (Meloy, 1988: 5; Schurman-Kauflin, 2008). Chapter 1 of Deborah Schurman-Kauflin's harrowing book *Disturbed: Terrorist Behavioral Profiles* provides an account of the Beslan siege in Russia in 2004 that leaves no doubt about the depravity of some terrorists. This is a clear statement that terrorists are born, not made. Accepting, for the moment, the possibility that some individuals are born this way, there is no reason why they end up engaging in terrorism when other, much easier, outlets for their violent tendencies are available; becoming a serial killer, for example (Leyton, 2003; Seltzer, 2013).

However, this does not negate the importance of personal subjectivity in relation to the explanation of terrorism. One can accept that terrorists are made, not born, but still incorporate that personal subjectivity into our explanatory accounts (Stahelski, 2005). In fact, research into radicalization is embedded within this belief, insofar as it assumes that terrorists have a subjectivity that has been constructed (radicalized) over time (Coolsaet, 2011; Ranstorp, 2010). Moreover, such research assumes that if we can identify the causes and processes of radicalization we can intervene to stop people being made in this way. Yet, no matter how far we want to attribute this radicalization to social conditions – economic, political, personal experience, peer pressure – the subjectivity of individuality, constructed or not, still plays a role in understanding terrorism. Thus, for example, attempting to explain the rise of al-Qaeda without mentioning the personal characteristics of bin Laden would leave much unexplained. Individuals matter, but they are not the sole locus of explanation, unless we adopt a strong version of methodological individualism.

However, much of the literature dealing with terrorism tends towards individualistic explanations, often based on psychological factors (Hacker, 1976). There is good reason for this and researchers face substantial problems in gaining access to, and understanding, group dynamics. Yet, given the dynamics of group identification, and the process of 'deindividuation' mentioned above, the commitment to the justice of the cause and the belief that violence is the only option is actually embedded within group norms, not simply individual traits. Terrorists are indeed made, not born (Stahelski, 2005). This holds true even if we accept there are individuals born evil. For such individuals could find multiple outlets for their aggression, and what turns them to terrorism is a belief in the cause. There is no model terrorist, and any attempt to understand why people engage in terrorist acts will have to grapple with both the structural and individual factors (Crenshaw, 2000: 409; Wight, 2004, 2009).

The closeness of the group, the lack of contact with wider community and social norms, and the secrecy on which the group depends ensure that alternative visions of the world that might provide a counter to the ideology of the group are at best marginalized, and at worst never engaged with. Thus, the logic of the cause becomes an unchallengeable truth for members of the group, and this is reinforced by the dynamics of the resort to violence. Once violence has been accepted as a legitimate course of action, it serves to bind the group into an insider versus outsider mentality, even though the aims of the group might have originally been orientated around helping the wider community in which they are embedded. Once violence is embraced it becomes difficult to step outside its possibility and reflect critically on both means and ends.

Moreover, this in-group dynamic produces an absolutist mind-set with little or no room for compromise and every aspect of life understood as a Manichaean struggle between good and evil. This absolutist mind-set, of course, is reinforced when religion plays a major role in the group ideology. In an almost perfect enactment of Carl Schmitt's (1996) concept of the political, the world is divided into two camps and the necessity of labelling enemies ensures that the terrorists move ever closer to becoming true believers. Thus, the dynamics within the group reinforce the commitment to the one truth and make the identification of an enemy deserving of violent responses an easy process. In many respects, terrorism represents an extreme form of idealism. Group members are committed to the 'ideal' and are prepared to go to any lengths to achieve it. The 'ideal' becomes a motivating factor that overrides all other considerations. This idealist aspect leads some to conclude that terrorists are often young (Laqueur, 2003: 15).

The old adage that young people tend to be more romantic and idealistic than older people certainly has a ring of truth to it, which is nicely captured by the quote from Churchill:; 'If you're not a liberal at twenty you have no heart, if you're not a conservative at forty you have no brain.' The adage is not strictly true, however, and many terrorist leaders are clearly not young. Bin Laden was 54 when he was killed, and the current supposed leader of al-Qaeda, Ayman al-Zawahiri, is 63 (as at 2015). Many other terrorist organisations have a leadership that can hardly be described as young. It is true, however, that many of the terrorists who carry out the actual acts often are young, and post 9/11 images of British youths being radicalized, and in particular, the 7/7 London bombers, and recruits to IS, do lend support to the view that terrorism is a young person's game. However, we can accept this without accepting claims, such as that made by Jonathan R. White, that 'young people are particularly suscepti- ble to extremist beliefs' (White, 1997: 27).

An influential typology of terrorists comes from Frederick J. Hacker (Hacker, 1976). Hacker argues that terrorists can be grouped into three kinds; criminals, crazies and crusaders. An organization prepared to use terrorism could contain a mix of any of the three. Whilst many critics have argued that Hacker's approach is far too simplistic, American police hostage negotia- tors have used his typology (Welch, 1984). My own view is that Hacker's typology is not only simplistic, but also tautological; ter- rorism is by definition a criminal activity, anyone who intention- ally targets non-state actors would most probably be considered crazy by most of the population, and a the fact that a deep com- mitment to their own truth characterizes most forms of terrorism means that the term crusader accurately applies. Hence, Hacker's category tells us nothing new and suggests that these 'personality types' are mutually exclusive, when, in fact, they might be mutu- ally reinforcing. That said, the fact that Hacker's typology has been so influential demands that it be addressed.

Criminals are the first of Hacker's categories. In many respects, this is the least useful category of Hacker's typology, since all forms of terrorism are by definition criminal. However, Hacker is drawing attention to the fact that some criminals can be attracted to groups. This group of people are already outsiders in society and the potential of financial gain through membership of a ter- rorist group provides an additional incentive. The group provides a means through which the criminal can become part of a wider group identity and structure that then provides resources (social and material) that help fund further criminal activity. Organized crime, even though it often involves the production of terror, should not be categorized as terrorism since criminals use terror to enact revenge or for economic gain. There is no doubt that all terrorists are criminals, so in this very limited respect, Hacker's category has some resonance.

Crazies are Hacker's second category. By a crazy Hacker means a mentally unstable violent person. The motivations driv- ing such people are varied, but according to Hacker they all seek some sort of psychological reward through terrorism. This group of people are not necessarily political terrorists, but they may be used by terrorist groups in a very instrumental manner. What drives this kind of person to join such groups, argues Hacker, is the psychological gratification, and the feeling of power violence provides. Often people like Charles Manson are cited as good examples of Hacker's crazies. However, as should be clear, the lack of an overt political programme to Manson's violence means that he would not qualify as a terrorist under my definition. Equally, we might want to say that people who deploy violence for no other reason than some pleasure they derive from the violence are crazy, but this hardly serves as an accurate description of the pursuance of violence for political ends. Some individuals with violent tendencies might find membership of a terrorist group attractive in terms of satisfying their violent desires, but once in the group, the logic of the cause becomes the primary driver.

Hacker's third category is that of crusaders. According to Hacker crusaders constitute the majority of political terrorists, and he describes them as people using terrorism to change society. Most crusaders will have accepted the 'doctrine of necessity' and they feel that they use violence to bring about much needed social and political change. The terminology of crusader, however, is a distraction in the current context of the war on terror. The historically embedded nature of the term confuses the issue. Moreover, it is difficult to see what benefits it brings above and beyond what we can achieve simply thinking in terms of commitment. The term crusader is simply too embedded in a particular historical narrative to be of any use in the contemporary debate surrounding terrorism. However, it is certainly true that the vast majority of terrorists display a deep commitment to the cause, as well as an almost unshakeable belief in the truth of their worldview.

Despite these limitations, individual personality types can play a role in explaining terrorism, but only when placed within the broader social and political context. In this respect, the second level of social being outlined above that clearly plays an explanatory role is that of 'material transactions'. Humans are materially embodied and exist in material circumstances that play some role in how social behaviour unfolds. In addition, social actors do not get to choose the material conditions of their existence and are born in particular locations and settings, which to a large extent determine their life possibilities. Children born in comfortable Western societies are afforded more possibilities and have greater life expectancy rates than those born into less developed parts of the world. One does not have to be a Marxist to agree that the need to meet basic needs (food, shelter, water, security) alters how societies are ordered depending on the material conditions under which such needs can be satisfied. In societies where the basic needs are already largely provided for, then other less pressing needs can be accommodated; education, entertainment, and so on. Those foregrounding the relationship between economic conditions, such as poverty, and terrorism are highlighting one aspect of these material transactions.

For example, in January 2001, former US president Bill Clinton described terrorism as the 'dark side of globalization'. He argued that one-half of the world's population survives on less than $2 per day, and urged American policy makers to promote national security by easing growing international disparities in wealth (Clinton, 2001). The presumed relationship between poverty and terrorism seems intuitive, but it is not universally accepted. James Piazza, for example, has argued that the link between poverty and terrorism may be illusory (Piazza, 2006: 161). Poverty and other associated economic conditions undoubtedly provide an environment in which terrorists can gain support for their cause. But poverty is rarely a direct cause of terrorism. Poverty provides the conditions under which terrorists can gain easy support from a community, and hence tackling it may undercut the support terrorists rely on from vulnerable communities. However, poverty, by itself, is rarely, if ever, the sole cause of terrorism. Many people live their lives in conditions of extreme poverty today, but only a handful of them turn to terrorism. Nonetheless, insofar as material conditions affect the perception of the terrorist cause among a population then it may, potentially at least, play a major role in any explanation, and certainly cannot be left out of any coherent account.

The next level of explanation is that of intersubjective relations. Here I mean the whole range of human understandings and beliefs that structure the conditions under which people live. These can range from politics and language to culture and identity. Humans make sense of their world through these intersubjective relations that structure every aspect of their lives. In many respects, these intersubjective relations are a necessary component in understanding the material relations. The material world is not given to us directly in experience but has to be interpreted, and we do so by placing it within a web of understanding that, in part, structures what we can and cannot do with it. Many of the material conditions we confront, such as poverty, are directly related to, and only understandable within, intersubjective relations. Capitalism, for example, clearly has objective material consequences, but it is dependent upon a set of human understandings concerning money, profit, loss, wealth, and so on. The intersubjective relations are also a crucial aspect of any understanding of terrorism in terms of conflicting beliefs about the world. They underpin religion, politics and ideology. If, as I have claimed elsewhere, that politics is the terrain of competing ontologies, then intersubjective structures are implicated in the construction of these ontologies (Wight, 2006).

Next are social relations. These differ from intersubjective relations insofar as they can exist without the agents being aware of their existence, whereas intersubjective structures rely, in part, on agents being aware of some aspect of them. Social relations specify relations between groups and communities in a society or domain. Examples here might be race, ethnicity, class, or the relations between differing genders. Gender provides a good example of the necessity of distinguishing social relations and intersubjective structures. All societies, can, and probably do, have gendered relations, but how those relations are mediated is dependent upon the intersubjective structures that dominate the society. Thus, the social relations between men and women can remain constant, but how we deal with those relations is dependent upon the intersubjective structures. Equally we can imagine a set of social relations that distinguish between the powerful and the powerless, but the intersubjective structures may not lead to terrorism in order to redress this balance. Likewise, we can think of the relationship between those in power and those not in power and explore this relationship through the changing intersubjective understandings of how power is legitimized or not. The idea of social relations as distinctive from intersubjective understandings is important so that intersubjective relations are not taken to exhaust the social.

In terms of understanding terrorism, social relations are crucial when it comes to placing it in a wider context. The development of the modern state system, for example, has clearly led to a certain set of social relations that structure the global environment. States at the core of the international system are situated in a set of social relations that allow them greater levels of freedom than states at the margins of that system. Those core states, largely through a series of historical accident, but also the use of force, have defined the rules that those on the margins follow. These social relations specify social status, social access, social standing and political, cultural and economic possibilities, as well as barriers. Although we distinguish between political, economic and cultural worlds, what binds them all together are social relations.

Finally, social roles. Social roles specify those roles individual actors play in certain circumstances. Social roles are contingent. I, as a particular individual, can occupy the position of a university professor, but once I leave that post, I no longer occupy that social role, even though the social role continues. Groups that use terrorism also have clear social roles. They have leaders, and depending on how the group is structured, other social roles; internal discipline, deputy leadership, bomb making, weapons procurement, finance management. Wherever organized groups emerge, social roles likewise do so. Social roles do not determine how people act. Nothing in social life is determined, in the sense we ordinarily use that word. However, social roles do set the boundary conditions for what the people occupying those roles can do. Only certain political leaders can press a nuclear button, and that power is defined by the social role they occupy and the intersubjective structures that govern how those roles are played. And of course, the material conditions reappear here insofar as not every political leader has access to nuclear weapons.

We can see how all of these fit together by examining bin Laden. He represents our first level of that individual subjectivity. He has a unique biographical narrative that constructed him as an individual like no other in terms of the development of al-Qaeda. However, bin Laden the individual was shaped by many factors: the material conditions of his birth, as well as the changing material conditions he encountered as his life developed. In addition, the intersubjective structures prevailing in the society he was born into, Islam in this instance, form an important horizon of possibility for what he was to become. Likewise, the social relations he encountered (as a male) shaped his worldview and altered his life chances in particular ways. Finally, once he occupied the important role of leader of al-Qaeda, he was afforded opportunities, and possibilities, denied to others not occupying that role (Scheuer, 2011).

Conclusion

Any explanation of a group that uses terrorism, such as al-Qaeda, requires that we pay attention to all aspects of the assemblage. Certainly we might want to highlight some factors over others in particular instances, but no one area can be ruled out a priori. The structural context, both in its material and intersubjective aspects, are clearly important, as are the social roles, social relations and the individuals occupying them. In the final analysis, the explanation depends on the question under consideration. If we want to explain why X individual turned to terrorism, our focus will be on the personal biography and circumstances of that individual and the structural context that has shaped them. On the other hand, if we want to explain a given terrorist event, we would need to look not only at the individuals involved in the event, but also the broader issues surrounding it, including the political and ideological context, the prevailing political and economic conditions, and the specifics of the situation that led to the act. However, if we want to explain terrorism itself, rather than individual instances of it, then we have to look towards the structural relationship between politics, violence and the state in the contemporary international political system. The state is part of any explanation for terrorism. Without the state, we may well have violence conducted against individuals, but we could not have violence conducted by non-state actors against non-state actors, which is one of the defining characteristics of terrorism.

This also helps us understand the many justifications for terrorism also fail. There may well be good reasons why individuals and groups feel they have legitimate grievances against states. However, if so, those grievances need to be addressed and raised with the state, and not by using citizens of that state as information ciphers.

7

Terrorism: Types, Effects and Organization

According to George Ritzer, 'the differential distribution of authority invariably becomes the determining factor of systematic social conflicts' (Ritzer, 2008: 266). All social orders are conflictual, and violence has, unfortunately, become the ultimate source of exerting authority in such conflicts (Collins and Sanderson, 2009). Violence and the state are intimately related. This does not mean that we valorize violence, or that we find the persistence of violence to be a cause for celebration. However, in the modern-state system it is a fact that social conflicts are ultimately decided through the use of violence. Over the course of history, the state has gained a distinct advantage in this conflict. The state not only attempts to exercise control over the use of violence; it claims ownership of it. This means that all non-state violence begins from the assumption that it is illegitimate. Terrorism is one illegitimate form of political violence, but it is not the only one. As a specific form of political violence, however, terrorism has particular characteristics that enable us to identify aspects of it that are important, and examine its goals, modes, justifications and means of employment. Terrorism is a distinctive form of political violence, but it is not the worst, nor the most destructive.

In the previous chapter, we explored some of the justifications for terrorism and the minimum explanatory context that it needs to be embedded within. In this chapter, I explore some of the differing ways in which terrorism has been characterized, the impact it has on the social order and the structural forms through which groups using terrorism organize themselves.

Types of Terrorism

A common tactic for authors keen to avoid the definitional problem is to construct typologies of terrorism. Yet, typologies are not unproblematic. Indeed, given that a typology is a system used for putting things into types according to how they are similar, then without a coherent answer to the similarity issue (the definitional problem), any typology of terrorism would suffer from the same problems facing the definition. Indeed, it would seem impossible to construct a typology of terrorism in the absence of a definition; we would need some means of knowing that these were different types of the same thing. Moreover, terrorism is not a static strategy or tactic, but rather, it changes over time. It is dynamic. Typologies are generalizations of a phenomenon that highlight particular aspects deemed to be important, whereas terrorist incidents must be understood in their specific social, historical, economic and political context. This indicates some potential problems with typologies of terrorism.

First, once the typology has been developed there is always the temptation to try and fit reality into the typology. This is what Pierre Bourdieu refers to as the synoptic illusion; the confusion of a model of reality with that reality (Bourdieu, 1977: 97–109). This is a particular danger in relation to the demands of policy makers who seek models of terrorism that can then be applied in real-world situations. But academics also can construct sophisticated typologies and then attempt to push differing types of terrorism into them. We should be wary of assuming that our typologies are accurate accounts of the reality of terrorism.

Second, typologies simplify a complex reality, and policy makers can use typologies to provide an academic justification for political ends. Third, as a simplification of a complex reality, typologies can distort our understandings and can elide details, differences and nuances among social practices that may seem similar, but which are, in fact, different. According to Peter Fleming, Michael Stohl and Alex Schmid, the uncritical use of typologies often reflects the bias of the researchers rather than illuminating factors related to the phenomena under examination (Fleming, Schmid and Stohl, 1988: 154). Notwithstanding all of these problems, however, typologies of terrorism can provide useful ways of framing the issues and help illuminate some of the differences between groups that use terrorism as a tactic, or strategy.

In particular, it is useful to cluster terrorism into types according to what it is the particular groups are aiming to achieve. However, since terrorism is constantly developing, some of the types I discuss below are less prevalent in the contemporary world than in previous eras. This highlights the fact that it is the structural configuration within which terrorism emerges that helps account for the form it takes. Moreover, although the types of terrorism discussed below are common in the literature, it is imperative to remember that groups using terrorism can belong to more than one category. So, for example, some groups that use terrorism can be both nationalistic and religious. Hence, terrorist typologies have to be treated with care and do not represent hard and fast categories, but rather complex associations of overlapping aims and goals underpinning the use of terrorism.

Prior to 9/11, the two groups most responsible for placing terrorism at the forefront of international public discourse were the Palestine Liberation Organization (PLO) and the Irish Republican Army (IRA). Ironically, both groups are also, arguably, the most successful movements to have used terrorism throughout history (Cobban, 1984; O'Brien, 1995, 2007). Yet, after 9/11, the cause of the Palestinians in particular has become confusingly linked with religious forms of terrorism, but this ignores the fact that the original impetus for the PLO was, and still is, national self-determination. Nationalist forms of terrorism can attempt to achieve many goals related to national identity, but perhaps the primary one is that of self-determination or autonomy for a perceived national group. For example, the IRA sought a united Ireland and the PLO national self-rule for the Palestinian people.

Nationalist groups that use terrorism often oppose what they consider to be occupying, imperial or otherwise illegitimate political powers controlling their destiny. The high point of nationalist terrorism is typically said to have been during the post-1945 decolonization period, as newly emerging national identities became aware that the age of colonization was over (Burleigh, 2009: 88–151; Springhall, 2001). However, much of the literature that discusses political violence in the era of decolonization tends to adopt a very broad definition of terrorism, hence it is easy to assume that levels of it were high. If my deflationary account is accepted, on the other hand, then many of the acts that might be thought to be terrorism during decolonization could turn out not to be. The key point, however, is that groups asserting their right to national self-determination have indeed used terrorism as a deliberate tactic in pursuance of their goals. It is not inevitable that they do so, however, and many nationalist movements have not deployed terrorism.

A second type of terrorism can be described as revolutionary. Revolutionary terrorist campaigns are intended to bring about a fundamental change in the distribution of wealth, power and status in a society (Geifman, 1995; O'Neill, 2005). Revolutionary terrorism and nationalist terrorism are often closely linked. Groups pursuing nationalist objectives can assert their revolutionary commitments. Often when they do so the aim is to increase the support base of the movement. Equally, many groups advocating revolutionary change do so from a nationalist basis. In some instances, forms of economic exploitation are commonly associated with the presence of foreigners; foreign-owned multinational corporations, and often a foreign military presence, for example. Hence, for many revolutionary terrorists there is often a close link between economic exploitation and a foreign presence. The link between anti-American nationalism and social revolution has been particularly strong in Latin America, where opposition to American imperialism has been a central theme in the doctrines of many left-wing political movements (Castro, 1999; Gott, 1970). Many of the world's major industrial democracies have experienced revolutionary terrorism (Wilkinson, 1986). Despite the close link between nationalist and revolutionary forms of terrorism, however, the two are quite distinct. Revolutionary terrorism seeks the overthrow of the system within a state, whereas nationalist forms of terrorism commonly seek a breakaway from a particular state in the hope of forming their own sovereign entity. Revolutionary terrorism also spans the political spectrum. Many revolutionary movements have been inspired by left-wing ideologies, but right-wing revolutionary groups prepared to use terrorism have also emerged (Taylor, Holbrook and Currie, 2013). In addition, counter-revolutionary groups can, and will, sometimes use terrorism as a specific tactic.

In general, however, where left-wing terrorists typically want an overthrow of the capitalist system, right-wing terrorists can be considered reactionary. Often such right-wing groups will engage in terrorist acts to force states to crack down on other groups within society who may be agitating for major social and economic change (Chomsky and Herman, 1973). Interestingly, some right-wing terrorism that has emerged in the United States is embedded in deeply religious structures as well as a deep-seated suspicion of the state. These have often been lone individual acts of terrorism, for example, Timothy McVeigh (Wright, 2007). McVeigh was a former US army veteran who detonated a bomb in front of the Alfred P. Murrah Federal Building in Oklahoma City on 19 April 1995. This was the most deadly terrorist attack on American soil prior to 9/11 and 168 people were killed and over 800 people injured. McVeigh had hoped that his actions would incite an uprising against what he considered to be a tyrannical federal government.

In addition to nationalist forms of terrorism, and revolutionary terrorism in both its right-wing and left-wing variants, some analysts refer to single-issue types of terrorism (Posłuszna and Posłuszny, 2013; Smith, 1998). These might be attacks on abortion clinics, or laboratories using animals for research. There is no doubt that such forms of violent action can spread terror through the affected population. However, given their focus on particular issues that may, or may not be, political in nature, then they are not terrorism as defined here.

Certainly, these focused groups do attack non-state actors, but their primary motivation for doing so is to spread terror throughout the community engaged in the practice to which they object. Hence, for example, violent attacks on laboratories conducting research on animals can be interpreted as attempts to spread fear among the community of researchers and firms employing them. Nonetheless, it is possible that such attacks can be attempts to alter the political and public environment surrounding such issues in the hope of effecting change in some policy. Thus, attacks on abortion clinics can be attempting to persuade politicians that laws against abortion are required. As such, these single-issue types of terrorism are not attacks on the state; although this does not rule out the possibility that they may be. However, such an assessment can only be made on a case-by-case basis.

The final type of terrorism I discuss, and possibly the most contentious, is religious terrorism (Berman, 2009; Perlmutter, 2004). Since 9/11, debate surrounding this issue seems to have ossified into two opposing camps. On the one hand, there are those writers such as Mark Juergensmeyer (2003), Charles Selengut (2008), Jessica Stern (2003) and James Jones (2008) who see religious terrorism not only as a valid category, but perhaps the dominant form of terrorism in the contemporary age. On the other hand, authors such as Richard Jackson and colleagues (Jackson, Jarvis and Gunning, 2011), Robert Pape (Pape, 2005) and Terry Nardin (Nardin, 2001) see little value in the concept. According to these critics the separation of the political from the religious is always difficult to make, and whilst particular groups may espouse religious motivations, these often conceal political ends. Many of the disagreements between these positions are based on fundamental misunderstandings. Few of those prepared to accept the possibility of religious terrorism would want to argue that religion is the only factor. Mark Juergensmeyer, for example, argues that 'religion is not innocent. But it does not ordinarily lead to violence. That happens only with the coalescence of a peculiar set of circumstances – political, social, and ideological – when religion becomes fused with violent expressions of social aspirations, personal pride, and movements for political change' (Juergensmeyer, 2003: 10). This is a clear acknowledgement that it is the combination of religion with other factors that creates a particular mind-set. However, without religion, that mind-set would be different, so excluding religion would be an error.

In the final analysis, some of the most violent groups that have turned to terrorism have emerged out of religious motivations. There is no doubt that contemporary Islamic terrorism grounds its practice and justification in religious understandings, even if these are then manipulated and used to support non-religious ends. Religion and politics are often deeply implicated in one another. For example, although the IRA was essentially a nationalist organization whose aim was a united Ireland, most of its support was generated from the Catholic community in Northern Ireland. Most of the Protestant community in Northern Ireland, on the other hand, was keen to remain part of Britain. Yet this religious divide was not the driving force of the 'Troubles'; this was the British presence and control of a part of Ireland that was deemed to be, by Catholics at least, under occupation. However, to leave out religion of any description of this conflict would be to misdescribe it. Likewise, although the Palestinian liberation struggle has primarily focused on the pursuit of Palestinian statehood and an ending of the Israeli occupation, it too has become fused with a religious overlay. Thus, it is difficult not to see Hamas, for example, as both engaged in a project aimed at the removal of Israel from Palestinian territory (and possibly the eradication of Israel itself), but also engaged in a religious/political project of ensuring that whatever Palestinian state emerges is based on Islamic principles (Caridi, 2012: Ch. 1; Milton-Edwards and Farrell, 2010: 1–30; Tamimi, 2007). Likewise, al-Qaeda has made clear its commitment to a religious renewal across the Islamic world and, in some instances, beyond it (Alexander and Swetnam, 2001; Bergen and Cruickshank, 2007; Burke, 2003). Calls for Sharia law, an Islamic caliphate and appeals to the Umma (the collective community of Islamic peoples) all reflect this religious aspect, and it would be foolish to deny it.

It needs to be noted, however, that the more radical Islamic positions are both political and religious at the same point in time and reflect a major point of departure between Western and Islamic understandings of politics. According to the more radical versions of Islamic political theology, sovereignty ultimately rests with Allah, not with the state, the monarch or the people. As Iilyas Ahmad puts it:

> Though Muslim writers have given us the legal view of Sovereignty, it is not the Islamic view, for in Islam, even from the point of view of Law, the Sovereignty of Allah is to be recognised, and it is His Authority alone for which the word Sovereignty can be used. (Ahmad, 1958: 244)

Thus, for these forms of radical Islam, Western attempts to constitute the state on secular grounds are an attempt to wrest sovereignty from its rightful location in religious authority. Hence, al-Qaeda is not simply a movement orientated against particular states, but rather is a religious/political project aimed at overturning the Western state system. Or to put it another way: al-Qaeda and other radical forms of Islamic political activity can only be understood as non-religious from a secular perspective that already accepts the separation of religion from politics. That said, whilst it is obviously difficult to separate religion and politics, the Western secular movement is predicated on the idea that politics and religion not only can be separated, but ought be so(Hurd, 2008). Obviously, political leaders, such as George Bush and Tony Blair may have deeply held religious convictions, but according to the Western political tradition these religious convictions can play no role in determining political outcomes (Cliteur, 2010: 172–280; Koppelman, 2013: 166–78).

The Political and Social Effects of Terrorism

Once again, when considering the political and social effects of terrorism, ontology is our starting point. Ontology forces us to think about effects on what? Given the definition I have outlined in previous chapters, we are, as a first cut, interested in the effects of terrorism on the non-state actors who are instrumentally attacked and manipulated as a transmission mechanism for a broader political message. The primary audience of acts of terrorism, however, are state managers. However, acts of terrorism clearly send a message, not just to state managers, but also to the wider social community. The aim of the terrorist is to either change the behaviour of state managers, or to make the community put pressure on state managers in the hope of bringing about political or social change. An important aspect of this is, of course, the media, which play a major role in spreading the message for the terrorists. Terrorists attempt to spread fear and hence, the social and political effects of terrorism go beyond that inflicted on those who suffer directly from it.

In terms of any assessment of the effect on victims, the definition of terrorism clearly plays a major role. Although now dated, some analysis by Weinberg and Davis in 1989 makes the point here (Weinberg and Davis, 1989). Weinberg and Davis attempt to quantify the number of deaths from terrorist incidents over a given period (1968–80). Using 1980 data from the Washington National Foreign Assessment Centre, under the label 'Patterns of International Terrorism 1980', Weinberg and Davis suggest that there had been 2863 terrorist attacks on US citizens or property between 1968 to 1980. This can be broken down in the following way:

Attacks on diplomatic officials or property	805 (28.1%)
Attacks on military officials or property	456 (15.9%)
Attacks on other US government officials or property	344 (12%)
Attacks on business facilities or executives	901 (31.5%)
Attacks on private citizens	357 (12.5%)

When combined with other data drawn from the geographic distribution of international terrorist incidents, and data based on deaths by domestic terrorism in selected countries, Weinberg and Davis claim that 'we can say with some certainty ... that a minimum of approximately 16,000 people have lost their lives since 1968 as a result of terrorism' (Weinberg and Davis, 1989: 119–21). It should be clear why the definitional question cannot simply be left aside. For on my account of terrorism, the figures would be substantially lower, since attacks on diplomats, military and US government officials would not count as terrorism. In fact, when considered on a global level, even Weinberg and Davis's figures make clear that terrorism is not a major cause of death in the international system. Indeed, states have caused far more deaths over the same period in efforts to suppress their own populations. One could also point to deaths from car accidents, smoking, poverty, malnutrition, and so on (Chapman and Harris, 2002).

Of course, terrorists do not only aim to kill non-state actors to send their message, and hostage taking and kidnapping clearly also have a deep effect on victims and populations that perceive themselves to be under attack. The point is not that the victims do not suffer terribly, but rather it is that when considered in purely numerical terms, terrorism is not a significant threat to most people, or even most states (although there is a very special case, to be discussed in the next chapter, that could potentially, at least, constitute a major threat to both individuals and the state that arises from contemporary forms of terrorism) (Meuller, 2006). And, of course, there is the wider psychological effect on the community after terror attacks. However, this is a double-edged sword for the terrorists.

Often a community that is subject to terrorist attacks can gain increased cohesion as a result of the attacks and such crises can generate positive emotions among the community (Fredrickson et al., 2003). A good example here might be the #illridewithyou hashtag that emerged on Twitter after the Sydney siege of December 2014. During the siege there were fears that it could lead to deterioration in relations between the mainly white Australian community and the Muslim community in Sydney. In fact, the reverse happened, and the two communities came together to express their common rejection of the siege. Once a society perceives itself to be under attack it can produce forces that generate resilience and resistance to the terrorists rather than fear. In this respect, it is often difficult, if not impossible, for the terrorists to control the public reaction to the message. The aim of the terrorist is to put pressure on the government or society to change policy in some way, but the effect of any terrorist incident may harden attitudes and decrease the likelihood of the terrorist achieving their aims (Abrahms, 2006: 76). Nonetheless, in the immediate aftermath of terrorist attacks it is clear that communities can suffer a deep collective sense of shock and fear. It is equally clear, however, that these quickly subside as the demands of everyday life become pressing, and people move back into what is considered to be normality.

The purpose of all terrorism is to send a message. How this message is transmitted and communicated to the audience is, therefore, important to consider. In this respect, the media play a major role, in both television and print forms (Archetti, 2013; Freedman and Thussu, 2012; Nacos, 2007; Norris, Kern and Just, 2003; Paletz and Schmid, 1992; Schmid and Graaf, 1982). Moreover, in a global age when media images circulate almost instantaneously, it has become increasingly difficult for states to control and stop the terrorists propagating their message. It is also true, however, that terrorists do not always trust the media, and hence, in certain instances, they have developed their own independent channels for communicating with the public. This could be simply the distribution of pamphlets that describe the group's political aims or, as in the case of the PLO, the emergence of its own radio station (The Voice of Palestine). Indeed, contemporary terrorists have become highly sophisticated in spreading their message via the internet (Bockstette, 2008: 14–17) and other social networking sites (Weimann, 2006). This makes it extremely difficult for states to control the dissemination of the terrorists' message, and terrorists are increasingly producing highly sophisticated forms of message transmission.

Nonetheless, and despite the possibilities afforded by the internet and other new communications platforms, such as Facebook and Twitter, the global media still play a major role, often inadvertently, in transmitting the terrorists' message. Violence, whether we like it or not, is newsworthy, and terrorist violence against non-state actors particularly so. Humans, it seems, are fascinated by bad, not good news (Kottler, 2011; Mount, 2012). Acts of terror targeted at non-state actors attract our attention in ways that other developments, perhaps of a longer-term importance, do not. Terrorism, as the saying goes, sells newspapers and attracts audiences. Moreover, acts of terrorism offer the possibility of commercial spin-offs. Films, such as *Die Hard*, or television programmes such as *Homeland* and *24*, for example, provide the public with added symbolic resources through which to (mis-) understand terrorism (Hammond, 2011). Equally, the number of books on terrorism written specifically for public, rather than academic, consumption has grown exponentially since 9/11. Given the competitive environment in which the media operate, both with money to be made and the careers of individual journalists to be advanced, the global media compete with one another to present terrorist events in the most dramatic fashion possible. In this context, appeals from the state and other interested parties for media self-restraint often fall on deaf ears, and although we should be wary of overstating the potential impact of terrorism on a society, censorship of the media is not a valid approach in democracies (Schlesinger, 1981).

Given this, it is hardly surprising that the mass media have had multiple influences on the development of contemporary terrorism. Of course, journalists will argue that all they do is report events as they occur. In this sense, the journalists are simply the bearers of bad news, and just as we would not blame the journalists for an earthquake, we should not hold them responsible for terrorism. The issue is more complicated than this. Terrorists intend to spread a message, and the media constitute the vehicle for that message. As such, the relationship between terrorism and the media is not the same as that between the media and natural disasters. Some people have also claimed that the mass media helps legitimize groups that use terrorism by providing a platform for their spokespeople. Often this is implicit rather than explicit, and reporters asking for the views of group will often display the same objective attitude to that of the terrorist as they do towards state officials who have been critical of the act. Of course, for the journalist this is simply a case of maintaining good journalistic standards, whereas, for the state, it seems to imply that the terrorist viewpoint is equally valid (Schlesinger, Murdock and Elliott, 1983: 84).

Perhaps the most pernicious effect of media coverage of terrorism is what is known as the contagion effect (Midlarsky, Crenshaw and Yoshida, 1980). The coverage of terrorist acts, it is argued, can encourage some to emulate those acts. In this way, it is argued, the mass media help to spread terrorism. Likewise, by publicizing the activities of such groups the media can, potentially at least, perform a recruitment function. In addition, by closely monitoring media responses to their actions, groups prepared to engage in terrorism may refine and improve their techniques so as to create the widest effect and abandon others that have the least impact. The problem for the media in relation to terrorism is that communication is the ultimate aim of the individual acts. Indeed, for many contemporary terrorists media coverage is itself a victory. Killing schoolchildren will not weaken the armed forces of the state, but it will win considerable publicity for the group. This has led some to argue that the mass media is deeply implicated in terrorist events, since media coverage is what the terrorist craves (Eid, 2014: xvi, 33–44).

Another way in which media coverage might contribute in a direct way to terrorism is the manner in which live reporting of state attempts to deal with the terrorists potentially affects the outcome. Media-savvy terrorists will often tune in to major radio stations, watch live broadcasts and monitor police and security-service radios. Thus, live television pictures showing military or police units moving into position to storm a building in which hostages were being held can help the terrorist prepare for any rescue operations. Likewise, media selectivity of which images to broadcast, perhaps focusing on particular parts of the globe, whilst neglecting terrorist attacks in other parts of the world, can distort public perceptions of terrorism. Thus, for example, public perceptions of an assumed link between Islam and terrorism are fuelled by the media focus on groups that are Islamic, and thus contribute to the spread of Islamophobia (Allen, 2010). Of course, after 9/11 and the subsequent 'war on terror' it is understandable that the media should focus on this particular type of terrorism; however, to do so at the expense of other forms distorts the overall picture, and Islamic terrorism is not the only type that is practised today. In fact, there is evidence to suggest that right-wing extremism represents a greater threat to US citizens than Islamic extremism (Bergen and Sterman, 2014; Michael, 2003).

In addition to the effects of terrorism on the media are also wider social effects that result from incidences and campaigns of terrorism. If terrorist attacks are sporadic, and do not constitute a sustained campaign against a population, then the effect on society can be very transient and vary with each attack. On the other hand, if the campaign is well organized, coordinated and sustained, the effect on society can be quite dramatic and goes well beyond the immediate and visible consequences. There is evidence, for example, that as a result of the Troubles in Northern Ireland there were large increases in alcohol- and drug-related problems, and many people suffered post-traumatic stress disorder (Campbell, 2008). Moreover, there are numerous studies that demonstrate a clear link between acts of terrorism and social dysfunction (Njenga et al., 2004; Salib, 2003). In addition, a public subjected to a sustained campaign of terrorism can be a potent source of information and support to the state. Clearly, a society where the threat of terrorism is pervasive becomes a society that learns to deal with the possibility of terrorist attacks, and such a society will differ from one in which there are no such attacks. There is no doubt, for example, that Israeli society has developed particular procedures to deal with the ever-present possibility of terrorist attacks (Sharkansky, 2003).

Of course, perhaps the biggest impact on the public as a result of terrorist attacks is the added security and even perhaps changing attitudes towards civil liberties, as the state attempts to control the activities of those groups and lessen the possibility of future attacks. This not only changes behaviour and extra security at airports, but can lead to state agents fundamentally altering the relationship between the state and the individual. Fingerprinting at airports, body scans, restrictions on the fluids that can be carried on aircraft and generally, increased security measures, are simply some of the effects that terrorism can have on a society (Cole and Dempsey, 2006; Grayling, 2009; Hardin, 2004). Politically, there is no doubt that terrorism, whatever political leaders say about it, has been successful in bringing particular causes to the attention of the public (Dershowitz, 2002b: 31).

In the final analysis, the effects of terrorism on individuals caught up in it and societies in which it emerges are varied, and we have only addressed some of them here. In the immediate aftermath of terrorist attacks the effects are clear to see, with increased media reporting, perhaps immediate restrictions on the activities of the public until the authorities feel they have gained control of the situation, and widespread fear amongst the public about the possibility of further attacks (Meade and Molander, 2006). Depending on the scale of the attack, the number of casualties, and the perception of whether or not this is an isolated incident, the effects can be much longer-lasting, and in many respects damaging to social cohesion, individual wellbeing and the very values a society holds.

The Structure and Organization of Groups that Use Terrorism

Like any other kind of human collective or institution, groups prepared to use terrorism are socially organized, and structured in particular ways (Shapiro, 2013). Likewise, although there may be minor differences, it is often the case that the structures of such groups, in different parts of the world, often bear a close resemblance to one another (Centre of Excellence Defence Against Terrorism, 2008). This is so for at least two main reasons. First, groups who turn to terrorism are known to interact with one another. They provide resources to each other, and they often provide training to one another (Karmon, 2005). Even though the causes to which they are committed may differ, they share a belief that violence against non-state actors is a valid means to an end. Hence, it is not surprising that such groups learn from one another about what is successful in terms of the optimal structural organization to deploy. At a deeper level, however, the structural organization of these groups can resemble one another even when there has been little or no contact between them. How is this possible, and why does it come about?

The answer to this question lies in the fact that the structural environment all terrorists face is very similar. This environment, of course, is the state system. Even though the form of the state in different parts of the globe may vary, the fundamentals of state sovereignty have been globalized. Hence, terrorists always face a situation where politics is organized through the state. Interacting with the state, attempting to attack it, and attempting to evade its intelligence and security apparatus require groups that deploy terrorist tactics to adopt very similar modes of structural organization. Equally, the fact that violence is the chosen mode of protest against the state provides an added impetus towards structural similarity. The successful deployment of violent protest in a state system that has been globalized means that the groups only have a few models of structural organization on which to draw. But it also means that as the structure of the international system changes then the structure of groups using terrorism in that system must also change. Nothing illustrates this better than the structural organization adopted by al-Qaeda, which looks very different to the structural organization of traditional terrorists (Sageman, 2004, 2008). The success of al-Qaeda can largely be explained due to its formidable ability to integrate itself with the structural environment from which it emerged. So perfectly does the al-Qaeda structural configuration fit the era of globalization that it is difficult to speak of an organizational form at all. Al-Qaeda has adapted to the prevailing social, political and economic circumstances of its age, rather than adopting the structural form of prior terrorists.

Al-Qaeda could not have been as successful as it has been if it had not adapted itself to the form globalization was taking (Moghadam, 2008: 2–3; Roy, 2004; Stapley, 2006). Indeed, al-Qaeda has been so successful that newly emerging groups such as IS may adopt its model, and in the era of globalization if they fail to do so then their success may well be limited. What this also means is that any attempt by states to deal with al-Qaeda can only be successful if located at the global level. The al-Qaeda cause is not driven by antipathy to any particular state but by a rejection of the Western state system per se; although obviously they attack the most powerful states responsible for the contemporary configuration of that system. It is for this reason that the war on terror is also a war on globalization; it is an attempt to address and attack the structural context that both facilitates the emergence of groups like al-Qaeda as well as allowing their strategies to be successful (Moghaddam, 2008). However, this is an issue that will be tackled in more depth in the following chapter. For now it is important to note that the following analysis is concerned primarily with more traditional forms of terrorism.

In an influential analysis James Frazer and Ian Fulton (Fraser and Fulton, 1984) argue that there are two factors to understanding how groups that use terrorism are organized. These are the structure of its organizational framework and the structure of its support. According to Frazer and Fulton, the most common type of structural organization within these groups resembles that of a four-level pyramid. At the top of the pyramid is the Command level, which makes policy, devices plans and provides general direction and ideological leadership. At the next level is the Active Cadre, who carry out the missions of the organization. The next level down consists of Active Supporters, who provide safe houses, intelligence logistical support, and so on. Finally, at the bottom level of the pyramid are the Passive Supporters, who, whilst not actively providing material support for the group, nonetheless produce a supportive and favourable political climate within which the group can operate. Membership of the various groups within terrorist organizations varies according to the structural level on which they are located. Thus, groups who turn to terrorism generally have many more passive supporters than those in command or those involved in actual operations. Many more people are needed to provide support terrorist operations than to carry them out. These passive supporters also do not need to be members of groups committed to using terrorism, and the support they give can be implicit rather than explicit. Indeed, passive supporters may agree with the aims of the group but not the tactics. Passive supporters commonly provide political and ideological support for the group, but rarely material support. However, at times, perhaps through fundraising events, such as by the IRA in the United States, political support can translate into material support.

At the second level of the pyramid are the active supporters who, according to Frazer and Fulton, are the most important level for any terrorist organization. A small group of committed terrorists may be able to carry out a limited bombing campaign or engage in a series of kidnappings, for example, but to maintain a sustained terrorist campaign requires a number of active supporters who provide logistical support, such as communication channels, intelligence gathering and the supply of materials, often including, of course, bomb-making material and/or weapons. What Frazer calls the Active Cadre is the group we commonly refer to as terrorists in public discourse. These are the people who carry out the actual missions, and they can have a range of skills depending on the size of the group. So, for example, some may be bomb-making experts; others may have important electronics expertise. Still others could have skills in chemical manipulation and others could be drivers, and so on. The division of labour within the group provides an important limitation/enablement as to the tactics the group employs. The tactics chosen by the group will depend upon the skill set in the group. By far the smallest group within Frazer and Fulton's pyramid is the Command level. The commanders provide overall strategic direction of the group, oversee the planning of operations, and in general enforce discipline within the group.

Most groups that turn to terrorism, because of the need for secrecy, have tended to remain small, often numbering fewer than fifty people (Robb, 2004). As we have seen, according to the pyramid model we can group these people according to the tasks they complete for the group. Frazer and Fulton provide another way of looking at this through an analytical typology that looks at what the groups must do and how they are related. A command structure is a necessary component of any social group. However, groups will also need internal discipline, training, logistics, intelligence, financing, and then the active cells themselves. Considered, for the moment, as simply a social group that has to fulfil these tasks, we can see how organizations deploying terrorism are structured in particular ways. Another vital aspect of the group if it is to remain successful is that of secrecy. Anthony Burton (Burton, 1975: 70–2) argues that the high levels of secrecy needed by terrorists can best be maintained under two structures. Perhaps the most prevalent is the cell-type structure.

Cells are normally very small groups of people, often numbering fewer than ten. The less, the better, if secrecy and group success are to be achieved and maintained. Each cell will often have its own special set of skills, and the ultimate aim is the maintenance and security of the individual cell, and preserving its ability to carry out its tasks; in principle, cells may be aware of the existence of other cells, but owing to the need for secrecy they rarely know little more than that other cells exist. In theory, cell members should only contact other members of the same cell and communication with the command level is achieved through the deployment of active supporters, who have often escaped the attention of security services. This cell-type structure ensures that the terrorist organization is not threatened if one cell is discovered and disrupted by the authorities. According to Jonathan White, groups of cells create columns, each column being a semi-autonomous collection of cells with a variety of specialities and a single command structure (White, 2014: 54–85).

This organizational structure presents terrorists with particular problems. The first, of course, is the need to maintain secrecy, and this dominates all aspects of such groups and is not something faced by more open organizations in society (Mobley, 2012: 1–19). This makes the study of them extremely difficult, but over time analysts have attempted to grasp how these groups organize in order to deal with particular problems related to their particular structures. Secrecy is both a necessary element of terrorism, and if successfully maintained, provides the mechanism of their success (Mobley, 2012: 1). It also, however, presents the group with particular problems. Whilst terrorism demands secrecy, secrecy can also prevent effective communication; the structure gives the group protection, but it is also a barrier to effective communication and control. Each cell needs to be protected from discovery, and the organization as a whole has to be aware of possible infiltration by the security services. Under the cell structure, even if a state agent manages to infiltrate one cell, because the cell does not know the overall structural context within which it operates, it is difficult for a state agent to gain any intelligence other than that relating to the specific cell.

Another negative aspect of such a cell-type structure is that the internal dynamics of each group can differ, and this can lead to the emergence of ideological differences. The provisional IRA is a classic example here, with constant factional infighting and groups within the organization breaking off to form their own small units. Often these breakaway groups would use violence against elements in the larger group who disagreed with them (Coogan, 2002: 42). It is hardly surprising, given the commitment to terror as a legitimate tactic, that factionalism and ideological differences are controlled through strict internal discipline, itself often involving the use of terror. For organizations already pre-disposed towards terror, it is an effective internal control mechanism. This can, however, often have the opposite effect. After all, those drawn to terrorism have reached an accommodation with the use of violence, hence, when their commanders use violence against them in order to enforce group cohesion and control it is always possible that they will react with violence against the group leaders. It is for this reason that large terrorist organizations tend to display fragmentary tendencies (Hellmich, 2011: 17).

Another problem with this cell/column structure is that of logistics. Cells need resources in order to complete their missions. Here again, the active supporters play a major role, and often the biggest problem that commanders of groups that use terrorism face is ensuring that they have a large group of active supporters able to support the individual cells. Training provides another problem, and the need to maintain secrecy often means that individual cell members have to go overseas to receive training in techniques required for the completion of missions. Thus, all groups using terrorism face major coordination and management problems. They all survive only with political support, planning, organization and adequate resources. Running an organization committed to terrorists is big business, and often such groups will begin to develop structures that look like bureaucratic organizations.

Groups that use terrorism, although similar to big businesses in many crucial respects, differ in important ways. Terrorists have no shareholders, which means they do not need to provide dividends from their funds. However, without profits terrorists need a means to fund their activities, and those in charge of the group have to find a way to finance it (Costigan and Gold, 2007). Often, these groups may be funded by some state that wishes to sponsor their activities (Ehrenfeld, 2003). However, this level of dependency is not ideal for many terrorist organizations that prefer to remain autonomous from state control, even if they are prepared to accept state sponsorship for strategic reasons. In an influential book, James Adams (1986) argues that the nature of terrorism changed between the 1960s and 1980s, but most security forces analysis was still based on an outdated belief that terrorists were largely funded by sponsoring states. Yet, according to Adams, most of the major terrorist organizations of the time were independent of states and had created their own independent financial networks (Adams, 1986: 3).

Adams's work is still relevant today, and according to many analysts the most efficient way to defeat terrorism is to destroy the financial networks that they use to maintain themselves. In a globalized world with financial flows increasingly difficult to control, however, this has become a major issue for state security services. Moreover, it helps explain the rafts of legislation aimed at controlling the financial resources of terrorist organizations (Biersteker and Eckert, 2008: 1–16). It is for this reason that being labelled an organization that uses terrorism at the international level is so important; it forces all states to take economic action against the assets of the group.

So how do terrorists fund themselves? Assuming that the PLO at times used terrorism, then they provide one important example. The PLO had a high level of passive support and established an economic wing known as SAMED (more correctly known as the Palestine Martyrs Works Society) in 1970. SAMED developed into a sophisticated business enterprise in order to support the PLO, developing large agricultural and manufacturing facilities. Ostensibly, these were formed to help fund the Palestinian people; however, money was also channelled to those parts of the PLO engaged in acts of political violence, at it is clear that once an organization has generated funds it is difficult to check on how those funds are distributed within the group (Ehrenfeld, 2003: Ch. 3). Other sources of terrorist finances include funding support from the passive supporters, but most importantly, crime. The IRA is a classic example of this, running an organized crime network in Northern Ireland. Interestingly, the IRA blurred the distinction between the legal generation of funding and criminal activity. They quickly learned that a successful legal business could be criminally maintained. Thus, for example, the IRA took over the running of taxis in parts of Northern Ireland and used criminal activity to drive competitor firms out of business (Horgan and Taylor, 2003). This proved to be very lucrative for them. The scope of terrorist criminal activity can include bank robberies, kidnappings, extortion, protection rackets and drugs. The complexity of the contemporary international financial system also makes money laundering, and the transferring of funds for operations, much easier. More recently, Gretchen Peters has argued that al-Qaeda has moved into the production of heroin as a way to maintain its funding (Peters, 2012).

The importance of understanding how terrorists finance themselves has become a crucial aspect in the war on terror, since terrorists emerge in the structural context that provides both social and material resources that allow the group to function. Finance is a key aspect of these resources, as are the humans required to both support and carry out terrorist operations. Every organization prepared to turn to terrorism requires financing, and in the context of a complex global economy counter-terrorist operations also need a global reach. Thus, states cannot act in isolation against contemporary terrorists. Combating terrorism in the contemporary age can only be achieved through a coordinated global response.

Conclusion

Accepting the need to arrive at a definition of terrorism should not lead us to assume that it is all of a kind. Terrorism is a specific form of political violence, but once it has been identified we can see that it comes in differing forms, pursues differing goals and aspires to differing ends. Often, the various types of terrorism have differing dynamics. Groups that use terrorism to advance very specific and limited political aims are often much easier to deal with than those with grandiose political blueprints for complete political reorganization. Groups that use terrorism without clearly defined goals are often difficult to deal with. The type of terrorism often dictates the kinds of responses that are appropriate to deal with it. Likewise, the specific structural organization of differing groups that use terrorism requires a differentiated response to them. Effective responses to such groups demand an understanding of their internal organizational structures, their hierarchical organization, and an awareness of their most common tactics. Although we can define the general category of terrorism, it is important to differentiate between its various manifestations.

It is important, in this respect, is to gain some understanding of the wider effects terrorism has on society at large. Once these effects are understood it is possible to consider ways to mitigate those effects and potentially, at least, decrease the effectiveness of terrorism. In addition, a better understanding of the aims and effects of terrorism can itself allow society a means through which to lessen the generation of fear that surrounds such acts. And if the fear can be controlled, responses can be more measured, and hopefully, the main aims of terrorism – the production of fear – might be reduced. In this sense, as far as terrorism goes, knowledge is power.

8
Contemporary Terrorism and the War on Terror

Terrorism, as I have defined it, is an emergent structural consequence of the way human societies organize their political relationships. As long as some exercise power over others there will always be groups, and individuals, that object to that rule. Insofar as the right to rule is historically embedded within a political configuration (the state system) founded on violence, then those objecting to the prevailing order may feel that it is legitimate to use violence against that order. If those political protesters lack the means to effectively and openly articulate a non-violent challenge to the prevailing order, then they may attempt to change that order by attacking that which the order values; its people. This does not validate terrorism; it explains it. Terrorism, then, is a structural product of the political system and historically it will occur whenever rule emerges (Onuf, 1989).

Given my deflationary definition of terrorism, however, any history of the practice that I might outline would look very different from that articulated by many other books that deal with the issue. It is interesting, however, that so many books on terrorism include chapters that deal with the history of terrorism without specifying how the term is being defined. But one cannot possibly look at the history of a practice in the absence of a definition of what that practice is. In many cases, the history is used to form the concept; as if we could simply look historically at certain practices in the attempt to decide what those practices are; in effect derive the concept, or definition, from the history. But how can we look at the history of terrorism without a definition of what it is we are looking at? History cannot provide us with a definition of terrorism; only conceptual analysis can. Hence, conceptual analysis is prior. Some authors (Laqueur, 2001) provide a history of so-called terrorism by including acts that would not be considered terrorism under different definitions. For example, it is common to find histories of terrorism that include acts against state actors, such as political assassinations, as instances of terrorism (Laqueur, 1996). An alternative definition of terrorism would provide an alternative history. The deflationary account of terrorism developed here rules out all histories of terrorism that include violent acts committed against the state or state actors. However, violent acts against non-state actors with the express aim of using those subject to the attack as transmission mechanisms to convey a political message also have a long history.

Despite this, terrorism does undergo change over time; there is change within continuity (Wight, 2001). The social and political causes of groups using terrorism change, as do the methods. Public awareness of terrorism fundamentally changed after 9/11. The question is, did the practice of terrorism change? Does 9/11 represent a 'new' form of terrorism? At its most basic level, the answer to this question has to be no. The horrific attacks of 9/11 were still politically motivated acts of violence directed against non-state actors with the aim of using those actors in an instrumental manner to transmit a political message. However, when viewed from another perspective, 9/11 does represent a fundamental change in how terrorists, the public and states view the phenomenon.

Contemporary Terrorism

Terrorism today, or what I call contemporary terrorism, differs in substantial ways from terrorism in previous eras. I want to avoid many of the debates surrounding whether or not there is something called 'new terrorism' (Cetina, 2005; Crenshaw, 2003; Duyvesteyn, 2004; Laqueur, 1996, 1999; Neumann, 2009), by simply examining the form that terrorism takes today; whether it is deserving of the label 'new' is something I will leave others to decide. All social practices undergo change. Whether the label 'new' can be validly applied to these changes is a question that can only be answered on the basis of some agreement of what the older forms of that practice were. In the absence of an agreed definition of terrorism, it is impossible to say if there is anything 'new' about the form terrorism takes today (Bolanos, 2012; Duyvesteyn and Malkki, 2012). Given the stress I have placed on understanding terrorism as a context-bound and structurally produced social practice, we would expect terrorism to be different in 2011 from what it was in 1911. If the context has changed, so will the practice. However, in order to say that something has changed we need a robust account of the thing that we are claiming has changed. Terrorism is still terrorism, according to the very restricted definition I am using here. Hence, the form that terrorism takes today may not be 'new', but it has certainly changed, and we need to consider what those changes are and how we might understand them.

The idea that new forms of terrorism were emerging can be dated back to the late 1990s. In this respect, 9/11 simply repre-sents that moment when the new terrorism was thrust onto the public stage. However, authors had already begun to identify the parameters of the 'new' terrorism (Laqueur, 1999; Lesser et al., 1999). One of the key characteristics of contemporary terror-ism is the growing influence of religion as a source of motivation among terrorists (Jones, 2008; Juergensmeyer, 2003; Perlmutter, 2004; Stern, 2003). Indeed, in public discourse, and among many analysts, it is the religious aspect that marks contemporary ter-rorism as being essentially different from terrorism of previous eras. All contemporary terrorism, however, is not necessarily religiously motivated. Many groups that employ terrorism as a tactic still pursue nationalist or revolutionary aims. The form of terrorism that has gripped the public imagination, and which has been the impetus for the exponential rise in books and articles on the issue, has been Islamic terrorism.

This is not an unproblematic label. While some authors (Gabriel, 2002: 23–32) have been keen to demonstrate a sup-posed culture of violence at the heart of Islam itself, it is clear that Islam and the Qur'an are subject to multiple interpretations (Lewis, 2003: 3–28). Christianity, particularly when based on Old Testament principles, also has its violent proclivities. Some of the more radical versions of Islam do valorize violence and struggle; IS, for example. One simply cannot deny that there are passages of the Qur'an that suggest violence is not only acceptable, but is demanded. Of course, such passages do not demonstrate that Islam advocates violence, but the fact of their existence does mean they can be subject to interpretation by those that would wish to use the Qur'an to support the use of violence. bin Laden, for example, is explicit about this:

> Our encouragement and call for Muslims to enter jihad against the American and the Israeli occupiers are actions which we undertake as religious obligations. God Most High has commanded us in many verses of the Qur'an to fight in His path and to urge the believers to do so. These are his words: 'So [Prophet] fight in God's way. You are accountable only for yourself. Urge the believers on. God may well curb the power of the disbelievers, for He is stronger in might and more terrible in punishment' and His words: 'Why should you not fight in God's cause and for those oppressed men, women and children who cry out, "Lord rescue us from this town whose people are oppressors! By your grace, give us a protector and helper!"?', and His words: 'When you meet the disbelievers, strike them in the neck ...' We have given an oath to God to continue and the struggle as long as we have blood coursing through our veins or a seeing eye, and we beg of God to accept and to grant a good outcome for us and for all the Muslims. (bin Laden, 2005: 41)

Given this, it is difficult to deny that there is something called Islamic terrorism, or at least, that Islam has been invoked in the cause of terrorism. This does not mean, however, and should not be taken to mean, that Islam itself is necessarily predisposed towards violence, or that all Muslims support the use of violence. When I use the term Islamic terrorism I simply refer to that specific group of people who are prepared to use terrorism, as I have defined it, and base that use of terrorism on a very particular, and arguably distorted, version of Islam (Sutton and Vertigans, 2005: 1–9).

However, some authors continue to blur the boundaries of this issue. Scott Atran, for example, suggests that religion actually plays a minor role in the motivations of those drawn to terrorism:

> When you look at young people like the ones who grew up to blow up trains in Madrid in 2004, carried out the slaughter on the London underground in 2005, hoped to blast airliners out of the sky en route to the United States in 2006 and 2009, and journeyed far to die killing infidels in Iraq, Afghanistan, Pakistan, Yemen or Somalia; when you look at whom they idolize, how they organize, what bonds them and what drives

them; then you see that what inspires the most lethal terrorists in the world today is not so much the Koran or religious teachings as a thrilling cause and call to action that promises glory and esteem in the eyes of friends, and through friends, eternal respect and remembrance in the wider world that they will never live to enjoy ... Jihad is an egalitarian, equal-opportunity employer: ... fraternal, fast-breaking, thrilling, glorious, and cool. (Pinker, 2011: 639)

Atran seems to be sitting on the fence somewhat. On the one hand, he is saying that it is 'not so much the Qur'an or religious teachings' but the adoption of a 'thrilling cause or call to action', yet on the other, he is admitting the place of religion in this cause. This equivocation has led some to suggest that Atran supports a view that 'Islamic faith has little to do with the modern jihadist movement' (Hasan, 2014). However, this runs counter to what Atran has said elsewhere based on interviews he conducted with terrorists and families of terrorists (Atran, 2006). In this, the ability of religion, what Atran calls 'sacred values', plays a role that overrides all other considerations. Hence, according to Atran, 'sacred values' are 'not very sensitive to standard calculations regarding cost and benefit, to quantity' (Atran, 2006: 6). Indeed, the excerpts from the interviews that Atran quotes prove, with a high degree of certainly, that the religious aspect of this phenomenon overrides all other considerations. It is worth quoting these at length:

'So what if your family were to be killed in retaliation for your action?' or 'What if your father were dying and your mother found out your plans for a martyrdom attack and asked you to delay until the family could get back on its feet?' To a person they answered along lines that there is duty to family but duty to God cannot be postponed. 'And what if your action resulted in no one's death but your own?' The typical response is, 'God will love you just the same.' For example, when these questions were posed to the alleged Emir of Jemaah Islamiyah, Abu Bakr Ba'asyir, in Jakarta's Cipinang prison in August 2005, he responded that martyrdom for the sake of jihad is the ultimate fardh 'ain, an inescapable individual obligation that trumps all others, including the four of the five pillars of Islam (only profession of faith equals jihad). What matters for him as for most would-be martyrs and their sponsors I have interviewed is the martyr's intention and commitment to God, so that blowing up only oneself has the same value and reward as killing however many of the enemy. (Atran, 2006: 6)

Notwithstanding the methodological and epistemological problems interviews pose, taken at face value, these excerpts suggest that religion is clearly a factor in contemporary Islamic terrorism. However, there is a more difficult problem.

For many of the more radical forms of political Islam, the Qur'an is literally the word of God; it was revealed and dictated to the Prophet; he was not divinely inspired to compose it himself. And the desire for a return to the original meaning of the text lies at the heart of many of the more radical political forms of Islam today (Heffelfinger, 2011; Sookhdeo, 2008) Hence, in many instances violent passages in the Qur'an are simply quoted verbatim by radical clerics and are not put into any kind of historical or social context, or subject to interpretation.

From the perspective of radical Islam, however, the idea of putting the Qur'an into a historical and social context is to misunderstand what the Qur'an is. The Qur'an is the word of God, and no historical or social context can alter what the words mean; 'We Muslims believe The Qur'an to be the book of divine guidance and direction for mankind, consider the text in its original Arabic to be the literal word of Allah (God)' (Islam.com, 2014). The re-emergence of political Islam as a major political force in the world, and the associated emergence of groups within that movement prepared to use violence to challenge the prevailing order, means that religiously motivated terrorism, however misguided, is a characteristic of contemporary terrorism. According to Ian O. Lesser et al. (1999: 17–20), the percentage of religiously inspired groups in relation to the total number of terrorist organizations grew from less than 4 per cent in 1980 to over 40 per cent by the mid-1990s. Moreover, while still not in the majority, it is the high visibility of al-Qaeda, in particular, - clearly a religiously motivated movement, which suggests that religion is now a key factor in contemporary terrorism (Hoffman, 1995). Moreover, as the events of 2014 demonstrate, new forms of violent Islamic dissent are emerging; as groups such as the Islamic State in Iraq and al-Sham (IS) and Boko Haram in Nigeria clearly show.

There is another aspect to this. According to some of the more radical versions of Islam, sovereignty can only reside with God and attempts to place sovereignty in some other entity – popular sovereignty, for example – is heresy. This is most clearly articulated through the words of Sayyid Quṭb (Quṭb, 1993; Quṭb and Bergesen, 2008). Quṭb was an Egyptian government bureaucrat, author, literary critic and Islamic political leader, but is most famous as an Islamist theoretician. His most famous, widely read and influential book is *Milestones*. There is no doubt it has influenced al-Qaeda, and Islamic fundamentalists across the world, and bin Laden references it approvingly (bin Laden, 2005: 16, 41, 58, 229).

Milestones covers many issues, however. In relation to sovereignty Quṭb is clear. Anyone who does not obey traditional Sharia, or 'God's rule on earth', is by definition not a Muslim. The problem is 'not that they believe in other deities besides God or because they worship anyone other than God, but [that] their way of life is not based on submission to God alone. Although they believe in the Unity of God, still they have relegated the legislative attribute of God to others and submit to this authority' (Quṭb, 1993: 82). For Quṭb, this situation cannot be tolerated, and all Muslims have an obligation to engage in '[o]ffensive Jihad to ensure the establishment of the sovereignty of God' and the 'implementation of the rule of the Divine Shari'ah in human affairs' (Quṭb, 1993: 61). This is necessary, according to Quṭb, because human freedom is linked to the restoration of God's sovereignty; 'When, in a society, the sovereignty belongs to God alone, expressed in its obedience to the Divine Law, only then is every person in that society free from servitude to others, only then does he taste true freedom' (Quṭb, 1993: 94). Thus all Muslims, insofar as they are to be considered 'true' Muslims, must

> challenge … all kinds and forms of systems which are based on the concept of the sovereignty of man; in other words, where man has usurped the Divine attribute. Any system in which the final decisions are referred to human beings, and in which the sources of all authority are human, deifies human beings by designating others than God as lords over men. This declaration means that the usurped authority of God be returned to Him and the usurpers be thrown out – those who by themselves devise laws for others to follow, thus elevating themselves to the status of lords and reducing others to the status of slaves.
> (Quṭb, 1993: 58)

These quotations provide some support to those, such as Juergensmeyer (2003), who argue that there is a relationship between religiously inspired forms of terrorism and the increasing lethality of terrorist attacks. For many religiously motivated groups that deploy terrorism, the sacred nature of the cause demands greater sacrifices, and they are seemingly prepared to accept ever-greater casualties among the targets of attacks. Religion is also said to affect the use of violence by making the violence more indiscriminate as a result of the demonization or dehumanization of the other (Bolanos, 2012: 31). Whole communities are demonized when they are deemed to be unbelievers and thus become legitimate targets. In this sense, whilst the primary aim of most Islamic terrorism is the destruction of the Western state system, those who acquiesce in the maintenance of this system, or do not directly challenge it, become legitimate targets. This, it is argued, means that religiously inspired contemporary terrorist organizations do not seem to be prepared to limit the use of force against populations. There used to be a rather pithy phrase that characterized terrorists as 'wanting a lot of people watching, but not a lot of people dead' (Jenkins, 1975: 15). This was a necessary component of most forms of terrorism since they aimed, in part, to gain the support of the population at large, and too many casualties might negatively affect the level of this support. Contemporary terrorism, on the other hand, does not seem to hold to the same ideals, and Daniel Benjamin and Steven Simon argue that the objectives of the new terrorism are 'not to influence, but to kill, and in large numbers' (Benjamin and Simon, 2000).

However, whilst there is something to this argument, it is not unique to religious forms of terrorism and ideologically motivated forms of terrorism can also dehumanize the other. A better explanation, based on principles of retributive justice, might be that the injustices of the current system are perceived to be so great that the terrorists believe that they can only be redressed through inflicting large numbers of casualties on those that benefit from the system. Equally, the terrorists' assessment of who the enemy is might be playing a major role here. It used to be the case, when considering traditional forms of terrorism, that a sharp distinction could be made between domestic terrorism and international terrorism (Dugan, LaFree and Fogg, 2006). Domestic terrorism was typically conceived as acts of terrorism that were targeted against domestic populations of particular states in order to highlight a distinct political grievance, the aim being to get the state in which the terrorism occurred to change its practices. International terrorism, on the other hand, was typically defined as domestic terrorism that had moved onto the international stage in order to publicize its cause to a wider audience. Contemporary Islamic terrorism, however, is not attempting just to publicize particular domestic grievances on the international stage, but rather, challenges the international order itself. Certainly, such terrorist organizations will have grievances against specific states in the system, but the overall strategic target is the complete destruction of the international state system itself, and its replacement with a system based on Islamic principles (Gow, 2005: 61–2). That is why no government can consider its population safe from attack.

However, how can a relatively small group of fanatical believers possibly hope to bring down a global political system? Part of the answer here relates to the increasing levels of lethality that contemporary terrorism displays. The terrorists cannot hope to confront the system on its own terms. However, if they can provoke the system to engage in acts that contribute to its own demise then the aims will be achieved. Contemporary Islamic terrorism, then, aims to engage in just those acts that will lead to the system destroying itself. This requires that the terrorist acts be of such a magnitude and frequency that the system is forced to act against itself as it attempts to secure itself. Whilst it has often been thought that contemporary terrorism is irrational, nihilistic and essentially evil, contemporary Islamic terrorists do have very specific aims. These are: (1) to pull states within the system into unnecessary and costly conflicts (Iraq and Afghanistan, and possibly Iran); (2) one of the spin-offs from these costly wars, the terrorists hope, will be pressure on the international financial system; and (3) that in attempting to secure their populations from attack and safeguard the system as a whole the values the system purports to uphold will be overturned and ignored in the search for security (Wright, 2006b). As of July 2014, this looks like 3–0 to the terrorists. However, whilst we can be rightly critical of the responses to terrorism thus far, there is an additional issue that places states in the international political system in a particularly difficult situation in terms of their responses to contemporary terrorism.

It is not only the willingness to kill in large numbers on the basis of religious beliefs that makes contemporary terrorism different from previous forms, and hence so difficult to deal with;

it is the fact that terrorists increasingly have the means to do so. This is one of the main problems state managers face when attempting to assess terrorist threats. Increasingly, in a globalized world, the terrorists have access to all kinds of resources (information, knowledge and materials). Given this, and the increased proclivity they demonstrate to kill large groups of people indiscriminately, the fear is always that they may gain access to weapons of mass destruction. This fact has fundamentally changed the way state managers think about contemporary terrorism. This is the essence of what has come to be known as the 'one-percent doctrine', which is the belief that if there is a one-per cent chance of terrorists acquiring weapons of mass destruction, then states have to act on the basis of that possibility (Suskind, 2006: 62).

The fear is that if terrorists could gain nuclear, biological or chemical weapons they would use them. Traditional models of state military deterrence are useless here, not only because contemporary terrorists seem devoid of rational calculations concerning their own wellbeing, but also because they are not state actors who could be easily punished if they deploy such weapons. In fact, on one level, the use of weapons of mass destruction by terrorists could seem to be perfectly rational from their perspective. Setting aside the deep moral questions about the use of such weapons, which after 9/11 it can reasonably be assumed would not worry the terrorists, what could the United States, for example, do in response to such an attack? Engage in more costly wars around the world? Retaliate with nuclear attacks of their own, but against whom? Withdraw from the international political system? Engage in a global war against Islam? The possible responses that any state might engage in after a terrorist attack that had used weapons of mass destruction seem decidedly limited.

In addition, state sponsorship of contemporary terrorism could mean that states sympathetic to the Islamic cause could supply such groups with weapons of mass destruction. Such fears have already been expressed in relation to Pakistan (Gregory, 2009), but also underpin some of the efforts to ensure Iran does not gain access to nuclear material (Alam and Islamia, 2009). This may be the real axis of evil; (1) religiously motivated groups prepared to use terrorism to kill non-state actors on a massive scale; (2) rogue or failed states that lend support to terrorists or are unable to stop them operating on their territory; (3) the possibility of terrorists acquiring weapons of mass destruction. It is this triple aspect of the contemporary world that really defines terrorism today.

In addition, there is one final aspect of contemporary terrorism that marks it out as being different from previous forms. This is the organizational or structural form it takes. A growing number of terrorist organizations, al-Qaeda being perhaps the best example, are no longer organized in a typical cell/column structure as detailed in the previous chapter. The typical model of al-Qaeda today is said to be that of a network with decentralized decision-making structures (Burke, 2003; Sageman, 2004, 2008). Networks have particular characteristics, and I shall discuss some of them below. However, contemporary terrorism is not only comparable to a network, and other metaphors also provide useful ways to understand it.

As well as a network, al-Qaeda can be understood, in part, as a complex self-organizing system (Bousquet, 2012; Marion and Uhl-Bien, 2003: 56–7). All social systems, although complex, are not chaotic or disordered. As such, they can be understood as a form of organized complexity (Byrne, 1998; Cilliers, 1998; Harrison, 2006). The question is, how does this particular form of organization occur and what form does it take? For al-Qaeda the answer seems clear, and this is their propensity to self-organize. Self-organization can be defined as the spontaneous creation of a globally coherent pattern out of local interactions. Self-organizing systems can be characterized as bottom-up systems (Holland, 1998). The organization that emerges in such systems comes about through the interactions of a mass of individual elements rather than the following of a plan or the influence of a single intelligent executive branch, or architect. In open systems the dynamics of self-organization can be affected through internal change in the system, or through changes in the environment. Although many systems are self-organizing, they do not all display the same kind of characteristics or internal structure. Good examples here are the political system and the economic system.

An economic system is self-organizing insofar as it changes its internal behavioural patterns and structure in response to a large number of factors (money supply, rate of growth, political context, resource availability, etc.). Individual responses to these factors vary across actors, with no single actor possessing complete knowledge of the complexity of the overall situation. Nonetheless, even though individual action only takes place within a limited understanding of its place in outcomes, order does emerge at the system level.

However, evolved social systems such as the economy do exhibit some control mechanisms that attempt to steer the direction of the system as a whole. Governments, political elites, intellectuals, spiritual leaders and business leaders all attempt to exercise control on the system through the implementation of policies on the basis of some understanding of perceived outcomes. The effects of these interventions, however, are only predictable in the short term, since the spontaneous adjustment of the system involves the complex interaction of too many factors; many of which cannot be controlled at all. The fact that social systems do attempt to react in specific ways to changes within the system or the environment, however, does mean that they can be considered as complex adaptive systems (Miller and Page, 2007). I say in part because social systems are not wholly self-organizing, and the steering mechanisms in them may have a major impact in determining how such systems evolve and behave.

There is no doubt that the leadership of al-Qaeda that emerged in Afghanistan after the Soviets left played a major role in structuring the organization (Alexander and Swetnam, 2001; Burke, 2003; Hellmich, 2011). Moreover, the role played by this leadership has been imprinted on the organizational form Islamic terrorism takes today. Even after the death of bin Laden in 2011 (Bowden, 2012; Owen and Maurer, 2012), his presence still continues to shape the ideology and organizational form of the movement. After the invasion of Afghanistan, the leadership was dispersed to various parts of the globe but it still maintained substantial links and hubs of organizational activity in Pakistan and the more remote areas of Afghanistan (Celso, 2014: 10, Ch. 19). There is also no doubt that this leadership still plays a role in directing some aspects of many of the terrorist operations that go under the name al-Qaeda. In this respect, the al-Qaeda leadership fulfils many functions.

First, there is evidence to suggest the leadership is still involved in the planning and carrying out of specific terrorist attacks in a manner that is wholly consistent with more traditional forms of terrorism. For example, in London in 2009, Tanvir Hussain, Assad Sarwar and Ahmed Abdullah Ali were convicted of conspiring to detonate bombs disguised as soft drinks on aircraft. Both British and US officials have claimed that the plan was directly linked to al-Qaeda and guided by senior Islamic militants in Pakistan (Sandford, 2009). And, of course, al-Qaeda has claimed direct responsibility for the attacks of 2002 in Mombasa, Kenya (*New York Times*, 2002).

Second, whilst direct coordination for terrorist attacks from the al-Qaeda leadership is difficult to establish, the relationship between various parts of the al-Qaeda network and certain terrorist acts is much easier to find. For example, the Bali bomb attacks of 2002, which killed 202 people, were carried out by Jemaah Islamiyah, a violent Islamic group with clear links to al-Qaeda, links that were clearly demonstrated when Al Jazeera broadcast a recording of bin Laden claiming that the Bali bombings were in direct retaliation for Australia's support for war on terror, and its role in the liberation of East Timor (bin Laden, 2005: 173–5). Then there are the activities of al-Qaeda in the Arabian Peninsula (AQAP), a militant Islamist organization, primarily active in Yemen and Saudi Arabia. By 2010, it was considered the most active of al-Qaeda's offshoot organizations; often referred to as 'franchises' (Fishman, 2008: 47; Hellmich, 2011; *Wall Street Journal*, 2013).

This idea of al-Qaeda as a franchising organization is an important part of how we understand it today. Al-Qaeda is multifaceted and is not susceptible to any single organizational structural principle. Emerging and existing in an era of globalization, one would expect al-Qaeda to display elements of complexity. Despite this, there is no doubt that the leadership is organized. According to Rohan Gunaratna (Gunaratna, 2002: 54–94) the structure includes: a military committee responsible for training operatives, acquiring weapons and planning attacks; a money/business committee; a law committee which appraises Sharia law, and determines whether particular courses of activity conform to the law; an Islamic study committee that issues religious edicts; a media committee, which handles public relations; and, in 2005, al-Qaeda formed As-Sahab, to control its public relations and produce various forms of media and video publications.

In addition, however, al-Qaeda also has branches or franchises, in various parts of the world, such as al-Qaeda in the Arabian Peninsula, and the al-Qaeda Organization in the Islamic Maghreb (Gunaratna, 2002: 95–166). However, in addition to these well-organized groups there are a range of Islamic fundamentalist groups that draw on al-Qaeda for inspiration, but which are not directly linked in any organizational way. These groups are generally committed to the cause of Islamic revivalism but not necessarily affiliated formally to al-Qaeda. These loose relationships can work to the advantage of both al-Qaeda and these associated groups, for they allow al-Qaeda to claim responsibility for the acts committed by these groups if it wishes to do so, yet it can distance itself if it believes the acts do not serve its cause, as it has done with the emergence of the Islamic State of Iraq and the Levant (IS) (Mendelsohn, 2014). Thus, in many respects, al-Qaeda is better thought of as an idea rather than as an organization. Groups, or individuals, can carry out acts in its name without any direct input from any organizational entity we could call al-Qaeda. In fact, and despite the many cleavages within Islam, al-Qaeda has come to represent any group, movement or individual that wishes to work towards an Islamic caliphate based on the principles of Sharia. Moreover, with its network of groups and operatives scattered around the world, those committed to the idea of al-Qaeda can access resources and training for any particular acts they wish to commit.

In the final analysis, then, al-Qaeda is an organization that displays elements of self-organization as well as possessing a clearly defined hierarchical structure; it is a network, it is a global franchise, and it is an idea. We do not yet have a terminology that can capture all of this in one pithy term, such as 'the state'. Al-Qaeda is a hybrid organization that is yet to coalesce into a form that makes a clear social-scientific designation appropriate. However, insofar as the state can be considered a complex institutional ensemble, and insofar as al-Qaeda can be considered a complex institutional ensemble, then it can be considered a 'counter-state'. Or as Philip Bobbitt has put it, al-Qaeda can be considered to be a 'virtual state' (Bobbitt, 2002: 820). And of course, this clearly applies to IS, who have made their claim to statehood explicit. In this respect, both are fully adapted to the context out of which they emerged, and in many respects, their flexibility allows them to adapt much more quickly than the dominant state form, which emerged out of a previous era. The context out of which al-Qaeda emerged is globalization, and it is for that reason that the war on terror can also be considered to be a war on globalization.

The War on Terror

In this section, I want to deal with the war on terror in a very generic fashion. I have no desire to get into minute detail, attempting to unpack why the war has developed in the way it has, or to attempt to deal with the minutiae of what drove the international system into the currently confused state it now finds itself. There are already plenty of excellent books that cover this ground in a comprehensive manner (Booth and Dunne, 2012; Clarke, 2004). Rather, my aim is to look structurally at the war on terror as a response to the emergence of a particular kind of contemporary terrorism as detailed in the previous section. Let me begin by situating my position on the war on terror. When directly compared to the strategic goals of al-Qaeda, it appears to be an unmitigated disaster. Our political leaders seem to be sleepwalking (Clark, 2012) into the very situation that al-Qaeda is attempting to construct. However, one wonders, when faced with the possibility, and indeed the actuality, of such violence, what alternatives they have. Part of the rationale for the acceptance of state ownership of violence is the idea that the state will use that violence when its populations come under attack, or a threatened attack.

It might be possible to support a war on terrorism (at least as I have defined it), although a war on terror is impossible to support. Terror can no more be eradicated than can any other human emotion. Moreover, the structural relationship that exists between the state and violence means that the deliberate production of political terror could only be achieved if political organization were to cease. As we have seen in previous chapters, terror is intrinsic to the act of governing. Terrorism, on the other hand, can be defeated and largely expunged from the human condition with a comprehensive global strategy; terror cannot (Bobbitt, 2002: 180–237). But, then again, most people, I suspect, would support a war (broadly defined) on poverty, a war against oppression anywhere it occurs, and all manner of wars that attempt to improve the human condition. Of course, I am using the term war in a very loose manner here, meaning something like 'a systematic programme of activity orientated around the eradication of some or other phenomenon'. Understood this way, a war on poverty, for example, would be 'a systematic programme of activity organized around the eradication of poverty'.

Ideally, such wars could be non-violent, but we have to accept that this may not always be the case. However, this is hardly a problematic statement for anyone but the most fervent pacifist. For example, even the criminal justice system, which few object to, rests on the ultimate use of violence in the final analysis. After all, criminals have to be ultimately restrained, and forced into captivity. If something is worth pursuing it is also worth fighting for (Bufacchi, 2007: 164–86). Hence, it is impossible, apart from on purely ideological grounds, to simply be against the war on terror. Like all wars, the contemporary war on terror is multifaceted, and some aspects of it are laudable; most deplorable. The fact that we might stand against the production of political terror does not mean that we stand with the means chosen to deal with it; not least because the war on terror has had to engage in the deliberate production of terror even as it attempts to eradicate it. In this sense, the war on terror simply represents an ongoing conflict over who has the right to produce terror and who does not.

Take, for example, the attack on Afghanistan in the immediate aftermath of 9/11. We can call this the immediate response to 9/11. I call it an attack because invasion does not seem right word, and to all intents and purposes, and apart from some special forces on the ground, the United States subcontracted this attack to local Afghani warlords (Rashid, 2009: 125–44). The attack began on 7 October 2001, as the United States, the United Kingdom, Australia and the Afghan United Front (Northern Alliance) launched Operation Enduring Freedom. Allegedly, the aim of the invasion was to find, arrest or kill bin Laden and other high-ranking al-Qaeda members, and to destroy the operational capability of al-Qaeda, but also, to remove the Taliban regime that supported and gave safe harbour to bin Laden and his associates. The latter aim was most probably a symbolic gesture to the rest of the watching world, in order to lend support to George W. Bush's view that the United States would not distinguish between terrorist organizations and nations or governments that harboured them. Or as Bush had put it, 'No group or nation should mistake America's intentions: We will not rest until terrorist groups of global reach have been found, have been stopped, and have been defeated' (US Government, 2003).

In Operation Enduring Freedom, which was launched in October 2001, ground forces of the Afghan United Front working with US and British Special Forces, and with substantial US air support, removed the Taliban regime from power in a matter of weeks. The majority of senior Taliban leaders escaped to neighbouring Pakistan. With the collapse of the Taliban regime, the democratic Islamic Republic of Afghanistan was established, and an interim government under Hamid Karzai was created. By December 2001, the UN Security Council had authorized the establishment of an International Security Assistance Force (ISAF), the main aim of which was to secure Kabul and the surrounding areas. In 2003, NATO took over control of ISAF, which by that time included forces from 42 countries, with NATO members providing the bulk of the force (Ripley, 2011). In reality, the Americans did little other than provide massive air support, supply Special Forces on the ground to coordinate the activities of the Afghan United front, and fund the removing the Taliban from power.

In the context of 9/11, it is difficult to see how any major power could have done anything other than attack a regime that was harbouring the main suspect. If Bush had not been president of the United States, would an alternative leader at the time of the 9/11 attacks have taken a different course of action? Had Al Gore, for example, won the presidential elections of 2000 would he have acted differently in the aftermath of the 9/11 attacks? It is difficult to say, but it seems reasonable to conclude that any president of a major superpower would have been forced to take action against the perceived perpetrators of the act. The sheer scale of the attacks meant that some immediate reaction was inevitable. What was not inevitable, however, was the long-term development of the war on terror, and it would seem that the sheer scale of the 9/11 attacks had so damaged the American psyche that it was not until some years later that a more balanced account of these long-term reactions could emerge. Yet even now, as IS rampages over vast swathes of Iraq, Syria is engulfed in a vicious civil war, various Islamist groups are causing havoc across the world, and the Israel–Palestine conflict remains unresolved, some remain prepared to defend the war on terror, taking a general interventionist approach to international politics to attempt to rid the world of terrorism (McTague, 2014).

If a violent war against terrorism has failed, however the attempt to deal with terrorist finances seems to be a valid and essential tool in the fight against such organizations (Biersteker and Eckert, 2008; Costigan and Gold, 2007; Ehrenfeld, 2003; Pieth, 2002). However, such efforts have not been without their critics. Ibrahim Warde argues that many of the assumptions underpinning attempts to cut off terrorist financing fail owing to the nature and motivation of terrorists, the amount of money they need to carry out their terrorist acts, and the channels through which they can acquire the necessary funds. According to Warde, although governments have deemed the financial war on terrorism to be a success, the persistent ability of terrorist organizations to recruit and carry out their activities suggests that the impact of the financial war is less than that claimed (Warde, 2007: 3–22, 153–62). At the same time, the collateral damage, both in terms of deaths and financial hardship to innocent parties as a result of the war, has been considerable, building resentment at home and abroad, and in effect, acting as a recruiting drive for the terrorists.

There are other aspects to the war on terror that are equally problematic. No doubt in the immediate aftermath of the 9/11 attacks there was considerable pressure on governments to find mechanisms to detect terrorists before they could act. After 9/11 it seemed reasonable to ask how it was possible that the vast sums spent on intelligence gathering by modern states did not identify the terrorists before they could act (Gertz, 2003). Someone, or something, must be to blame. In the modern world, we have become so accustomed to believing that we can exercise almost total control over all events. However, this is a myth, a residual leftover of outdated modes of Enlightenment thinking. The stark and unpalatable truth is that no matter how good our intelligence agencies are, and no matter how many resources we put into target hardening, intelligence gathering, and counter-terrorism we can never guarantee that the terrorists will not evade our efforts. But more importantly, the intelligence failures surrounding 9/11 are not really about apportioning blame, but about understanding the structural environment in which the intelligence agencies operate (Gertz, 2003: 1–6; Scott and Hughes, 2008). There are two important aspects here. First, inter-service rivalry could well have meant that, although all the pieces of the jigsaw required to identify the 9/11 attacks in advance of them happening were in place, the lack of cooperation between intelligence services, both domestically in the United States, and globally among states, meant that no agency possessed the full story.

Perhaps more importantly, it could well be the case that there was simply too much information. Information is not knowledge, and the problem for intelligence agencies today is that the scale of communications that they need to monitor has grown exponentially. Certainly intelligence agencies are increasingly developing sophisticated computer programmes and monitoring techniques to filter out much of the extraneous noise that is generated by this rising pattern of communications activity, but it poses a major problem for them nonetheless (Silver, 2013). But even if we accept this, however reluctantly, we surely have to continue to try to gather intelligence on terrorist activity, and, where possible, control the movements of terrorists around the globe. Of course, identifying the terrorists from the general public is not easy, and in the effort to do so civil liberties and human rights have been trampled (Gani and Mathew, 2008; Grayling, 2009).

In part, this plays directly into the hands of the terrorists. The terrorist threat, and the associated axis of evil as I have detailed it above, have led democratic governments to limit human rights and civil liberties up to the point where they are in danger of abandoning the very values the terrorists wish to attack. In this sense governments are doing the terrorists' work for them. It is always admissible in times of emergency for democratic governments to limit for certain rights in order to protect other rights. However, security in a post-9/11 environment has taken on an almost absolute priority at the expense of all other rights. This has led many to equate the war on terror with a war on freedom (Freedom, 2014).

For example, the right to privacy has come under serious attack, with CCTV surveillance now ubiquitous, and DNA databases an everyday fact of life for most in the Western world (Lyon, 2003). In addition, as became clear after the revelations of National Security Agency (NSA) mass surveillance programmes, eavesdropping and wiretapping have to a large extent become accepted as valid forms of intelligence gathering by the security services (Greenwald, 2013, 2014; Greenwald, MacAskill and Poitras, 2013). Security and border agencies coordinate their activities and produce lists of individuals who face restriction on flights. Whilst such restrictions can serve to limit terrorists' freedom of movement, they can also be targeted at individuals critical of the government or those who attend peace protests. Hate-speech laws have been introduced in an attempt to silence the radical Islamic hate preachers, but these can be seen as an attack on the fundamental right of freedom of speech (Gelber, 2002; Gelber and Stone, 2007; Waldron, 2012). Racial and ethnic profiling also have the potential to turn innocent people into possible suspects, and habeas corpus has been limited, with extended periods of detention without charge introduced, sometimes indefinitely for those whose legal status is deemed undecidable (Bravin, 2013). Extraordinary rendition has been covertly practised as a means of extracting information through the use of torture, by relocating suspects to territories outside the judicial control of the democratic system. And extraterritorial prisons have been created, such as in Guantánamo Bay, where suspects can be held indefinitely and where Geneva conventions supposedly do not apply (Coates, 2004; Grey, 2006). Denied legal status, the inmates of such 'illegal' prisons do not exist in any legal sense.

In addition, Islamophobia has been gaining a hold throughout the Western world and threatens to undermine the values of tolerance and multiculturalism that most liberal societies profess to hold (Gottschalk and Greenberg, 2008). Of course, for the Islamic radicals this is to be expected and even encouraged. Their Manichaean worldview demands that the non-believers seem to be a constant threat to all Muslims. Thus a 'culture of fear' has been created by terrorists but also nurtured by irresponsible Western politicians. This fear has damaged democracy, and not only have the media relinquished their traditional role as watchdogs, but politicians also have abused the fear of terrorism to harness support for policies that prioritize security over rights. Given all of this, it is now widely believed, even in US government circles, that the war on terror is counter-productive, and President Obama has even stopped using the term (Fox News, 2009). In particular, the wars in Iraq and Afghanistan, the torture in Abu Ghraib and the detentions in Guantánamo have produced a backlash and have increased rather than reduced the terror threat. As the Director of US National Intelligence has put it, '[t]he Iraq conflict has become the "cause célèbre" for jihadists, breeding a deep resentment of US involvement in the Muslim world and cultivating supporters for the global jihadist movement' (Office of the Director of National Intelligence, 2006).

In the face of this, then, what is to be done? The answer to this question requires a deeper understanding of what the war on terror actually represents. And understanding this requires some context. All historical starting points are, to a certain extent, arbitrary. But in terms of the current war on terror, 1979 represents an important marker because of the occurrence of two major events that led to the re-emergence of more radical forms of political Islam. The first was the Iranian revolution in January 1979, although protests against the American-backed regime of the Shah had actually begun in October 1977 (Kurzman, 2004; Wagner, 2010). The revolution clearly caught the world by surprise. The normal drivers of social upheaval, such as a disastrous foreign policy, a national security threat, a financial crisis, a peasant revolt or a dissatisfied military, were not major factors in pre-revolutionary Iran. Moreover, it seemed to reverse a long-standing trend in global politics, insofar as a Westernized monarchy, albeit one lacking in many the features necessary for a well-functioning state, was replaced by a theocracy based on Islamic principles and governed by theological leaders. Ayatollah Khomeini, who was much more a spiritual leader than that of a political one, led the emergent Islamic Republic (Willett, 2004). The revolution was in part a conservative backlash against the Westernizing and secularizing efforts of the Shah to construct a state based on a Western model, as well as a deep-seated dissatisfaction with the prevailing social conditions and a perceived sense of injustice and regime corruption (Kurzman, 2004; Wagner, 2010)

The second event was the Soviet invasion of Afghanistan in December 1979 (Grau and Gress, 2002). The Soviet war in Afghanistan took place at the height of the Cold War and it can only be understood in that context. It quickly developed into a nine-year conflict involving the Soviet Union, who supported the Marxist–Leninist government of the Democratic Republic of Afghanistan, against the Afghan resistance movement and foreign Arab–Afghan volunteers. The Afghan resistance, or mujahedeen as they were known, received unofficial military and/or financial support from a variety of countries including the United States, Saudi Arabia, the United Kingdom, Pakistan, Israel, Indonesia and China (Loyn, 2009). In addition to the distorting influences of the Cold War, however, there was an added deep historical cleavage that was brought to the fore with the emergence of the Islamic Republic in Iran, and the ongoing conflict in Afghanistan.

This is the third issue, and it refers to the Shia/Sunni split in Islam that can be dated back to the seventh century, but which has occasionally emerged as a potential source of conflict in Islamic societies (Hazleton, 2009; Nasr, 2006). The original split between Sunnis and Shia occurred soon after the death of the Prophet Muhammad, in AD 632. It emerged as a result of a disagreement in the community of Muslims based in what today is Saudi Arabia. The dispute centred on the question of succession; or, more simply, who was to be the rightful successor to the Prophet Muhammad. The majority of the Prophet's followers wanted the community to determine who would succeed him; these have come to be known as the Sunni Muslims. A smaller group thought that the line of succession would be based on familial ties, and they favoured Ali ibn Abu Talib, who was married to Muhammad's daughter, and also his cousin, and these are known as the Shia. Fundamentally the Shia believe that leadership should stay within the family of the Prophet, whereas the Sunnis believe that leadership should fall to the person who was deemed by the elite of the community to be best able to lead the community (Hazleton, 2009). Although relations between the two groups of Muslims have had long periods of relative peace, and even close cooperation, there have been periods of intense violent conflict between the two groups, and this is certainly an aspect of contemporary international terrorism (Nasr, 2006). As Nazeer Ahmed argues:

> If a traveler from outer space were to visit planet earth, he/she would be astonished at the sheer tenacity of the passions and prejudices that govern human life. And the Shia–Sunni conflict would easily top the list of issues that arouse ugly passions. (Ahmed, 2008)

Some, such as Murtaza Hussain, have argued that the Sunni–Shia split is a myth, constructed by the Western powers to 'to perpetuate conflict and maintain a Middle East which is at once thoroughly divided and incapable of asserting itself' (Hussain, 2013). According to Hussain, this idea of a historical split between Sunni and Shia is an 'absurd falsehood' since the present-day conflicts between these groups are embedded within contemporary circumstances, not history. There is something to this argument, but it misses some fundamental points. First, it cannot be denied that there is a historical split and that this divide has regularly surfaced over the course of history and is the source of violent conflict and oppression between the groups (Gonzalez, 2009; Hazleton, 2009; Nasr, 2006). Second, although there have been long periods of stability, peace and cooperation among the Sunni and Shia, the underlying theological differences were never resolved and disputes about the theological veracity of the claims made by each group have been vehemently rejected by the others.

Third, Abdullah Hamidaddin argues that the Sunni–Shia split is a historical event that can have little consequence in the contemporary world (Hamidaddin, 2013). But this misses the point. The Sunni–Shia split has consequences today precisely because of its historical resonance. Yes, such a historical event will have a contemporary framing, but the history is never left behind, and the fact that many Muslims today embed their understandings in the history of the Sunni–Shia schism is evidence of this fact. When such disputes emerge the participants are not trying to resolve the historical conflict, but are using it. In addition, within Islamic thought in particular, the historical point plays a particularly significant role, because many of the more radical Muslim clerics are advocating a return to that historical era. In which case, the specifics of that history and its consequences for Muslims today become the focal point for conflict, precisely because what it is that should be returned to is subject to heated and highly contested debate. Fourth, to point out the origins of a particular split in Islam is simply to provide an explanation of that split and is not an attempt to suggest that historical split is a historically unmediated cause of conflict.

Moreover, when faced with the emergence of an Islamic regime in Iran, Sunni leaders looked on with dismay. Likewise the more radical of the Sunni groups, and in particular, those committed to Salafism, perceived this is a fundamental conflict about who would lead the Islamic world; the Sunnis or the Shia. This was a conflict about the most authentic reading of the Qur'an and a battle for the radical leadership of the Islamic community. Neither side can afford to lose. This is what is really at the heart of the concept of 'outbidding' in terrorism studies; the attempt to 'outbid' other organizations in order to situate oneself as the radical edge of Islamic resistance (Kydd and Walter, 2006).

Hence, in a limited sense the West has stepped into a civil war, and this has to be taken into account when attempting to understand how to deal with contemporary terrorism. It also makes it extremely difficult for Western security services to understand the complex web of relationships that exist between the various Islamic groups. Sometimes they will reach accommodations with each other and provide support, whereas at other times the

Sunni–Shia split, such as in Iraq, threatens to break out into all-out war (Chotiner, 2014).

In addition, the war in Afghanistan against the Soviets drew thousands of Islamic volunteers keen to defend the wider Islamic community against the atheist socialists. For the Americans this conflict, although they had no genuine desire to align themselves with Islamic fundamentalists, presented an opportunity to thwart Soviet ambitions in the region (Loyn, 2009). Thus the Americans provided both material and expertise to the Afghanis engaged in conflict against the Soviets (Chossudovsky, 2002). Once the Soviets were forced to withdraw this meant that there was a large collection of radicalized, well-armed and well-trained Muslims in the area, many who fell under the control of bin Laden and al-Qaeda.

Another event that was to play a role in how the war on terror would unfold was the Iranian hostage crisis. From November 1979 to January 1981, 52 Americans were held hostage for 444 days, after a group of Iranian students and militants overran the American Embassy in Tehran during the Iranian Revolution (Bowden, 2006). The revolution removed the US-backed Shah of Iran with an Islamic republic led by Ayatollah Khomeini. After initial diplomatic attempts to free the hostages failed, the US military attempted a rescue operation. Known as Operation Eagle Claw, and carried out on 24 April 1980, the mission was an abject failure and left eight American servicemen and one Iranian civilian dead, and led to the destruction of two US aircraft (Ryan, 1985). Coming on the back of the humiliation of American defeat in Vietnam, the chaotic withdrawal of American troops in 1975, the Iranian hostage crisis and the inability of the United States to support the Shah were devastating blows to American prestige. The most powerful state in the world seemed impotent in the face of aggression against its diplomats and citizens.

This perception of a superpower unable to exercise its power was further enhanced when two truck bombs caused extensive damage to an American Marines barracks, housing US and French military forces, who were in Lebanon as part of a peace-keeping operation. Suicide bombers detonated each of the bombs and the killing of 241 American servicemen was the highest single-day death toll for the US military since the Tet Offensive during the Vietnam War, and the deadliest single attack on Americans overseas since the Second World War. The blasts led to the withdrawal of the international peacekeeping force from Lebanon (Petit, 1986). Another important event was the disastrous US involvement in Somalia that began in 1992. The then US President George H.W. Bush announced that US military transports would support the multinational UN relief effort in Somalia. Known as Operation Provide Relief, the mission was initially framed as an attempt to provide support for humanitarian aid that was sent to Somalia (Clarke and Herbst, 1997). The Mission changed from support, however, to active engagement, when warlords, particularly Mohamed Farrah Aidid, attacked the food convoys and used the stolen goods to buy arms. When the United States attempted to arrest Aidid the mission went catastrophically wrong and, in what has come to be known as the Battle of Mogadishu, in 1993, the US lost two Black Hawk helicopters (Bowden, 1999). This left 18 American soldiers dead and 73 wounded. After a national security policy review of the incident on 6 October 1993, US President Bill Clinton ordered a cessation of all actions of US forces against Aidid apart from those necessitated for reasons of self-defence. He also announced that all US forces would withdraw from Somalia, and by 6 March 1994 all of remaining UN troops were withdrawn.

The mission in Somalia was seen as an abject failure and a clear warning that the use of American troops for humanitarian purposes was something that should only be employed in extreme circumstances. The Clinton administration in particular endured considerable criticism for the outcome of the operation. The administration's decision to leave the region before completing the humanitarian and security objectives of the operation, as well as the perceived failure to recognize the threat al-Qaeda elements posed in the region, as well as the threat against US security interests at home, were a sad indictment of superpower impotence. Critics claim that bin Laden and other members of al-Qaeda provided support and training to Aidid's forces (Patman, 2010). Bin Laden refers to the Somalia episode at length, drawing attention to how the world's major superpower was forced into the region and stating that it displayed 'the weakness, and cowardliness of the American soldier' (bin Laden, 2005: 82). Again the symbolism was important. Here we have the world's major superpower, seemingly unable to force its will on much weaker non-state actors. This perception of imperial impotence was further enhanced by the October 2000 attack on the *USS Cole* while it was harboured and refuelling in the Yemeni port of Aden. This left 17 Us sailors dead and injured 39. al-Qaeda once again claimed responsibility for the attack and claimed it demonstrated the impotence of American power (bin Laden, 2005: 193).

These events, and many others, portrayed the United States as a waning superpower, unable to defend its interests abroad or force its will on what was in reality a loose network of poorly armed Islamic radicals. All of this was to change after 9/11. The fact that the terrorists had brought the fight to the American homeland, and the sheer number of casualties and the scale of destruction, ensured that the United States would have to strike back using the full spectrum of its military capability (Mahajan, 2003). At the same time, US intellectuals and policy elites, who had come to be known as the neoconservatives, had already begun to reflect on the effects of this supposed American impotence on America's place in the world. These neoconservatives took the view that America must reassert itself on the global stage if American values and democracy were to be promoted, and that any attempt to stop this process must be dealt with by the use of military force (Halper and Clarke, 2004). It is possible that these people sincerely thought that they knew best, that they had a view of the world that they were fundamentally committed to; a vision of the world that would both safeguard America's predominant position in the global order, whilst at the same time improving, where possible, the lives of others. This would be the charitable reading; many others have suggested less altruistic motivations (Peleg, 2009; Sniegoski, 2008). So strongly were they committed to this view that it is appropriate to see them as mirror images of the dogmatic beliefs that drove bin Laden and his associates.

Only this context helps explain why America invaded Iraq in March 2003. After the attacks of 9/11 the American people, the political elites and the neoconservatives came together in an understandable alliance that firmly believed it was no longer possible for America to simply wait for its enemies to come to them. The mission in Afghanistan had largely been a success, but it had been a success from a distance. Iraq represented a symbolic opportunity to display to the world that America was indeed a superpower prepared to use its military force to its utmost extent. When the Americans had retreated from Vietnam there was much talk of the body-bag syndrome; the idea that Americans were not prepared to see their sons and daughters come home in body bags (Boot, 2002). bin Laden expressed just this belief in his taunting of the American retreat from Somalia. For the neoconservatives and the Bush administration what was needed now was a demonstration of American power that clearly showed to the world both the strength of that military might, and the resolve of the United States to use it, even if it meant the deaths of its own soldiers.

In a context in which George W. Bush had declared that you are either 'with us or with the terrorists', the hope was that this would signal to all states in the world that if they were unable to control the activities of terrorists within their own territory, then the United States would come and do it for them. It is in this sense that the war on terror is also a war on globalization. To many analysts one of the most pressing negative effects of globalization is an erosion of state sovereignty (Ohmae, 1995). Under conditions of globalization, it is argued, it is difficult for states to secure their borders, or even to control what goes on inside them. For the neoconservatives this process has gone too far. Globalization in terms of the economic sphere and to a certain extent in terms of cultural homogenization, was to be applauded since it facilitated American economic imperialism and the spread of the American values throughout the world. Political globalization, on the other hand, had to be rolled back. Non-state actors capable of inflicting the kind of damage witnessed in the 9/11 attacks could not be tolerated. This meant that states had to be forced to regain sovereignty over what went on in their territory. In terms of the axis of evil as I have described it above, the Americans would attempt to tackle the spread of Islamic fundamentalism by forcibly taking democracy into the hearts of those regions where Islamic fundamentalism was strongest. Equally, they would attempt to control the potential spread of weapons of mass destruction in the hope of stopping such weapons falling into the hands of the terrorists. And finally, the message of Iraq was that 'we can and we will'.

Yet the war on terror has been an unmitigated disaster. American military power may be unchallenged, but its normative power and ability to shape world politics have been fundamentally curtailed. US foreign policy is almost universally treated with suspicion; everyone becomes a sceptical realist as far as the United States is concerned. The explanations differ – oil, imperial hubris, stupidity, support for Israel – but whatever America does, it does so to serve American interests, not some notion of the wider global community of states. In addition, whilst the Arab Spring initially suggested the spread of democracy across the Middle East, various forms of authoritarianism now seem to be re-emerging. Alongside these developments the wars in Iraq and Afghanistan seem to have only increased Islamic radicalization as more and more groups emerge that are committed, in their own way, to some notion of an Islamic resurgence.

Conclusion

Terrorism is a tactic deployed by groups and individuals that feel they have no other option but to spread their message via the deliberate targeting of non-state actors. It is not the only form of political violence, and it is not necessarily the worst. Violence is a structural aspect of the contemporary political system, and it is only within that context that terrorism can be understood. Part of the context of contemporary forms of terrorism is undoubtedly the resurgence of religious extremism, emanating from all religions. It would be a mistake to reduce all terrorism post-9/11 to this religious dimension, just as it would be a mistake to ignore it. Islamic terrorism is simply the most troubling and most visible form we face at the beginning of the twenty-first century, but there is no reason to assume it will continue to be so.

More important than this religious aspect is the manner in which the conditions of the new century, and in particular, globalization, provide an environment in which all forms of terrorism now take on a global dimension. Domestic terrorism may still emerge, but it is doubtful its effect can be isolated to just the context out of which it emerges. All terrorism is now, potentially at least, international terrorism. Thus if the idea of new terrorism has any 'essential' characteristic, it is in its global potential.

Conclusion
Rethinking Terrorism

The academic study of terrorism has, even among its practitioners, always been the subject of profound critique. This critique is not without merit. The subject has struggled to constitute itself as a coherent academic field of study because there is no consensus on what the object of inquiry is. If we cannot agree on the object/process/phenomenon we wish to study, we cannot begin to ask questions about how to study it, or how we might validate knowledge claims about it. Science is a social practice, and without some consensus on the object of analysis, results cannot be checked, verified or replicated. Likewise, in the absence of even a minimal consensus on what is, and is what is not, included in the study of terrorism, it is impossible to develop theories about it. A field of inquiry that fails to agree on what it should study cannot fail to be fragmented. Granted, terrorism is not the only social concept that is 'essentially contested', but the debate around this issue has also suffered from the intense 'politicization' of the term. Again, granted, in political science all concepts are politicized to a degree, but with the concept of terrorism this process has so distorted the field that scholars are generally engaged in promoting a particular view of political violence rather than studying it. Some would say that this is all we can do. I think we can do better.

Moreover, the lack of agreement on a definition has meant that terrorism is studied across multiple disciplines, which only adds to the absence of a coherent approach to the subject. In addition, state imperatives to control terrorism provide a siren call to those prepared to provide advice to state institutions on how to deal with it. This has meant that many of those best placed to contribute to the academic study of terrorism are attracted to do so outside an academic context, in which the imperatives of 'policy relevance' dominate. Add to these problems the difficulties of gaining access to empirical data due to the secrecy of state institutions when national security is at stake, and the natural reluctance of groups using terrorism to provide access, it is little wonder that it is an area of study that has very particular, and enduring, difficulties.

However, as a form of violent political communication political science must be involved in the study of terrorism. In addition, in a globalized world where the boundaries between domestic and international politics are increasingly blurred, the distinction between domestic and international terrorism is difficult to maintain. This does not mean that the recourse to terrorism does not have domestic roots, but these domestic sources almost inevitably have international consequences. Hence, the subject of contemporary terrorism is also a concern for the study of IR.

More than this, however, it is the structural relationship between the state and terrorism that demands that political science and international relations are the natural home of terrorism studies. Placing the state at the centre of terrorism ensures that we reject all attempts to view terrorists as irrational, or evil, madmen (*sic*) operating outside rational parameters. Psychological approaches have their place, but provide us with limited insights into the political context of the issue. Even the definition of terrorism has to commence with the state, because at its very core terrorism is a form of violent political protest against the state. We may not agree with the means employed to pursue these political ends, but its political nature requires us to understand the political motivations and structural causes that produce it.

The state is founded on violence, and political disputes are ultimately resolved by violence. State violence may not always be exercised, but it provides the foundation for the state itself and the law. The law does not resolve disputes in a non-violent way; it sets the conditions under which violence is allowed, and the state decides where that line is drawn. The state threatens the exercise of violence against individuals or groups when it decides no alternatives remain. These threats are often made manifest. The state also retains the right to decide when this position has been reached. Importantly, the state also denies other actors the use of violence, particularly when such violence is directed against states themselves. In a curious twisted logic, states have codified, and accepted, rules regarding the use of violence against other states; only states have a legitimate recourse to violence against other states. States legitimate violence between them, and all non-state violence is deemed illegitimate.

However, violence is not the only way of resolving political disputes. Yet, because of the role that violence has played in the development of the state, and the role it continues to play in the maintenance of political order – even if only as a threat – it should come as no surprise that some non-state actors resort to violence when they object to state policies, or even the legitimacy of the state's governing institutions. The place of violence in the formation and maintenance of the state requires us to accept the possibility that some instances of violence against it might be legitimate, and morally appropriate, to redress inappropriate uses of state violence. What we do not have to accept is the use of violence against non-state actors, unless it can be shown that those actors are intimately involved in the maintenance of the state. Thus, placing the state at the centre of terrorism studies supplies us with the means to finally deal with the definitional issue and move the study of terrorism forward in productive ways.

I have attempted to rethink terrorism by placing it in the context of the state, political violence and protest. To restate the argument: terrorism is a form of political protest, and the state is the dominant institutional form through which politics is organized today. Terrorism is also a form of violent political protest. This should not be surprising; violence is at the heart of the modern state system. The state was founded on violence, ultimately its predominant place in the social field as the major political actor remains dependent upon violence, and it uses violence to claim sole ownership of violence. Groups that use violent political protest against the state are a direct challenge to that claim to ownership.

I have placed this control of violence within a history of the development of the state (Chapter 1). I then demonstrated (Chapter 2) how the perspective one takes on this history colours the account of the state that is embraced. Those who have gained most out of state-ownership of violence will tend towards an acceptance of our contemporary political discourses. Those who feel they have suffered will adopt a more critical stance to the state and, potentially at least, consider protest against it.

That protest does not have to be violent, and I demonstrate (Chapter 3) the differing forms that protest against the state can take. The distinctions introduced in this chapter are in many ways artificial, and many of these types of protest blend, or mutate, easily into one another. The messy, dynamic and fluid nature of political protest should not restrict our attempts to build coherent analytical models. Moreover, given that violent political protest is best considered a continuum, it becomes an interesting question as to why some groups reject alternative types of protest and embrace terrorism. The following four chapters all attempt to rethink terrorism in this context of the state, political violence and protest. Ultimately, I argue that we have choices we can make about how to define terrorism, and that political practice and academic standards would be improved if we adopted the definition advocated here.

No doubt many will disagree. Mainstream terrorist scholars may take issue with the very restrictive definition of terrorism; for it means that much that has traditionally been considered to be terrorism is not. Likewise, I also expect that some will read the book as advocating violence. It does not. It does, however, argue that, at times, violent political protest against the state may be justified. Any political entity that maintains its control over the use and ownership of violence through the use of violence should not be surprised that protest against it occasionally takes violent forms.

Scholars, who see themselves working in a more critical tradition, will no doubt disagree with the rejection of the concept of state terrorism. The concept of state terrorism is hopelessly confused. It fails to distinguish between terror and terrorism, brings an explicit, politically charged way of talking into the study of the subject, flattens out differences between differing forms of violence, inflates the amount of so-called terrorism encountered in the world and, essentially, equates all state practices with terrorism. In short, the concept of state terrorism acts as a barrier to our understanding of the phenomenon and serves to make the resolution of political problems more difficult. And for what? What exactly do we gain by using the term state terrorism? Proponents of it will claim that it allows us to place state violence on an equal footing with violence committed by non-state actors. Supposedly, it enables us to see how state violence is far more effective in producing terror than non-state actors. On all of these points I agree, but do not agree that the concept of state terrorism is needed to achieve these aims. Yes, we need to place the state at the heart of the study of terrorism; not in terms of a discourse of state terrorism, but by recognizing that the state is a condition of possibility for the existence of terrorism. We cannot understand terrorism until we place the state (its history, development and form) at the centre of the analysis.

In many respects, the book can also be considered as an attempt to think through the difficult problem of how we judge our definitions. This issue has received scant attention. Social science definitions have to serve ends, have to have some purchase on what the actors engaged in a practice, and those commenting on the practice, mean when using the term, and, have to capture as accurately as possible the variety of activity we would meaningfully accept as being a practice of that form. Definitions also have to be subject to application, and should allow us to ask of any instance of a given practice (in this case terrorism) whether or not it falls under the definition. Sometimes we may not like the answers. But if the definition is sound, we should be able to see why the answer is as it is, even if we do not like the consequences of that answer. To that end, I want to conclude by considering some high-profile cases that have been deemed to be terrorism and to use these to highlight how this rethinking of terrorism might be put to work.

The Islamic State

In many respects, the Islamic State (IS) stands as the archetypical Islamic terrorist group. Its emergence and development are long and convoluted (Sekulow, 2014). Initially affiliated with al-Qaeda, IS emerged in Iraq after the invasion of 2003, and despite some setbacks in Iraq, has become a major player in the Syrian civil war (2011–). It now controls major tracts of territory in Syria and Iraq and is attempting to spread its influence across the region. The media regularly refer to it as a terrorist organization and the UN and many states have designated it one. However, the situation in relation to IS is not as straightforward as it seems. It certainly presents some problems for my definition of terrorism, but it is also a good test case for how the definition might be applied.

Formerly known as the Islamic State of Iraq and the Levant (ISIL), IS is probably best viewed as a militia, or insurgent group (Vick and Baker, 2014). Indeed, Jessica Lewis, a former US army intelligence officer who served in Iraq and Afghanistan, has described ISIL as 'not a terrorism problem anymore', but rather 'an army on the move in Iraq and Syria, and they are taking terrain. They have shadow governments in and around Baghdad, and they have an aspirational goal to govern' (Vick and Baker, 2014). However, more than just an insurgent group, IS are a successful insurgent group. In fact, they have been so successful they have proclaimed themselves to be a state. And for all intents and purposes they operate as a state in the areas they control. They are in the process of establishing all the necessary components of a functioning political institution.

As a nascent Islamic state, however, they reject the Western state model and are attempting to set up an Islamic Caliphate, which, by definition, rejects the state boundaries forced on the Middle East by the European powers. As they have put it, 'The legality of all emirates, groups, states and organizations becomes null by the expansion of the khilāfah's [caliphate's] authority and arrival of its troops to their areas ... Support your state, which grows every day – by Allah's grace – with honor and loftiness, while its enemy increases in retreat and defeat' (ISIL, 2014). Whether they will be successful in the long term remains to be seen, but there is no doubt that that the idea of an Islamic caliphate has widespread support among many Muslims. However, on the other hand, the regimes currently in power in the Middle East have rejected IS, and virtually all Islamic theological authorities have declared their version of Islam to be a deviant distortion of the core principles of the religion (Kirkpatrick, 2014). As yet they have no international legitimacy and little domestic legitimacy. However, to attempt to apply these standards of legitimacy to IS is exactly what they would reject:

> If your leaders whisper to you claiming it is not a khilāfah, then remember how long they whispered to you claiming that it was not a state but rather a fictional, cardboard entity, until its certain news reached you. It is a state. Its news will continue to reach you showing that it is a khilāfah, even if after time. (ISIL, 2014)

Viewed from the perspective of the history of the development of the state, this is precisely the kind of claim that was made by lords and kings during the early period of European state growth. To apply Western notions of state legitimacy to IS is to miss the point. They simply do not care about such recognition, for to seek

it is to accept the very parameters of a political order they seek
to challenge:

> Whom would we consult? They never recognized the Islamic
> State to begin with, although America, Britain and France
> acknowledge its existence. Whom would we consult? Should
> we consult those who have abandoned us? Those who have
> betrayed us? Those who have disowned us and incited against
> us? Those who have become hostile towards us? Those who
> wage war against us? Whom would we consult, and whom did
> we step over? (ISIL, 2014)

It is clear that IS use terror to spread their message and to exercise control over the territories they control. They also explicitly
use violence as a form of political communication and deliberately target non-state actors. But insofar as they are assuming the
mantle of statehood then their violent actions, although brutal in
the extreme, are not terrorism. Of course, not just any entity can
declare itself to be a state and thus avoid the charge of terrorism.
However, the analysis of the state contained in Chapters 2 and 3
provided a means by which we can assess claims to statehood. In
this respect, IS meet many of the necessary conditions for statehood; they control large areas of territory, their rule is accepted
and supported by large sections of the population in those areas,
they have a military force, a governance structure, they provide
welfare services (albeit limited) and they have a legal system. As
such, much as I find the conclusion troubling, to maintain consistency I have to conclude that their actions are not forms of
terrorism, but abhorrent state violence. And indeed, the international community now treats those actions as war crimes, and not
acts of terrorism (BBC News, 2014; Al Jazeera, 2014).

The Killing of Fusilier Lee Rigby

Lee Rigby was a member of the Royal Regiment of Fusiliers.
He was a drummer and a machine-gunner and had served in
Afghanistan. On 22 May 2013, he was returning to his mili-
tary barracks in Woolwich, south-east London, when Michael
Adebolajo and Michael Adebowale, two Nigerians who had con-
verted to Islam, killed him. The two men deliberately ran him

down with their car, then proceeded to cut him to death with knives and a meat cleaver, and attempted to behead him. They then dragged his body into the road and stayed at the scene until the police arrived. Whilst waiting they informed passers-by that they had killed the soldier to avenge the killing of Muslims by the British armed forces:

> The only reason we have killed this man today is because Muslims are dying daily by British soldiers. And this British soldier is one ... By Allah, we swear by the almighty Allah we will never stop fighting you until you leave us alone. So what if we want to live by the Sharia in Muslim lands? Why does that mean you must follow us and chase us and call us extremists and kill us? (*Daily Telegraph*, 2013)

This case seems straightforward in terms of the definition of terrorism advanced here. Although it contains many of the essential elements of terrorism, the fact that Rigby was a soldier and hence a state agent places this event outside a terrorism discourse. This fact was recognized when the two men were charged with murder, and not offences under Terrorism Act.

The Sydney hostage siege, December 2014

This is another interesting and complicated example. The idea of a 'lone wolf' terrorist has been a concern for some time. The term is used by security and intelligence agencies to refer to individuals who carry out violent terrorist acts in the name of a wider cause, or group, but who in fact have had little or no contact with that group (Teich, 2013). Acting on his or her own initiative, the 'lone wolf' attempts to promote, communicate or advertise the ideological stance of an extremist group, outside of direct command or direction from the group. An important caveat needs to be discussed here. The concept of a 'lone wolf' explicitly refers to an individual, but the idea of coordinated groups acting on their own initiative to promote or communicate a cause is also possible. In fact, this could be the essential aspect of the 'franchise' model of terrorism we confront today (Fishman, 2008; Hellmich, 2011; *Wall Street Journal*, 2013). The idea that clear lines of command and control exist between the leadership and those carrying out terrorist acts only applies to older forms of terrorism. The new terrorism expects the ideology of the movement to be the primary motivating factor, with loosely aligned groups using the language of the cause, in the absence of direct control from the centre. This is what is meant when we use the term 'affiliates', and the level of contact between those acting in the name of a particular cause may be low or non-existent.

The Sydney hostage siege in December 2014, however, was a clear example of a lone actor claiming to be promoting the IS cause. Man Haron Monis held ten customers and eight employees of a Lindt café in Martin Place Sydney, Australia on 15–16 December 2014. Police and media treated the siege as a terrorist incident. Monis had been a vocal critic of Australian foreign policy, but even extremist Islamic groups in Australia shunned him. The siege ended with the deaths of two of the hostages and Monis, and four other people (one policeman) were injured. The authorities believed that it was a terrorist incident because Monis was wearing a black headband with the Arabic inscription: 'We are ready to sacrifice for you, O Muhammad' and he had forced the hostages to hold a black Islamic flag up against the window of the café, with the shahādah creed ('There is no God but Allah, and Muhammad is the messenger of God') written on it in Arabic. Monis also demanded that he be allowed to speak to Australian Prime Minister Tony Abbott on live radio, that an Islamic State flag be delivered to him, that there were four 'devices' located in Sydney, and he demanded that a hostage ask the media to broadcast that 'this is an attack on Australia by the Islamic State' (Begley, 2014).

There is no doubt that Monis was acting alone, and no evidence has emerged that he had been in contact with IS, or even extremist Islamic groups in Australia. In fact, both Shia and Sunni radicals in Australia had largely shunned him. Claims have emerged that he was mentally unstable, and he was facing charges relating to the murder of his ex-wife, as well as numerous allegations of sexual abuse. These aspects of Monis's character complicate the judgement of whether or not he was a terrorist. Some analysts claimed it was an act of terrorism, and some stated it was not (News.com.au, 2014). However, whatever else was going on in his life, Monis intended to portray his actions as being about the promotion of the IS cause. In addition, he attempted to communicate this cause through the use of violence, and those he held hostage were non-state actors. His mental state was clearly important, but on balance does not alter the fact of what he was trying to achieve: the use of violence against non-state actors to communicate a political message. Indeed, following the siege, IS stated that Monis's actions 'prompted mass panic, brought terror to the entire nation, and triggered an evacuation of parts of Sydney's central business district' (Knott, 2014). Likewise, al-Qaeda acknowledged his efforts in their self-produced magazine, *Inspire* (9News, 2014). This is not to say that Monis's mental state should be ignored, but as Max Abrahms has argued, such 'lone-wolf' terrorists are often deranged by definition. Abrahms has coined the term 'loon wolf' to describe this complex relationship of a mentally unstable individual who engages in acts of terrorism (Abrahms, 2014).

Another example of a 'lone wolf' who potentially fits this description might be that of Anders Breivik, a Norwegian man who bombed a government building and killed 69 young people who were attending a Workers' Youth League (AUF) camp on the island of Utøya on 22 July 2011. Breivik was clearly deranged, although the Norwegian court declared him to be sane, but he had produced a political manifesto and hoped that his actions would publicize it. The fact that Breivik first bombed a government building would suggest that that particular act was not terrorism. And it would be possible to argue that, given that those he killed on the island were youth members of the Norwegian Labour Party, this implicated them as state agents. On balance, however, of those he killed on the island, some may have gone on to take part in state-related activities, but some may have not, and there is no reason to regard them as state agents at the time they were killed.

9/11

If we accept that the attacks on 9 September 2001 were all connected and coordinated by al-Qaeda in some way, it seems inevitable that those attacks would be referred to as 'acts of terrorism'. Indeed, it seems absurd to suggest otherwise. If 9/11 was not terrorism, nothing was. However, the definition of terrorism suggested in this book allows us to deal with the attacks on the morning of 9 September 2001 in a more nuanced manner. First, as American Airlines flight 77 was intentionally flown into the Pentagon building, the headquarters of the US Department of Defense, this represented an assault on the US state. As such, this would not be considered an act of terrorism according to the logic of the definition advanced here.

However, the attack on the Twin Towers was a deliberate attempt to kill non-state actors. Of course, in statements delivered after 9/11, Bin Laden did attempt to justify the attacks on the twin towers by arguing that these were legitimate economic targets at the heart of US power (Lawrence, 2005: 107). Now whilst the World Trade Center buildings were clearly an important centre of economic power in the United States they were not part of the US state, unless one adopts an impossibly broad definition of the state. Equally, even though it might be possible to argue that certain individuals and firms might be closely related to parts of the security complex that allows a state to function, no such claim was made in relation to those people inside the Twin Towers when they were attacked. From everything we know about the attacks it seems clear that no specific individuals or firms were the target of the attacks; rather it was simply the symbolism of the Towers themselves, and those planning the attacks cared little for how many people would be killed as a result of the attacks. As such, the attack on the Twin Towers represents a classic case of terrorism, whereas the attack on the Pentagon does not.

These examples provide some indications of how this rethinking of terrorism could be put to use. Others, of course, are much clearer. The attack on the *USS Cole* in 2000, for example, is clearly not terrorism on my account. Nor would the 1983 bomb attack on the US barracks in Beirut that killed 299 American and French servicemen be considered an attack of terrorism. Likewise, the attempt by the IRA to kill Mrs Thatcher and her cabinet in Brighton in 1984 would also not be considered and act of terrorism, whereas the bombs placed in the Birmingham pubs in 1974 might be. However, it is instructive to note that both Sinn Féin and the IRA denied any involvement in the bombings. Indeed, a senior member of the IRA's Army Council, Dáithí Ó Conaill, said: 'if IRA members had carried out such attacks, they would be court-martialled and could face the death penalty. The IRA has clear guidelines for waging its war. Any attack on non-military installations must be preceded by a 30-minute warning so that no innocent civilians are endangered (Montreal, 1974).

The explicit recognition that military targets are legitimate in waging a war is clear evidence of how the account proposed in this rethinking of terrorism could go some way to placing terrorism in context, realizing it is minimal security threat to individuals, states or the international system, and could help facilitate better research on the subject. Much like the attempt to wage a war on terror, however, we will not be able to move forward until we allow the 'ism' to do its work and enable us to use it to distinguish the production of terror from the strategic use of terrorism.

Bibliography

9News. (2014) Extremists Urged to Follow Example of Martin Place Siege Gunman in ISIL Magazine. 30 December. Available at http://www.9news.com. au/national/2014/12/30/11/31/man-monis-praised-in-isil-magazine [accessed 19 February 2015].

Abrahms, Max. (2006) Why Terrorism Does Not Work. *International Security* 31(2): 42–78.

Abrahms, Max. (2010) Lumpers versus Splitters: A Pivotal Battle in the Field of Terrorism Studies. *Cato* (February).

Abrahms, Max. (2014) 'Loon' Wolf Terrorist Attacks to Become the Norm. *RT, Question More*, 16 December. Available at http://rt.com/op-edge/214711-sydney-hostage-lone-wolf-isis/ [accessed 31 December 2014].

Adams, James. (1986) *The financing of terror*, Sevenoaks: New English Library.

Addison, Paul and Crang, Jeremy A. (2006) *Firestorm: the bombing of Dresden, 1945*, Chicago: I.R. Dee.

Ahmad, Ilyas. (1958) Sovereignty in Islam (Continued). *Pakistan Horizon* 11(4): 244–57.

Ahmed, Nazeer. 2008. Shia versus Sunni, the World's Longest Running Feud. Available at http://www.irfi.org/articles/articles_551_600/shia_versus_sunni.htm [accessed 3 July 2014].

Alam, Anwar and Islamia, Jamia Millia. (2009) *Iran and post–9/11 world order: reflections on the Iranian nuclear programme*, New Delhi: New Century Publications.

Alexander, Yonah. (1986) *State sponsored terrorism*, London: Centre for Contemporary Studies.

Alexander, Yonah and Swetnam, Michael S. (2001) *Usama bin Laden's al-Qaida: profile of a terrorist network*, Ardsley, NY: Transnational Publishers.

Al Jazeera. (2013) Egypt: Crisis, Coup or Revolution? Available at http://www. aljazeera.com/programmes/insidestory/2013/07/2013727104242446430.html [accessed 1 August 2013].

Al Jazeera. (2014) UN Accuses Islamic State Group of War Crimes. Available at http://www.aljazeera.com/news/middleeast/2014/08/un-accuses-islamic-state-group-war-crimes-201482715354171063.html [accessed 28 December 2014].

Allen, Chris. (2010) *Islamophobia*, Farnham: Ashgate.

Allhoff, Fritz. (2012) *Terrorism, ticking time-bombs, and torture: a philosophical analysis*, Chicago, IL: University of Chicago Press.

Anderson, Perry. (1974) *Lineages of the absolutist state*, London: NLB.

Annan, Kofi. (2005) In *larger freedom: towards development, security and human rights for all*. Report of the Secretary-General. New York: United Nations.

Aragorn, Bang. (2012) *Occupy everything: anarchists in the occupy movement 2009–2011*. Berkeley, CA: LBC Press.

Archetti, Cristina. (2013) *Understanding terrorism in the age of global media: a communication approach*, New York: Palgrave Macmillan.

Arendt, Hannah. (1967) *The origins of totalitarianism*, London: Allen & Unwin.
Armstrong, Karen. (2014a) *Fields of blood: religion and the history of violence*, New York: Alfred A. Knopf.
Armstrong, Karen. (2014b) The Myth of Religious Violence. *Guardian*, 25 September.
Atran, Scott. 2006. What Would Gandhi Do Today? Non-violence in an Age of Terrorism. Available at http://sitemaker.umich.edu/satran/files/atran-gandhi_conference_120906.pdf [accessed 8 August 2014].
Avard, Christian. 2010. Reese Erlich: Stop Using the Word 'Terrorist'. 23 September. Available at http://www.huffingtonpost.com/christian-avard/reece-erlich-stop-using-t_b_737292.html [accessed 19 February 2015].
Badiou, Alain. (2012) *The rebirth of history*, London: Verso.
Baird, William E. (2012) *Madrid train bombings: a decision-making model analysis*, USA: BiblioScholar.
Bakunin, Mikhail Aleksandrovich. (1971) *God and the state*, Freeport, NY: Books for Libraries Press.
Barrow, Clyde W. (1993) *Critical theories of the state: Marxist, Neo-Marxist, Post-Marxist*, London: University of Wisconsin Press.
BBC News. (2014) UN 'May Include' Isis on Syrian War Crimes List. 26 July. Available at http://www.bbc.com/news/world-middle-east-28498661 [accessed 28 December 2014].
Beckett, Charlie and Ball, James. (2012) *Wikileaks: news in the networked era*, Cambridge: Polity Press.
Bedau, Hugo Adam. (1969) *Civil disobedience: theory and practice*, New York: Pegasus.
Bedau, Hugo Adam. (1991) *Civil disobedience in focus*, London: Routledge.
Begley, Patrick. (2014) Sydney Siege Over: Lindt Café Gunman Forces Hostages to Appear in Videos. *Sydney Morning Herald*, 26 December. Available at http://www.smh.com.au/nsw/sydney-siege-over-lindt-cafe-gunman-forces-hostages-to-appear-in-videos-20141216-127wgy.html [accessed 26 December 2014].
Benjamin, Daniel and Simon, Steven. (2000) The New Face of Terrorism. *New York Times*, 4 January.
Benjamin, Walter. (1996) *Critique of violence, selected writings; volume 1, 1913–1926*, London: Belknap Press of Harvard University Press.
Bergen, Peter and Cruickshank, Paul. (2007) The Iraq Effect – The War in Iraq and Its Impact on the War on Terrorism. *Mother Jones*, 1 March.
Bergen, Peter and Sterman, David. (2014) U.S. Right Wing Extremists More Deadly than Jihadists. CNN, 15 April. Available at http://edition.cnn.com/2014/04/14/opinion/bergen-sterman-kansas-shooting/ [accessed 19 February 2015].
Berki, R. N. (1989) Vocabularies of the State. In P. Lassman (ed.), *Politics and Social Theory*. London: Routledge, 12–29.
Berman, Eli. (2009) *Radical, religious, and violent: the new economics of terrorism*, London: MIT Press.
Bhaskar, Roy. (1993) *Dialectic: the pulse of freedom*, London: Verso.
Biersteker, Thomas J. and Eckert, Sue E. (2008) *Countering the financing of terrorism*, London: Routledge.
bin Laden, Osama, ed. Bruce B. Lawrence. (2005) *Messages to the world: the statements of Osama bin Laden*, London: Verso.
Bjørgo, Tore. (2004) *Root causes of terrorism: myths, reality and ways forward*, London: Routledge.
Blakeley, Ruth. (2009) *State terrorism and neoliberalism: the North in the South*, London: Routledge.
Bleiker, Roland. (2000) *Popular dissent, human agency, and global politics*, Cambridge: Cambridge University Press.

Bloch, Marc. (1989) *Feudal society*, London: Routledge.

Bobbitt, Philip. (2002) *The shield of Achilles: war, peace and the course of history*, London: Allen Lane.

Bockstette, Carsten. (2008) Jihadist Terrorist Use of Strategic Communication Management Techniques. *Marshall Center Occasional Paper Series*. Garmisch-Partenkirchen, Germany: George C. Marshall European Center for Security Studies.

Bolanos, Alejandro. (2012) The 'New Terrorism' or the 'Newness' of Context and Change. In R. Jackson and S.J. Sinclair (eds), *Contemporary debates on terrorism*, London: Routledge, 29–34.

Bongar, Bruce Michael. (2007) *Psychology of terrorism*, Oxford: Oxford University Press.

Boot, Max. (2002) *The savage wars of peace: small wars and the rise of American power*, New York: Basic Books.

Booth, Ken and Dunne, Timothy. (2012) *Terror in our time*, London: Routledge.

Booth, Ken and Wheeler, Nicholas J. (2008) *The security dilemma: fear, cooperation, and trust in world politics*, Basingstoke: Palgrave Macmillan.

Bosanquet, Bernard. (1899) *The philosophical theory of the state*, London: Macmillan.

Bourdieu, Pierre. (1977) *Outline of a theory of practice*, Cambridge: Cambridge University Press.

Bourdieu, Pierre. (2004) *Science of science and reflexivity*, Cambridge: Polity.

Bousquet, Antoine. (2012) Complexity Theory and the War on Terror: Understanding the Self-organising Dynamics of Leaderless Jihad. *Journal of International Relations and Development* 15(3): 345–69.

Bowden, Mark. (1999) *Black Hawk down*, London: Bantam.

Bowden, Mark. (2006) *Guests of the ayatollah: the first battle in the west's war with militant Islam*, London: Atlantic Books.

Bowden, Mark. (2012) *The finish: the killing of Osama bin Laden*, London: Grove.

Bravin, Jess. (2013) *The terror courts: rough justice at Guantánamo Bay*, London: Yale University Press.

Brenchley, Frank. (1984) *Diplomatic immunities and state-sponsored terrorism*, London: Institute for the Study of Conflict.

Buci-Glucksmann, Christine. (1980) *Gramsci and the state*, London: Lawrence & Wishart.

Bufacchi, Vittorio. (2007) *Violence and social justice*, Basingstoke: Palgrave Macmillan.

Bull, Hedley. (1977) *The anarchical society: a study of order in world politics*, London: Macmillan.

Burke, Jason. (2003) *Al-Qaeda: casting a shadow of terror*, London: I.B. Tauris.

Burleigh, Michael. (2009) *Blood and rage: a cultural history of terrorism*, London: Harper Perennial.

Burton, Anthony. (1975) *Urban terrorism: theory, practice and response*, London: Cooper.

Buzan, Barry and Lawson George. (2014) Rethinking Benchmark Dates in International Relations. *European Journal of International Relations* 20(2): 437–62.

Byman, Daniel. (2005) *Deadly connections: states that sponsor terrorism*, Cambridge: Cambridge University Press.

Byrne, David. (1998) *Complexity theory and the social sciences: an introduction*, London: Routledge.

Campbell, Bruce and Brenner, Arthur David. (2000) *Death squads in global perspective: mrder with deniability*, Basingstoke: Macmillan.

Campbell, Kate. (2008) *Trauma, alcohol and drug comorbidity: an investigation into the issues associated with post-traumatic stress disorder in terms of individual trauma, agency responses and community involvement in Northern Ireland*, Belfast, NI: Eastern Trauma Advisory Panel: Belfast Health and Social Care Trust.

Campbell, Tom. (2004) *Separation of powers in practice*, Stanford, CA: Stanford Law and Politics.

Caridi, Paola. (2012) *Hamas: from resistance to government*, New York: Seven Stories.

Castells, Manuel. (2012) *Networks of outrage and hope: social movements in the internet age*, Cambridge: Polity.

Castro, Daniel. (1999) *Revolution and revolutionaries: guerrilla movements in Latin America*, Wilmington, DE: SR Books.

Celso, Anthony. (2014) *Al-Qaeda's post-9/11 devolution: the failed jihadist struggle against the near and far enemy*, London: Bloomsbury.

Centre of Excellence Defence Against Terrorism, Ankara, Turkey. (2008) *Organizational and Psychological Aspects of Terrorism*. Amsterdam: IOS Press.

Cetina, Karin Knorr. (2005) Complex Global Microstructures: The New Terrorist Societies. *Theory, Culture & Society* 22(5): 213–34.

Chandrasekaran, Rajiv. (2007) *Imperial life in the Emerald City: inside Baghdad's green zone*, London: Bloomsbury.

Chapman, Clark R. and Harris, Alan W. (2002) A Skeptical Look at September 11th. *Skeptical Inquirer* 26(5). Available at http://www.csicop.org/si/show/skeptical_look_at_september_11th/ [accessed 19 February 2015].

Chenoweth, Erica and Stephan, Maria J. (2011) *Why civil resistance works: the strategic logic of nonviolent conflict*, New York: Columbia University Press.

Chomsky, Noam. (2001) The United States is a Leading Terrorist State: An Interview with Noam Chomsky. *Monthly Review* 53(6): 10–19.

Chomsky, Noam. (2014) The Leading Terrorist State. Available at http://www.truth-out.org/opinion/item/27201-the-leading-terrorist-state [accessed 1 December 2014].

Chomsky, Noam and Herman, Edward S. (1973) *Counter-revolutionary violence: bloodbaths in fact and propaganda*, Andover: Warner Modular Publications.

Chossudovsky, Michel. (2002) *War and globalisation: the truth behind September 11*, Shanty Bay, Ont.: Global Outlook.

Chotiner, Isaac. (2014) What in God's Name is Going on in Iraq? An Expert Explains. An Interview with Olivier Roy. *New Republic*, 16 June. Available at http://www.newrepublic.com/article/118198/olivier-roy-isis-iraqs-civil-war-and-sunni-shia-rift [accessed 19 February 2015].

Cilliers, Paul. (1998) *Complexity and postmodernism: understanding complex systems*, London: Routledge.

Clark, Christopher M. (2012) *The sleepwalkers: how Europe went to war in 1914*, London: Allen Lane.

Clarke, Richard A. (2004) *Against all enemies: inside America's war on terror*, London: Free Press.

Clarke, Walter S. and Herbst, Jeffrey Ira. (1997) *Learning from Somalia: the lessons of armed humanitarian intervention*, Boulder, CO: Westview Press.

Cline, Ray S. and Alexander, Yonah. (1986) *Terrorism as state-sponsored covert warfare*, Fairfax, Virginia: Hero Books.

Clinton, Bill. (2001) Terrorism must be addressed in parallel with poverty, underdevelopment and inequality, General Assembly is told. In GA9971 PR (ed.) United Nations News Service.

Cliteur, Paul. B. (2010) *The secular outlook: in defense of moral and political secularism*, Oxford: Wiley-Blackwell.

Coates, Ken. (2004) *America's gulag: full spectrum dominance versus universal human rights*, Nottingham: Spokesman for the Bertrand Russell Peace Foundation.

Cobban, Helena. (1984) *The Palestinian Liberation Organisation: people, power and politics*, Cambridge: Cambridge University Press.

Cole, David and Dempsey, James X. (2006) *Terrorism and the constitution: sacrificing civil liberties in the name of national security*, New York: New Press.

Collins, Randall and Sanderson, Stephen K. (2009) *Conflict sociology: a sociological classic updated*, Boulder, CO: Paradigm.

Conkin, Paul Keith. (1974) *Self-evident truths. Being a discourse on the origins and development of the first principles of American government – popular sovereignty, natural rights, and balance and separation of powers*, London: Indiana University Press.

Coogan, Tim Pat. (2002) *The IRA*, New York: St. Martin's Press.

Coolsaet, Rik. (2011) *Jihadi terrorism and the radicalisation challenge: European and American experiences*, Farnham: Ashgate.

Cooper, H.H.A. (1977) What Is a Terrorist? A Psychological Perspective. *Legal Medical Quarterly* 1: 8–18.

Corlett, J. Angelo. (2003) *Terrorism: a philosophical analysis*, London: Kluwer Academic.

Costanze, Letsch. (2013) Social Media and Opposition to Blame for Protests, Says Turkish PM. *Guardian*, 3 June.

Costigan, Sean S. and Gold, David. (2007) *Terrornomics*, Aldershot: Ashgate.

Crawford, Neta. (2013) *Accountability for killing: moral responsibility for collateral damage in America's post–9/11 wars*, New York: Oxford University Press.

Crenshaw, Martha. (2000) The Psychology of Terrorism: An Agenda for the 21st Century. *Political Psychology* 21(2): 405–20.

Crenshaw, Martha. (2003) 'New' Versus 'Old' Terrorism: Is Today's 'New' Terrorism Qualitatively Different from Pre-September 11 'Old' Terrorism? *Palestine-Israel Journal* 10(1).

Croucher, Sarah K. and Weiss, Lindsay. (2011) *The archaeology of capitalism in colonial contexts: postcolonial historical archaeologies*, New York: Springer.

Czander, William M. (1993) *The psychodynamics of work and organizations: theory and application*, London: Guilford Press.

Dabashi, Hamid. (2011) *The green movement in Iran*, Somerset, NJ: Transaction.

Dabashi, Hamid. (2012) *The Arab Spring: the end of postcolonialism*, London: Zed.

De Landa, Manuel. (2006) *A new philosophy of society: assemblage theory and social complexity*, London: Continuum.

Dean, Jodi. (2005) Communicative Capitalism: Circulation and the Foreclosure of Politics. *Cultural Politics* 1(1): 51–74.

Dershowitz, Alan M. (2002a) Want to Torture? Get a Warrant. *San Francisco Chronicle*, 22 January.

Dershowitz, Alan M. (2002b) *Why terrorism works: understanding the threat, responding to the challenge*, New Haven, CT: Yale University Press.

Donnelly, Jack. (2009) Rethinking Political Structures: from 'Ordering Principles' to 'Vertical Differentiation' – and Beyond. *International Theory* 1(01): 49–86.

Doyle, Michael W. (1986) *Empires*, Ithaca, NY: Cornell University Press.

Dugan, Laura, LaFree, Gary and Fogg, Heather. (2006) A First Look at Domestic and International Global Terrorism Events, 1970–1997. In S. Mehrotra, D. Zeng, H. Chen et al. (eds), *Intelligence and security informatics*. Berlin: Springer, 407–19.

Durkheim, Émile, Thompson, Kenneth and Thompson, M.A. (1985) *Readings from Émile Durkheim*, Chichester: Ellis Horwood.

Duyvesteyn, Isabelle. (2004) How New is the New Terrorism? *Studies in Conflict & Terrorism* 27(5): 439–54.

Duyvesteyn, Isabelle and Malkki, Leena. (2012) The Fallacy of the New Terrorism Thesis. In R. Jackson and S.J. Sinclair (eds), *Contemporary debates on terrorism*. London: Routledge, 35–41.

Easton, David. (1981) The Political System Besieged by the State. *Political Theory* 9(3): 303–25.

Eatwell, Roger. (1995) *Fascism: a history*, London: Chatto & Windus.

Ebtekar, Massoumeh and Reed, Fred A. (2000) *Takeover in Tehran: the inside story of the 1979 U.S. Embassy capture*, Vancouver: Talonbooks.

Ehrenfeld, Rachel. (2003) *Funding evil: how terrorism is financed – and how to stop it*, Chicago: Bonus Books.

Eid, Mahmoud. (2014) *Exchanging terrorism oxygen for media airwaves: the age of terroredia*, Hershey, PA: IGI Global.

Eisenstadt, Shmuel Noah (1963) *The political systems of empires*, London: Collier-Macmillan.

Esposito, John L. (1998) *Islam and politics*, Syracuse, NY: Syracuse University Press.

Evans, Peter B., Rueschemeyer, Dietrich and Skocpol, Theda. (1985) *Bringing the state back in*, Cambridge: Cambridge University Press.

Farber, Samuel. (1990) *Before Stalinism: the rise and fall of Soviet democracy*, Oxford: Polity.

Faulks, Keith. (2000) *Citizenship*, London: Routledge.

Fierke, K. M. 2013. *Political self-sacrifice: agency, body and emotion in international relations*. Cambridge: Cambridge University Press.

Figgis, John Neville. (1914) *The divine right of kings*, Cambridge: Cambridge University Press.

Fischer, George. (2012) *The Soviet system: models of a political society*, New Brunswick: Aldine Transaction.

Fishman, Brian. (2008) Using the Mistakes of Al Qaeda's Franchises to Undermine its Strategies. *ANNALS of the American Academy of Political and Social Science* 618(1): 46–54.

Fleming, Peter A., Schmid, Alex P. and Stohl, Michael. (1988) The Theoretical Utility of Typologies of Terrorism: Lessons and Opportunities. In M. Stohl (ed.), *The politics of terrorism*. New York: Marcel Dekker, 153–95.

Foran, John. (1997) *Theorizing revolutions*, London: Routledge.

Foran, John. (2003) *The future of revolutions: rethinking political and social change in the age of globalization*, London: Zed.

Foran, John. (2005) *Taking power: on the origins of third world revolutions*, Cambridge: Cambridge University Press.

Foucault, Michel, trans. Alan Sheridan. (1977) *Discipline and punish: the birth of the prison*, London: Allen Lane.

Fox News. (2009) Obama Scraps 'Global War on Terror' for 'Overseas Contingency Operation. Available at http://www.foxnews.com/politics/2009/03/25/obama-scraps-global-war-terror-overseas-contingency-operation/ [accessed 3 July 2014].

Franks, Jason. (2006) *Rethinking the roots of terrorism*, Basingstoke: Palgrave Macmillan.

Fraser, James and Fulton, Ian. (1984) Terrorism Counteraction. FC 100-37. Fort Leavenworth, KS: US Army Command and General Staff College.

Fredrickson, Barbara L., Tugade, Michele M., Waugh, Christian E. et al. (2003) What Good are Positive Emotions in Crisis? A Prospective Study of Resilience and Emotions Following the Terrorist Attacks on the United States on September 11th, 2001. *Journal of Personality and Social Psychology* 84(2): 365–76.

Freedman, Des and Thussu, Daya Kishan. (2012) *Media and terrorism: global perspectives*, London: Sage.

Freedom. (2014) Global issues. Available at http://www.globalissues.org/article/354/crackdown-on-civil-rights-war-on-freedom [accessed 3 July 2014].

Friedman, Jonathan. (2006) *Globalization and violence, vol. 3: globalizing war and intervention*, London: Sage.

Friedrich, Carl J. and Brzezinski, Zbigniew K. (1966) *Totalitarian dictatorship and autocracy*. 2nd edn. New York: Praeger.

Fuchs, Christian. (2012) Some Reflections on Manuel Castells' Book Networks of Outrage and Hope. Social Movements in the Internet Age. *Triple C* 10(2): 775–97.

Fukuyama, Francis. (1992) *The end of history and the last man*, New York: Free Press.

Gabriel, Mark A. (2002) *Islam and terrorism*, Lake Mary, FL: Charisma House.

Gallie, Walter Bryce. (1964) Essentially Contested Cconcepts. In W.B. Gallie (ed.), *Philosophy and the historical understanding.* London: Chatto & Windus, 157–91.

Galston, William A. (1991) *Liberal purposes: goods, virtues, and diversity in the liberal state*, Cambridge: Cambridge University Press.

Galtung, Johan. (1969) Violence, Peace, and Peace Research. *Journal of Peace Research* 6(3): 167–91.

Gandhi, Mahatma, ed. Dennis Dalton. (1996) *Mahatma Gandhi: selected political writings*, Indianapolis: Hackett.

Gani, Miriam and Mathew, Penelope. (2008) *Fresh perspectives on the war on terror*, Canberra: ANU E Press.

Gareau, Frederick H. (2004) *State terrorism and the United States: from counterinsurgency to the war on terrorism*, Atlanta, GA: Clarity Press.

Gearty, Connor. (1991) *Terror*, London: Faber & Faber.

Geifman, Anna. (1995) *Thou shalt kill: revolutionary terrorism in Russia, 1894–1917*, Princeton, NJ: Princeton University Press.

Gelber, Katharine. (2002) *Speaking back: the free speech versus hate speech debate*, Amsterdam: John Benjamins.

Gelber, Katharine and Stone, Adrienne. (2007) *Hate speech and freedom of speech in Australia*, Leichhardt, NSW: Federation Press.

Gellner, Ernest. (2006) *Nations and nationalism*, Oxford: Blackwell.

George, Alexander. (1991) *Western state terrorism*, Cambridge: Polity Press.

Gerbaudo, Paolo. (2012) *Tweets and the streets: social media and contemporary activism*, London: Pluto Press.

Gertz, Bill. (2003) *Breakdown: the failure of American intelligence to defeat global terror*, New York: Plume Books.

Gibbs, Jack P. (1989) Conceptualization of Terrorism. *American Sociological Review* 54(3): 329–40.

Giddens, Anthony. (1985) *A contemporary critique of historical materialism , vol. 2. the nation state and violence*, London: Polity.

Giddens, Anthony. (1998) *The third way: the renewal of social democracy*, Cambridge: Polity.

Gladwell, Malcolm. (2010) Small Change. Why the Revolution Will Not Be Tweeted. *New Yorker*, 4 October, 42–9.

Gleason, Abbott. (1995) *Totalitarianism: the inner history of the Cold War*, Oxford: Oxford University Press.

Golder, Ben and Williams, George. (2004) What is Terrorism? Problems of Legal Definition. *University of New South Wales Law Journal* 27(2): 270–95.

Goldfarb, Alex and Litvinenko, Marina. (2007) *Death of a dissident: the poisoning of Alexander Litvinenko and the return of the KGB*, London: Simon & Schuster.

Goldstone, Jack A. (1992) *Revolution and rebellion in the early modern world*, London: University of California Press.

Gonzalez, Nathan. (2009) *The Sunni-Shia conflict: understanding sectarian violence in the Middle East*, Mission Viejo, CA: Nortia Press.

Goodin, Robert E. (2006) *What's wrong with terrorism?*, Cambridge: Polity.

Gott, Richard. (1970) *Guerrilla movements in Latin America*, London: Seagull Books.

Gottlieb, Sherry Gershon. (1991) *Hell no, we won't go!: resisting the draft during the Vietnam War*, New York: Viking.

Gottschalk, Peter and Greenberg, Gabriel. (2008) *Islamophobia: making Muslims the enemy*, Plymouth: Rowman & Littlefield.

Gow, James. (2005) *Defending the west*, Cambridge: Polity.

Gramsci, Antonio. (1971) *Selections from the prison notebooks of Antonio Gramsci*, London: Lawrence & Wishart.

Grau, Lester W. and Gress, Michael A. (2002) *The Soviet-Afghan War: how a superpower fought and lost*, Lawrence: University of Kansas Press.

Grayling, Anthony Clifford. (2009) *Liberty in the age of terror: a defence of civil liberties and enlightenment values*, London: Bloomsbury.

Greenwald, Glenn. (2013) NSA Collecting Phone Records of Millions of Verizon Customers Daily. *Guardian*, 6 June.

Greenwald, Glenn. (2014) *No place to hide: Edward Snowden, the NSA and the surveillance state*, New York: Metropolitan Books.

Greenwald, Glenn, MacAskill, Ewen and Poitras, Laura. (2013) Edward Snowden: The Whistleblower Behind the NSA Surveillance Revelations. *Guardian*, 11 June.

Gregory, Shaun. (2009) The Terrorist Threat to Pakistan's Nuclear Weapons. *CTC Sentinel* 2(7).

Grey, Stephen. (2006) *Ghost plane: the inside story of the CIA's secret rendition programme*, London: Hurst.

Griffin, Roger and Feldman, Matthew. (2004) *Fascism*, London: Routledge.

Gross, Leo. (1948) The Peace of Westphalia. *American Journal of International Law* 42: 20–41.

Guardian. 2013. The NSA Files. Available at http://www.theguardian.com/world/the-nsa-files [accessed 13 November 2013].

Gunaratna, Rohan. (2002) *Inside Al Qae'da*, London: C. Hurst.

Hacker, Friedrich. (1976) *Crusaders, criminals, crazies: terror and terrorism in our time*, New York: Norton.

Hagopian, Joachim. 2014. US Terrorism From the Skies: The Truth Behind Drone Strikes as the President's Personal Choice of Warfare. Global Research. Available at http://www.globalresearch.ca/us-terrorism-from-the-skies-the-truth-behind-drone-strikes-as-the-presidents-personal-choice-of-warfare/5382279 [accessed 24 May 2014].

Hagopian, Patrick. (2009) *The Vietnam War in American memory: veterans, memorials, and the politics of healing*, Amherst: University of Massachusetts Press.

Hall, John A. (1994) *Coercion and consent: studies on the modern state*, Cambridge: Polity.

Halliday, Fred. (1987) State and Society in International Relations: A Second Agenda. *Millennium Journal of International Studies* 16(2): 215–30.

Halper, Stefan and Clarke, Jonathan. (2004) *America alone: the neo-conservatives and the global order*, Cambridge: Cambridge University Press.

Hamidaddin, Abdullah. (2013) Six Rules of Thumb for Writing on Sunni/Shiite Concepts. *Al Arabiya News*, 31 May.

Hammond, P. (2011) *Screens of terror: representations of war and terrorism in film and television since 9/11*, London: Arima.

Hardin, Russell. (2004) Civil Liberties in the Era of mass Terrorism. *Journal of Ethics* 8(1): 77–95.

Harrison, Neil E. (2006) *Complexity in world politics: concepts and methods of a new paradigm*, Albany: State University of New York Press.

Hasan, Mehdi. (2014) What the Jihadists Who Bought 'Islam for Dummies' on Amazon Tell Us About Radicalisation. *Huffington Post*, 2 August.

Hazleton, Lesley. (2009) *After the prophet the epic story of the Shia–Sunni split in Islam*, New York: Doubleday.

Heffelfinger, Christopher. (2011) *Radical Islam in America: salafism's journey from Arabia to the West*, Washington, DC: Potomac Books.

Held, David. (1989) *Political theory and the modern state: essays on state, power and democracy*, Cambridge: Polity.

Held, David. (1992) The Development of the Modern State. In S. Hall and B. Gieben (eds), *Formations of modernity*, Oxford: Polity, 71–126.

Hellmich, Christina. (2011) *Al-Qaeda: from global network to local franchise*, London: Zed.

Heribert, Adam. (2011) *Hushed voices: unacknowledged atrocities of the 20th century*, Highclere: Berkshire Academic Press.

Herman, Edward S. (1982) *The real terror network: terrorism in fact and propaganda*, Boston: South End Press.

Herngren, Per. (1993) *Path of resistance: the practice of civil disobedience*, Philadelphia, PA: New Society.

Higgs, Robert. (1987) *Crisis and leviathan: critical episodes in the growth of American government*, Oxford: Oxford University Press.

Hillyard, Mick and Edmonds, Tim. (1999) *Millennium trade talks and the 'battle in Seattle'*, London: House of Commons Library.

Hobbes, Thomas. (1946) *Leviathan: or, The matter, forme and power of a commonwealth ecclesiasticall and civil*, Oxford: Blackwell.

Hobsbawm, Eric. J. (1990) *Nations and nationalism since 1780: programme, myth, reality*, Cambridge: Cambridge University Press.

Hobson, John M. (2000) *The state and international relations*, Cambridge: Cambridge University Press.

Hobson, John. A. (1965) *Imperialism, a study*, Ann Arbor: University of Michigan Press.

Hoffman, Bruce. (1995) 'Holy Terror': The Implications of Terrorism Motivated by a Religious Imperative. *Studies in Conflict & Terrorism* 18(4): 271–84.

Hoffman, Bruce. (1998) *Inside terrorism*, London: Gollancz.

Holland, John H. (1998) *Emergence: from chaos to order*, Oxford: Oxford University Press.

Holsti, Kalevi. J. (1991) *Peace and war: armed conflicts and the international order 1648–1989*, Cambridge: Cambridge University Press.

Horgan, John. (2005) *The psychology of terrorism*, London: Routledge.

Horgan, John and Taylor, Max. (2003) Playing the 'Green Card' – Financing the Provisional IRA: Part 2. *Terrorism and Political Violence*, 15(2): 1–60.

Howard, Philip N. and Hussain, Muzammil M. (2013) *Democracy's fourth wave?: digital media and the Arab Spring*, Oxford: Oxford University Press.

Huntington, Samuel P. (1996) *The clash of civilizations and the remaking of world order*, New York: Simon & Schuster.

Hurd, Elizabeth Shakman. (2008) *The politics of secularism in international relations*, Oxford: Princeton University Press.

Hussain, Murtaza. (2013) The Myth of the 1,400 Year Sunni-Shia War. *Al Jazeera*, 9 July.

Ignatieff, Michael. (2001) It's War – But It Doesn't Have To Be Dirty. *Guardian*, 30 September.

Innes, Brian. (1998) *The history of torture*, London: St. Martin's Press.

Innes, Michael A. (2012) *Making sense of proxy wars: states, surrogates and the use of force*, Washington, DC: Potomac Books.

ISIL. (2014) ISIL Manifesto: This is the Promise of Allah. Baghdad: ISIL. Available at: http://msnbcmedia.msn.com/i/MSNBC/Sections/NEWS/z-pdf-archive/20140629-isil-manifesto.pdf [accessed 28 December 2014].

Islam.com. (2014) The Holy Qu'ran. Available at http://www.4islam.com/quran.shtml [accessed 1 November 2014].

Jackson, Richard. (2005) *Writing the war on terrorism: language, politics and counter-terrorism*, Manchester: Manchester University Press.

Jackson, Richard. (2008) The Ghosts of State Terror: Knowledge, Politics and Terrorism Studies. *Critical Studies on Terrorism* 1(3): 377–92.

Jackson, Richard. (2011) The Threat of Terrorism. In R. Jackson (ed.), *Richard Jackson Terrorism Blog.*

Jackson, Richard, Jarvis, L., Gunning, J. et al. (2011) *Terrorism: a critical introduction*, Basingstoke: Palgrave Macmillan.

Jackson, Richard, Murphy, Eamon and Poynting, Scott. (2010) *Contemporary state terrorism: theory and practice*, London: Routledge.

Jackson, Richard, Smyth, Marie and Gunning, Jeroen. (2009) *Critical terrorism studies: a new research agenda*, London: Routledge.

Jenkins, Brian Michael. (1975) International Terrorism: A New Mode of Conflict. In D. Carlton and C. Schaerf (eds), *International terrorism and world security*. London: Croom Helm.

Jessop, Bob. (1990) *State theory: putting the capitalist state in its place*, Cambridge: Polity Press.

Johnson, Chalmers. (2002) *Blowback: the costs and consequences of American empire*, London: Time Warner.

Jonas, Susanne. (1991) *The battle for Guatemala: rebels, death squads, and U.S. power*, Oxford: Westview Press.

Jones, James William. (2008) *Blood that cries out from the earth: the psychology of religious terrorism*, Oxford: Oxford University Press.

Juergensmeyer, Mark. (2003) *Terror in the mind of God: the global rise of religious violence*, London: University of California Press.

Kant, Immanuel. (1966) *The metaphysics of morals*, Cambridge: Cambridge University Press.

Karmon, Eli. (2005) *Coalitions between terrorist organizations: revolutionaries, nationalists and Islamists*, Leiden: Martinus Nijhoff.

Kase, Francis Joseph. (1968) *People's democracy. A contribution to the study of the Communist theory of state and revolution*: Leyden: A.W. Sijthoff.

Kepel, Gilles. (2006) *Jihad: the trail of political Islam*, London: I.B. Tauris.

Kimmel, Michael S. (1988) *Absolutism and its discontents: state and society in seventeenth century France and England*, New Brunswick: Transaction Books.

King, Martin Luther, Jr. (1968) *Letter from Birmingham Jail*, Stamford, CT: Overbrook Press.

Kirkpatrick, David D. 2014) 'ISIS' Harsh Brand of Islam is Rooted in Austere Saudi Creed. *New York Times*. Available at http://www.nytimes.com/2014/09/25/world/middleeast/isis-abu-bakr-baghdadi-caliph-wahhabi.html?_r=1 [accessed 24 September].

Knott, Matthew. (2014) Sydney Siege Gunman Man Haron Monis Glorified in Islamic State Propaganda Magazine *Dabiq*. *Sydney Morning Herald*, 30 December. Available at http://www.smh.com.au/federal-politics/political-news/sydney-siege-gunman-man-haron-monis-glorified-in-islamic-state-propaganda-magazine-dabiq-20141230-12fdg6.html [accessed 31 December 2014].

Koppelman, Andrew. (2013) *Defending American religious neutrality*, Cambridge, MA: Harvard University Press.

Kottler, Jeffrey A. (2011) *The lust for blood: why we are fascinated by death, murder, horror, and violence*, Amherst, NY: Prometheus Books.

Krasner, Stephen D. (1993) Westphalia and All That. In J. Goldstein and R.O. Keohane (eds), *Ideas and foreign policy: beliefs, institutions, and political change.* Ithaca, NY: Cornell University Press, 235–64.

Krasner, Stephen D. (1999) *Sovereignty: organized hypocrisy*, Princeton, NJ: Princeton University Press.

Kropotkin, Petr Alekseevich. (2002) *Anarchism: a collection of revolutionary writings*, New York: Dover Publications.

Krueger, Alan B. (2008) *What makes a terrorist: economics and the roots of terrorism*, Princeton, NJ: Princeton University Press.

Kurzman, Charles. (2004) *The unthinkable revolution in Iran*, Cambridge, MA: Harvard University Press.

Kydd, Andrew and Walter, Barbara. (2006) The Strategies of Terrorism. *International Security* 31(1): 49–80.

La Boétie, Estienne de and Kurz, Harry. (1975) *The politics of obedience: the discourse of voluntary servitude*, Montreal: Black Rose Books.

Langerbein, Helmut. (2004) *Hitler's death squads: the logic of mass murder*, College Station: Texas A&M University Press.

Laqueur, Walter. (1977) *Terrorism*, London: Weidenfeld & Nicolson.

Laqueur, Walter. (1986) Reflections on Terrorism. *Foreign Affairs* 65: 86–100.

Laqueur, Walter. (1987) *The age of terrorism*, London: Weidenfeld & Nicolson.

Laqueur, Walter. (1996) Postmodern Terrorism: New Rules for an Old Game. *Foreign Affairs*, 1 September. Available at http://www.foreignaffairs.com/articles/52432/walter-laqueur/postmodern-terrorism-new-rules-for-an-old-game [accessed 19 February 2015].

Laqueur, Walter. (1999) *The new terrorism: fanaticism and the arms of mass destruction*, London: Phoenix.

Laqueur, Walter. (2001) *A history of terrorism*, London: Transaction.

Laqueur, Walter. (2003) *No end to war: terrorism in the 21st century*, London: Continuum.

Le Bon, Gustave. (1977) *The crowd: a study of the popular mind*, New York: Penguin.

Leigh, David and Harding, Luke. (2011) *WikiLeaks: inside Julian Assange's war on secrecy*, London: Guardian.

Lenin, Vladimir Ilich. (1960) What Is To Be Done? In *Collected works.* Moscow: Foreign Languages Publishing House, 347–530.

Lenin, Vladimir Ilich. (2010) *Imperialism: the highest stage of capitalism*, London: Penguin.

Lesser, Ian O., Hoffman, Bruce, Arquilla, John et al. (1999) *Countering the new terrorism*, Santa Monica, CA: Rand.

Lewis, Bernard. (2003) *The crisis of Islam: holy war and unholy terror*, London: Weidenfeld & Nicolson.

Lewis, Michael. (2010) *The big short: inside the doomsday machine*, London: Allen Lane.

Leyton, Elliot. (2003) *Hunting humans: inside the minds of mass murderers*, New York: Carroll & Graf.

Loyn, David. (2009) *In Afghanistan: two hundred years of British, Russian and American occupation*, Basingstoke: Palgrave Macmillan.

Luders, Joseph E. (2010) *The civil rights movement and the logic of social change*, Cambridge: Cambridge University Press.

Luhmann, Niklas. (1993) Protest Movements. In N. Luhmann and R. Barrett (eds), *Risk: a sociological theory*. New Brunswick, NJ: Aldine Transaction, 125–44.

Luttwak, Edward. (1979) *Coup d'état: a practical handbook*, London: Wildwood House.

Lyon, David. (2003) *Surveillance after September 11*, Cambridge: Polity.

Lyons, David. (1998) Moral Judgment, Historical Reality, and Civil Disobedience. *Philosophy and Public Affairs* 27(1): 31–49.

Macpherson, C. B. (1977) *The life and times of liberal democracy*, Oxford: Oxford University Press.

Mahajan, Rahul. (2003) *Full spectrum dominance: U.S. power in Iraq and beyond*, New York: Seven Stories Press.

Manicas, Peter T. (2006) *A realist philosophy of social science: explanation and understanding*, Cambridge: Cambridge University Press.

Mann, Michael. (1984) The Autonomous Power of the State: Its Origins, Mechanisms and Results. *European Journal of Sociology* 25(02): 185–213.

Mann, Michael. (2005) *The dark side of democracy: explaining ethnic cleansing*, Cambridge: Cambridge University Press.

Mann, Michael. (2012) *The sources of social power: volume 3, global empires and revolution, 1890–1945*, Cambridge: Cambridge University Press.

Marchak, Patricia and Marchak William. (1999) *God's assassins: state terrorism in Argentina in the 1970s*, London: Queen's University Press.

Marion, Russ and Uhl-Bien, Mary. (2003) Complexity Theory and Al Qaeda: Examining Cmplex Leadership. *Emergence* 5(1): 54–76.

Markovits, Daniel. (2005) Democratic Disobedience. *Yale Law Journal* 114(8): 1898–1948.

Marx, Karl. 1870. The Character of the Commune: The Civil War in France, First Draft. Available at http://marxengels.public-archive.net/en/ME1511en_d1.html [accessed 1 August 2013].

Marx, Karl and Engels, Friedrich. (1964) *The German ideology*, Moscow: Progress Publishers.

Marx, Karl and Engels, Friedrich. (1967) *Capital: a critique of political economy*, New York: International Publishers.

Marx, Karl and Fernbach, David. (1973) *The revolutions of 1848: political writings, vol.1*, London: Allen Lane.

Mason, Paul. (2012) *Why it's kicking off everywhere: the new global revolutions*, London: Verso.

Mazzei, Julie. (2009) *Death squads or self-defense forces?: how paramilitary groups emerge and challenge democracy in Latin America*, Chapel Hill: University of North Carolina Press.

McTague, Tom. (2014) 'Intervene in Iraq and Syria or Britain Will Face Terror Attacks': Blair Warns UK Should Get Involved as He Defends Decision to Topple Saddam. *Daily Mail*, 15 June.

Meade, Charles and Molander, Roger C. (2006) *Considering the effects of a catastrophic terrorist attack*. Santa Monica, CA: RAND Center for Terrorism Risk Management Policy.

Meloy, Reid, J. (1988) *The psychopathic mind: origins, dynamics, and treatment*, Plymouth: Jason Aronson.

Mendelsohn, Barak. (2014) After Disowning ISIS, Al Qaeda Iis Back on Top: Here's Why That Isn't Necessarily Bad News. *Foreign Affairs*, 13 February.

Merari, Ariel. (1993) Terrorism as a Strategy of Insurgency. *Terrorism and Political Violence* 5(4): 213–51.

Mettam, Roger. (1988) *Power and faction in Louis XIV's France*, Oxford: Basil Blackwell.

Meuller, John. (2006) Is There Still a Terrorist Threat? The Myth of the Omnipresent Enemy. *Foreign Affairs*, September/October.

Michael, George. (2003) *Confronting right-wing extremism and terrorism in the USA*, London: Routledge.

Michels, Robert. (1966) *Political parties: a sociological study of the oligarchical tendencies of modern democracy*, New York: Free Press.

Midlarsky, Manus I., Crenshaw, Martha and Yoshida, Fumihiko. (1980) Why Violence Spreads: The Contagion of International Terrorism. *International Studies Quarterly* 24(2): 262–98.

Miller, John H. and Page, Scott E. (2007) *Complex adaptive systems: an introduction to computational models of social life*, Oxford: Princeton University Press.

Mills, C. Wright. (1957) *The power elite*, Oxford: Oxford University Press.

Milton-Edwards, Beverley and Farrell, Stephen. (2010) *Hamas: the Islamic resistance movement*, Cambridge: Polity.

Minnion, John. (1983) *CND story: the first 25 years of CND in the words of the people involved*, London: Allison & Busby.

Mobley, Blake W. (2012) *Terrorism and counter-intelligence: how terrorist groups elude detection*, New York: Columbia University Press.

Mockaitis, Thomas R. (2008) *The 'new' terrorism: myths and reality*, Stanford, CA: Stanford University Press.

Moghadam, A. (2008) *The globalization of martyrdom: al Qaeda, Salafi Jihad, and the diffusion of suicide attacks*, Baltimore, MD: Johns Hopkins University Press.

Moghaddam, Fathali M. (2008) *How globalization spurs terrorism the lopsided benefits of 'one world' and why that fuels violence*, London: Praeger Security International.

Montreal Gazette. (1974) Two-for-one Reprisal Vowed for Each IRA Member Hanged. 12 December. Available at http://news.google.com/newspapers?id=4pAjAAAAIBA J&sjid=v6EFAAAAIBAJ&pg=974%2C2948003 [accessed 1 December 2013].

Morozov, Evgeny. (2009) The Brave New World of Slacktivism. *Foreign Policy*, 19 May. Available at http://neteffect.foreignpolicy.com/posts/2009/05/19/the_brave_new_ world_of_slacktivism [accessed 19 February 2015].

Morozov, Evgeny. (2011) *The net delusion: how not to liberate the world*, London: Allen Lane.

Morreall, John. (1991) The Justifiability of Violent Civil Disobedience. In H.A. Bedau (ed.), *Civil disobedience in focus*. London: Routledge, 130–43.

Mosca, Gaetano. (1939) *The ruling class*, London: McGraw-Hill.

Mostov, Julie. (1992) *Power, process, and popular sovereignty*, Philadelphia: Temple University Press.

Mount, Harry. (2012) We're More Iinterested in Bad News than Good News. *Daily Telegraph*, 31 December.

Murphy, Jeffrie G. (1992) *Retribution reconsidered: more essays in the philosophy of law*, London: Kluwer Academic.

Nabavi, Negin. (2012) *Iran: from theocracy to the Green Movement*, Basingstoke: Palgrave Macmillan.

Nacos, Brigitte Lebens. (2007) *Mass-mediated terrorism: the central role of the media in terrorism and counterterrorism*, Plymouth, MA: Rowman & Littlefield.

Naimark, Norman M. (2001) *Fires of hatred: ethnic cleansing in twentieth-century Europe*, London: Harvard University Press.

Nardin, Terry. (2001) Review: Terror in the Mind of God. *Journal of Politics* 63(2): 683–4.

Nasr, Seyyed Vali Reza. (2006) *The Shia revival: how conflicts within Islam will shape the future*, London: W.W. Norton.

Neumann, Peter R. (2009) *Old and new terrorism: late modernity, globalization and the transformation of political violence*, Cambridge: Polity.

News.com.au. (2014) Man Haron Monis: Why Did He Carry Out Sydney Siege? 17 December. Available at http://www.news.com.au/national/nsw-act/man-haron-monis-why-did-he-carry-out-sydney-siege/story-fnj3rq0y-1227159748676 [accessed 23 December 2014].

New York Times. (2002) Threats and Responses: The Terror Network; Qaeda Claims Kenya Attacks; Promises More. 9 December.

Njenga, Frank G., Nicholls P. J., Nyamai Caroline, et al. (2004) Post-traumatic Stress After Terrorist Attack: Psychological Reactions Following the US Embassy Bombing in Nairobi: Naturalistic Study. *British Journal of Psychiatry* 185(4): 328–33.

Norris, Pippa, Kern, Montague and Just, Marion R. (2003) *Framing terrorism: the news media, the government, and the public*, London: Routledge.

Nozick, Robert. (1974) *Anarchy, state, and Utopia*: Oxford: Blackwell.

O'Brien, Brendan. (1995) *The long war: the IRA & Sinn Fein: from armed struggle to peace talks*, Dublin: O'Brien Press.

O'Brien, Brendan. (2007) *O'Brien pocket history of the IRA: from 1916 onwards*, Dublin: O'Brien Press.

Office of the Director of National Intelligence. (2011) Trends in Global Terrorism: Implications for the United States. National Intelligence Estimate 2006-02R, 30 September.

O'Neill, Bard E. (2005) *Insurgency & terrorism: from revolution to apocalypse*, Washington, D.C.: Potomac Books.

Ochoa-Espejo, Paulina. (2011) *The time of popular sovereignty: process and the democratic state*, University Park: Pennsylvania State University Press.

Ohmae, Kenichi. (1995) *The end of the nation state: the rise of regional economies*, London: HarperCollins.

Oliverio, Annamarie. (1998) *The state of terror*, Albany: State University of New York Press.

Onuf, Nicholas Greenwood. (1989) *World of our making: rules and rule in social theory and international relations*, Columbia: University of South Carolina Press.

Owen, Mark and Maurer, Kevin. (2012) *No easy day: the autobiography of a Navy SEAL: the firsthand account of the mission that killed Osama bin Laden*, London: Michael Joseph.

Oxford English Dictionary. (1989) Oxford: Oxford University Press.

Paletz, David L. and Schmid, Alex P. (1992) *Terrorism and the media*, London: Sage.

Pankhurst, E. Sylvia. (1911) *The Suffragettes: the history of the women's militant suffrage movement 1905–1910. [With illustrations.]*, New York: Sturgis & Walton Co.

Pape, Robert Anthony. (2005) *Dying to win: the strategic logic of suicide terrorism*, New York: Random House.

Pape, Robert Anthony. (2010) It's the Occupation Stupid. *Foreign Policy*.

Pape, Robert Anthony and Feldman James K. (2010) *Cutting the fuse: the explosion of global suicide terrorism and how to stop it*, London: University of Chicago Press.

Pareto, Vilfredo. (1963) *The mind and society. A treatise on general sociology*, New York: Dover.

Pareto, Vilfredo. (1968) *The rise and fall of the elites: an application of theoretical sociology*, Totowa, NJ: Bedminster.

Patman, Robert G. (2010) *Strategic shortfall: the Somalia syndrome and the march to 9/11*, Westport, CT: Praeger.

Peleg, Ilan. (2009) *The legacy of George W. Bush's foreign policy: moving beyond neoconservatism*, Boulder, CO: Westview Press.

Percy, Sarah V. (2007) *Mercenaries: the history of a norm in international relations*, Oxford: Oxford University Press.

Perlmutter, Dawn. (2004) *Investigating religious terrorism and ritualistic crimes*, London: CRC.

Perry, Lewis. (2013) *Civil disobedience: an American tradition*, New Haven CT: Yale University Press.

Peters, Edward. (1996) *Torture*, Pennsylvania: University of Pennsylvania Press.

Peters, Gretchen. (2012) *Seeds of terror: how drugs, thugs, and crime are reshaping the Afghan War*, Oxford: Oneworld.

Petit, Michael. (1986) *Peacekeepers at war: a Marine's account of the Beirut catastrophe*, London: Faber & Faber.

Piazza, James A. (2006) Rooted in Poverty?: Terrorism, Poor Economic Development, and Social Cleavages. *Terrorism and Political Violence* 18(1): 159–77.

Pierson, Christopher. (1996) *The modern state*, London: Routledge.

Pieth, Mark. (2002) *Financial terrorism*, London: Kluwer Academic.

Pinker, Steven. (2011) *The better angels of our nature: why violence has declined*, New York: Viking.

Poggi, Gianfranco. (1990) *The state: its nature, development and prospects*, Oxford: Polity.

Porter, Bruce D. (1994) *War and the rise of the state: the military foundations of modern politics*, Oxford: Free Press.

Posłuszna, Elżbieta. and Posłuszny Jacek. (2013) *Single-issue terrorism*, Kindle Edition: Youround Publishing.

Post, Jerrold M. (2007) *The mind of the terrorist: the psychology of terrorism from the IRA to al-Qaeda*, Basingstoke: Palgrave Macmillan.

Postmes, Tom and Spears, Russell. (1998) Deindividuation and Antinormative Behavior: A Meta-analysis. *Psychological Bulletin* 123: 238–59.

Poulantzas, Nicos. (1969) The Problem of the Capitalist State. *New Left Review* 58 (November–December).

Poulantzas, Nicos, trans. ed. Timothy O'Hagan. (1973) *Political power and social classes*, London: New Left Books.

Poulantzas, Nicos, trans. Patrick Camiller. (1978) *State, power, socialism*, London: New Left Books.

Primoratz, Igor. (1990) What Is Terrorism? *Journal of Applied Philosophy* 7 (2): 129–138.

Primoratz, Igor. (2004) *Terrorism: the philosophical issues*, Basingstoke: Palgrave Macmillan.

Proudhon, Pierre. Joseph. (1989) *The general idea of the revolution in the nineteenth century*, London: Pluto Press.

Przeworski, Adam. (2009) Conquered or Granted? A History of Suffrage Extensions. *British Journal of Political Science* 39(02): 291–321.

Putnam, Robert D. (1976) *The comparative study of political elites*, Englewood Cliffs, NJ: Prentice-Hall.

Quṭb, Sayyid. (1993) *Milestones*, Chicago: Kazi Publications.

Quṭb, Sayyid and Bergesen, Albert. (2008) *The Sayyid Quṭb reader: selected writings on politics, religion, and society*, New York: Routledge.

Ranstorp, Magnus. (2010) *Understanding violent radicalisation: terrorist and jihadist movements in Europe*, London: Routledge.

Rashid, Ahmed. (2009) *Descent into Chaos: The U.S. and the Disaster in Pakistan, Afghanistan, and Central Asia*, London: Penguin.

Rawls, John. (1971) *A theory of justice*, Cambridge, MA: Belknap Press of Harvard University Press.

Raz, Joseph. (1979) *The Authority of Law: Essays on Law and Morality*, Oxford: Clarendon Press.

Reich, Walter. (1990) *Origins of terrorism: psychologies, ideologies, theologies, states of mind*, Cambridge: Cambridge University Press.

Reicher, Steve and Stott Cliff. (2011) *Mad mobs and Englishmen*, London: Constable & Robinson.

Richards, Anthony. (2013) Conceptualizing Terrorism. *Studies in Conflict & Terrorism* 37(3): 213–36.

Richardson, Louise. (2006a) *The roots of terrorism*, London: Routledge.

Richardson, Louise. (2006b) *What terrorists want: understanding the terrorist threat*, London: John Murray.

Richardson, Robert D. (1986) *Henry Thoreau: a life of the mind*, London: University of California Press.

Ringmar, Erik. (1996) On the Ontological Status of the State. *European Journal of International Relations* 2(4): 439–66.

Ripley, Tim. (2011) *Operation Enduring Freedom: America's Afghan war 2001 to 2002*, Barnsley: Pen & Sword Aviation.

Ritzer, George. (2008) *Sociological theory*, Maidenhead: McGraw-Hill Higher Education.

Robb, John. (2004) The Optimal Size of a Terrorist Network. Available at http://globalguerrillas.typepad.com/globalguerrillas/2004/03/what_is_the_opt.html [accessed 1 November 2014].

Rodin, David. (2007) *War, torture, and terrorism: ethics and war in the 21st century*, Oxford: Blackwell.

Roy, Olivier. (2004) *Globalized Islam: the search for a new ummah*, New York: Columbia University Press.

Russell, Bertrand. (1961) Civil Disobedience. *New Statesman*, 14 November 2013.

Ryan, Paul B. (1985) *The Iranian rescue mission: why it failed*, Annapolis, MD: Naval Institute Press.

Sageman, Marc. (2004) *Understanding terror networks*, Philadelphia: University of Pennsylvania Press.

Sageman, Marc. (2008) *Leaderless jihad: terror networks in the twenty-first century*, Philadelphia: University of Pennsylvania Press.

Salib, Emad. (2003) Effect of 11 September 2001 on Suicide and Homicide in England and Wales. *The British Journal of Psychiatry* 183(3): 207–12.

Sandford, Daniel. (2009) UK Airline Plot: Al-Qaeda Connection. Available at http://news.bbc.co.uk/2/hi/uk_news/8221375.stm [accessed 20 June 2014].

Sarat, Austin. (2002) *Law, violence, and the possibility of justice*, Princeton, NJ: Princeton University Press.

Sassen, Saskia. (2006) *Territory, authority, rights: from medieval to global assemblages*, Princeton, NJ: Princeton University Press.

Sayer, Andrew. (2000) *Realism and social science*, Thousand Oaks, CA: Sage.

Schelling, Thomas C. (1982) Thinking about nuclear terrorism. *International Security* 6(4): 61–77.

Scheuer, Michael. (2011) *Osama bin Laden*, Oxford: Oxford University Press.

Schlesinger, Philip. (1981) Terrorism, the media, and the liberal-democratic state: a critique of the orthodoxy. *Social Research* 48(1): 74–99.

Schlesinger, Philip, Murdock, Graham and Elliott, Philip. (1983) *Televising 'terrorism': political violence in popular culture*, London: Comedia.

Schmid, Alex P. and Graaf, Janny de. (1982) *Violence as communication: insurgent terrorism and the Western news media*, London: Sage.

Schmid, Alex P. and Jongman, Albert J. (2005) *Political terrorism: a new guide to actors, authors, concepts, data bases, theories and literature*, Somerset, NJ: Transaction.

Schmitt, Carl. (1985) *Political theology: four chapters on the concept of sovereignty*, London: MIT Press.

Schmitt, Carl. (1996) *The concept of the political*, Chicago: University of Chicago Press.

Schurman-Kauflin, Deborah (2008) *Disturbed: Terrorist Behavioral Profiles*, Sun City: Violent Crimes Institute LLC.

Scott, Len. V. and Hughes, Gerald. R. (2008) *Intelligence, crises and security: prospects and retrospects*, London: Routledge.

Sekulow, Jay. (2014) *The rise of ISIS: the coming massacre*, New York: Howard Books.

Selengut, Charles. (2008) *Sacred fury: understanding religious violence*, Plymouth: Rowman & Littlefield Publishers.

Seltzer, Mark. (2013) *Serial Killers: Death and Life in America's Wound Culture*, London: Taylor & Francis.

Shapiro, Jacob N. (2013) *The terrorist's dilemma: managing violent covert organizations*, Oxford: Princeton.

Sharkansky, Ira. (2003) *Coping with terror: an Israeli perspective*, Lanham, MD: Lexington.

Sharp, G. (1968) The politics of nonviolent action: a study in the control of political power. Doctoral dissertation, University of Oxford [online resource].

Sharp, Gene. (1979) *Gandhi as a political strategist: with essays on ethics and politics*, Boston, MA: P. Sargent.

Sharp, Gene. (2012) *Sharp's dictionary of power and struggle: language of civil resistance in conflicts*, Oxford: Oxford University Press.

Shirky, Clay. (2008) *Here comes everybody: the power of organizing without organizations*, London: Allen Lane.

Shirky, Clay. (2010) The Political Power of Social Media: Technology, the Public Sphere and Political Change. *Foreign Affairs*, January/February. Available at http://www.foreignaffairs.com/articles/67038/clay-shirky/the-political-power-of-social-media [accessed 19 February 2015].

Sifry, Micah L. (2011) *WikiLeaks and the age of transparency*, London: Yale University Press.

Silke, Andrew. (2004) *Research on terrorism: trends, achievements and failures*, London: Frank Cass.

Silver, Nate. (2013) *The signal and the noise: the art and science of prediction*, London: Penguin.

Simon, Jeffrey. (2001) *The terrorist trap*, Bloomington: Indiana University Press.

Simpson, Gerry J. (2007) *Law, war and crime: war crimes trials and the reinvention of international law*, Cambridge: Polity.

Singer, Peter. (1973) *Democracy and disobedience*, Oxford: Clarendon Press.

Skinner, Rob. (2010) *The foundations of anti-apartheid: liberal humanitarians and transnational activists in Britain and the United States, c.1919–64*, Basingstoke: Palgrave Macmillan.

Skocpol, Theda. (1979) *States and social revolutions: a comparative analysis of France, Russia and China*, Cambridge: Cambridge University Press.

Skocpol, Theda. (1994) *Social revolutions in the modern world*, Cambridge: Cambridge University Press.

Smith, Anthony D. (2001) *Nationalism: theory, ideology, history*, Cambridge: Polity.

Smith, G. Davidson. (1998) *Single issue terrorism*, Montreal: Canadian Security Intelligence Service.

Smith, Graeme. (2008) *A short history of secularism*, London: I.B. Tauris.

Smith, Lyn. (2010) *Voices against war: a century of protest*, Oxford: ISIS.

Sniegoski, Stephen J. (2008) *The transparent cabal: the neoconservative agenda, war in the Middle East, and the national interest of Israel*, Norfolk, VA: Enigma Editions.

Sookhdeo, Patrick. (2008) *Global jihad: the future in the face of militant Islam*, McLean, VA: Isaac.

Springhall, John. (2001) *Decolonization since 1945: the collapse of European overseas empires*, Basingstoke: Palgrave Macmillan.

Spruyt, Hendrik. (2002) The Origins, Development, and Possible Decline of the Modern State. *Annual Review of Political Science* 5(1): 127–49.

Stahelski, Anthony. (2005) Terrorists are Made, not Born. *Cultic Studies Review* 4(1): 30–40.

Stapley, Lionel. (2006) *Globalization and terrorism: death of a way of life*, London: Karnac.

Stellato, Jesse. (2012) *Not in our name: American antiwar speeches, 1846 to the present*, University Park: Pennsylvania State University Press.

Stern, Jessica. (2003) *Terror in the name of God: why religious militants kill*, New York: Ecco.

Stohl, Michael and Lopez, George A. (1988) *Terrible beyond endurance?: the foreign policy of state terrorism*, New York: Greenwood Press.

Storing, Herbert J. (1991) The Case against Civil Disobedience. In H.A. Bedau (ed.) *Civil disobedience in focus*. London: Routledge, 85–102.

Stritzke, Werner G. K. (2009) *Terrorism and torture: an interdisciplinary perspective*, Cambridge: Cambridge University Press.

Sullivan, Andrew. 2009. The Revolution Will be Twittered. Available at http://www.theatlantic.com/daily-dish/archive/2009/06/the-revolution-will-be-twittered/200478/ [accessed 12 November 2013].

Suskind, Ron. (2006) *The one percent doctrine: deep inside America's pursuit of its enemies since 9/11*, London: Simon & Schuster.

Sutton, Philip W. and Vertigans, Stephen. (2005) *Resurgent Islam: a sociological approach*, Cambridge: Polity.

Taipei Times (2002) Mahathir lashes out at terrorist threat. 2 April Available at http://www.taipeitimes.com/News/front/archives/2002/04/02/0000130160 [accessed 1 November 2014].

Tamimi, Azzam. (2007) *Hamas: a history from within*, Northampton, MA: Olive Branch Press.

Taylor, Max, Holbrook, Donald and Currie, P.M. (2013) *Extreme right wing political violence and terrorism*, London: Bloomsbury.

Teich, Sarah. (2013) Trends and Developments in Lone Wolf Terrorism in the Western World: An Analysis of Terrorist Attacks and Attempted Attacks by Islamic Extremists. International Institute for Counter-Terrorism, Herzliya. Available at http://www.ict.org.il/Article.aspx?ID=691 [accessed 19 February 2015].

Daily Telegraph. (2013) Woolwich Attack: The Terrorist's Rant. 23 May. Available at http://www.telegraph.co.uk/news/uknews/terrorism-in-the-uk/10075488/Woolwich-attack-the-terrorists-rant.html [accessed 28 December 2014].

Teschke, Benno. (2003) *The myth of 1648: class, geopolitics, and the making of modern international relations*, London: Verso.

Thomas, Janet. (2000) *The battle in Seattle: the story behind the WTO demonstrations*, Golden, CO: Fulcrum.

Thompson, Paul. (2004) *The terror timeline: year by year, day by day, minute by minute: a comprehensive chronicle of the road to 9/11 and America's response*, New York: Regan Books.

Thoreau, Henry David. (1993) *Civil disobedience, and other essays*, New York: Dover Publications.

Tilly, Charles. (1985) War Making and State Making as Organised Crime. In P. Evans, D. Rueschemeyer and T. Skocpol (eds), *Bringing the state back in*. Cambridge: Cambridge University Press, 169–91.

Tilly, Charles. (1990) *Coercion, capital, and European states, AD 990–1990*, Oxford: Basil Blackwell.

Time. (2011) Person of the Year Issue: The Protester. December.

Tonkin, Hannah. (2011) *State control over private military and security companies in armed conflict*, Cambridge: Cambridge University Press.

Tormey, Simon. (2015) *Politics after Representation*, Cambridge: Polity.

Triska, J. F. (1969) *Communist party-states: comparative and international studies.* Indianapolis, IN: Bobbs-Merrill.

UN. (2002) Addressing Security Council, Secretary-General calls on counter-terrorism committee to develop long-term strategy to defeat terror. Available at http://www.un.org/News/Press/docs/2002/SC7276.doc.htm [accessed 24 April 2014].

UN. (2007) Definitions of terrorism. United Nations. [accessed 3 December 2013].

UN Statistics (2006) Demographic Yearbook. Available at http://unstats.un.org/unsd/demographic/sconcerns/mortality/mort2.htm [accessed 10 October 2014].

UN Security Council. (2001) Resolution 1373. United Nations, *S/RES/1373 (2001)*.

UN Security Council. (2004) Resolution 1566. United Nations, *S/RES/1566 (2004)*.

US Central Intelligence Agency. (2003) *National strategy for combating terrorism*. Washington, DC: CIA.

US Department of Defense. (2001) *Department of Defense Dictionary of Military and Associated Terms*, Joint Publication 1-02.

van Gelder, Sarah. (2011) *This changes everything: Occupy Wall Street and the 99% movement*, San Francisco: Berrett-Koehler.

van Gelderen, Martin and Skinner, Quentin. (2002) *Republicanism: a shared European heritage. Vol. 1, Republicanism and constitutionalism in early modern Europe*, Cambridge: Cambridge University Press.

Verton, Dan. 2014. Poll shows Americans More Concerned About Terrorism Than NSA Surveillance. Available at http://fedscoop.com/poll-shows-americans-more-concerned-about-terrorism-than-nsa-surveillance/ [accessed 29 August 2014].

Vick, Karl and Baker, Aryn. (2014) Extremists in Iraq Continue March Toward Baghdad. *Time*. 11 June. Available at http://time.com/2859454/iraq-tikrit-isis-baghdad-mosul/ [accessed 28 December 2014].

Wagner, Heather Lehr. (2010) *The Iranian revolution*, New York: Chelsea House.

Waldron, Jeremy. (2012) *The harm in hate speech*, Cambridge, MA: Harvard University Press.

Walker, Rob. B. J. (1993) *Inside/outside: international relations as political theory*, Cambridge: Cambridge University Press.

Wall Street Journal. (2013) The Al Qaeda Franchise Threat: Reports of the Terrorist Group's Imminent Defeat are Greatly Exaggerated. 30 April.

Wallerstein, Immanuel Maurice. (2004) *The modern world-system in the longue durée*, Boulder, CO: Paradigm.

Waltz, Kenneth Neal. (1979) *Theory of international politics*, Reading, MA: Addison-Wesley.

Walzer, Michael. (1978) *Just and unjust wars: a moral argument with historical illustrations*, London: Allen Lane.

Warde, Ibrahim. (2007) *The price of fear: Al-Qaeda and the truth behind the financial war on terror*, London: I.B. Tauris.

Weber, Cynthia. (1995) *Simulating sovereignty: intervention, the state, and symbolic exchange*, Cambridge Cambridge University Press.

Weber, Max. (1965) *Politics as a vocation*, New York: Fortress Press.

Weber, Max. (1978) *Economy and society: an outline of interpretive sociology*, Berkeley: University of California Press.

Weber, Max, Henderson, Alexander M. and Parsons, Talcott. (1964) *The theory of docial and economic organization*, New York: Free Press.

Weimann, Gabriel. (2006) *Terror on the Internet: the new arena, the new challenges*, Washington, DC: US Institute of Peace.

Weinberg, Leonard and Davis, Paul. (1989) *Introduction to political terrorism*, London: McGraw-Hill.

Welch, Michael. F. (1984) Applied Typology and Victimology in the Hostage Negotiation Process. *Journal of Crime and Justice* 7(1): 63–86.

Wellman, Carl. (1979) On Terrorism Itself. *Journal of Value Inquiry* 13(4): 250–8.

Wheaton, Bernard and Kavan, Zdenek. (1992) *The velvet revolution: Czechoslovakia, 1988–1991*, Oxford: Westview.

White, Jonathan Randall. (1997) *Terrorism: an introduction*, London: Wadsworth.

White, Jonathan Randall. (2014) *Terrorism and homeland security*, Belmont, CA: Wadsworth Cengage Learning.

Wight, Colin. (2001) The Continuity of Change, or a Change in Continuity? *International Studies Review* 3(1): 81–9.

Wight, Colin. (2004) State Agency: Social Action Without Human Activity? *Review of International Studies* 30(02): 269–80.

Wight, Colin. (2006) *Agents, structures and international relations: politics as ontology*, Cambridge: Cambridge University Press.

Wight, Colin. (2009) Theorising Terrorism: The State, Structure and History. *International Relations* 23(1): 99–106.

Wilkinson, Paul. (1974) *Political terrorism*, London: Macmillan.

Wilkinson, Paul. (1986) *Terrorism and the liberal state*, New York: New York University Press.

Wilkinson, Paul. (2011) *Terrorism versus democracy: the liberal state response*, London: Routledge.

Willett, Edward. (2004) *Ayatollah Khomeini*, New York: Rosen.

Willoughby, Westel Woodbury. (1896) *An examination of the nature of the stat: a study in political philosophy*, London: Macmillan.

Wilson, N and Thomson G. (2005) Deaths from International Terrorism Compared with Road Crash Deaths in OECD Countries. *Injury Prevention* 11(6): 332–3.

Wilson, Peter H. (2000) *Absolutism in Central Europe*, London: Routledge.

Wright, Lawrence. (2006a) *The looming tower: al-Qaeda's road to 9/11*, London: Allen Lane.

Wright, Lawrence. (2006b) The Master Plan. *New Yorker.* 11 September.

Wright, Stuart A. (2007) *Patriots, politics, and the Oklahoma City bombing*, Cambridge: Cambridge University Press.

Index

Printed by Printforce, the Netherlands